The Hygienic Apparatus

The Hygienic Apparatus

Weimar Cinema and Environmental Disorder

✦

Paul Dobryden

NORTHWESTERN UNIVERSITY PRESS
EVANSTON, ILLINOIS

Northwestern University Press
www.nupress.northwestern.edu

Printed in the United States of America

10 9 8 7 6 5 4 3 2 1

Library of Congress Cataloging-in-Publication Data

Names: Dobryden, Paul, author.
Title: The hygienic apparatus : Weimar cinema and environmental disorder / Paul Dobryden.
Description: Evanston, Illinois : Northwestern University Press, 2022. | Includes bibliographical references and index.
Identifiers: LCCN 2021057733 | ISBN 9780810144965 (paperback) | ISBN 9780810144972 (cloth) | ISBN 9780810144989 (ebook)
Subjects: LCSH: Motion pictures—Germany—History—20th century. | Health in motion pictures. | Environmental degradation in motion pictures.
Classification: LCC PN1993.5.G3 D63 2022 | DDC 791.43094309042—dc23
LC record available at https://lccn.loc.gov/2021057733

CONTENTS

ACKNOWLEDGMENTS

This book would have been unimaginable without the guidance of Johannes von Moltke and Anton Kaes. Johannes introduced me to film theory and German film studies. Working for him at the German Film Institute in 2004 opened up an intellectual world and sent me on a path I am still following. It was at that event that I met Tony, whom I later had the privilege of studying with at the University of California, Berkeley. His work on Weimar cinema has inspired me for nearly twenty years, and what I have achieved I owe in large part to his teaching, mentorship, and generosity.

I am thankful for the many people who commented on versions of this material over the years, both in writing and at conference presentations. Michael Cowan gave generous feedback on chapter 1. Carl Gelderloos and Harald Zils invited me to the "News from Nature" conference at SUNY Binghamton in 2018, where I first presented on *Kulturfilme*. Carl has been a model of scholarly generosity, commenting on drafts and walking me through crucial steps of the publication process. Seth Howes, whose camaraderie was a bright spot in a dark year, provided much-needed assistance with the final chapter. Kristin Schroeder, a fellow Michigan transplant to Virginia, gave valuable comments on an earlier version of what would become the chapter on *Faust*. Annika Orich and her colleagues hosted me at Georgia Tech to present material from the manuscript just days before all such travel was prohibited. The participants in the "Perceiving Disability" panel series at the 2020 German Studies Association conference provided a forum for my initial foray into the topic of disability. Over the past couple of years I have valued learning from and collaborating with Caroline Weist, whose comments on chapter 4 advanced it significantly. Rielle Navitski and Kristin Dickinson, whom I am lucky to have as friends and role models, helped me at various stages.

I am grateful to my colleagues at the University of Virginia. Chad Wellmon commented on the work and pushed me forward at a crucial time. I value Bill McDonald for his warmth and candor, and for always keeping his door open. Gina Hutton has been a lifesaver. I am especially thankful to Jeffrey Grossman, who as chair of the Department of Germanic Languages and Literatures supported me in ways too numerous to list. Furthermore, generous funding from the University of Virginia facilitated crucial periods of research. A Mellon Fellowship at UVA's Institute for the Humanities and Global Cultures and a Sesquicentennial Associateship from the College of

Arts and Sciences freed time for writing; A&S travel funding made it possible for me to do research in Germany; and a grant from the Buckner W. Clay Dean of Arts & Sciences and the Vice President for Research aided preparation of the manuscript.

Thanks go to Trevor Perri, my original editor at Northwestern University Press, for taking a chance on this book. I am glad to have gotten to work with him. Lisa Regan of Textformations was a wonderful reader, editor, and sounding board, who helped turn a collection of ideas into a book. Lisa's team also provided crucial translation assistance with some of the material, though any infelicities are my own.

I want to thank Bruce Levy for his assistance at the U.S. Holocaust Memorial Museum in Washington, DC, and Beatrix Haussmann for hers at the Bundesarchiv-Filmarchiv in Berlin. I am also grateful to Philipp Stiasny, who helped me get an appointment at the Bundesarchiv on outrageously short notice.

Most of chapter 3 was published as "Clouded Vision: Particulate Matter in F. W. Murnau's *Faust*," copyright © 2020 The Johns Hopkins University Press. This article first appeared in *Modernism/modernity*, volume 27, issue no. 4 (November 2020): 707–33. Portions of chapter 2 and chapter 5 were published in "Teaching Urban Hygiene in the Weimar *Kulturfilm*," copyright © 2021 Narr Francke Attempto Verlag GmbH + Co. KG. This essay first appeared in *Colloquia Germanica*, volume 52, issue no. 3–4, pp. 309–33. I am grateful for the permission to include them here.

In Charlottesville I've been blessed to know Samhita, Ali, Kristin, Ian, Sree, and Tracey. Without them, life here wouldn't have been nearly as rewarding. And the members of the Vanderchat have been an indispensable outlet for gossip and silliness—I've learned so much.

This book would have been impossible to write without the support of my family. Al and Mary Dobryden gave me the freedom to make what must have often seemed like strange decisions. I appreciate their love and generosity more with every passing year. I also owe Diana Ellis many debts of gratitude, and am happy she's been able to follow us from California to Charlottesville. Our cats Charlie, Sophie, and Tailor provided indispensable companionship (and entertainment) during long periods spent working from home. We miss you, Tailor. Finally, I could not ask for a better partner and interlocutor than Robin Ellis—there's nothing that isn't benefited by your presence, attention, and care. This book is for you.

The Hygienic
Apparatus

Introduction

Hygiene, Cinema, and German Modernity

German cinema had its premiere in a greenhouse. On November 1, 1895, the brothers Max and Emil Skladanowsky presented a series of short moving-picture subjects to a paying audience in Berlin's Wintergarten. Then a prominent variety theater, the Wintergarten had originally opened in 1880 as an actual "winter garden," that is, a greenhouse, attached to the newly established Central-Hotel on Friedrichstrasse. "The goal," reported a contemporary architectural journal,

> was to create a large concert and gastronomic establishment; which during any season of the year would offer a garden-like space that was decorated with greenery, well-lit and ventilated, and moderately warmed, in the style of Paris's Café Concerts; in which visitors, sitting at any table they like, can enjoy musical or theatrical performances any day of the week, independent of the fickle mood of the weather in our climate.[1]

Under its expansive, seventeen-meter-high vaulted glass ceiling, the Wintergarten housed palm trees and other non-European plants, two aquariums with exotic fish, and a stage for concerts and other performances. The space was to serve travelers as well as Berliners as an escape from the city's harsh and often gray weather; it was important for the architects that "even on the coldest days a temperature of twelve to twenty degrees Celsius will be set and held with certainty."[2] Both the hotel and its greenhouse were part of a larger effort to modernize Berlin's city center, which was seen as lagging behind the more cosmopolitan European capitals (especially Paris). In 1886, the Wintergarten was repurposed as a variety theater. In November 1895, audiences enjoyed the Skladanowskys' moving images while the temperature outside hovered around freezing.

Environmental control, like that of the Berlin Wintergarten, was a hallmark of modernity. Beginning in the nineteenth century, technological developments in energy, lighting, heating, cooling, ventilation, and construction transformed how people in Europe and beyond lived and worked. In

1909, the chemist Wilhelm Ostwald wrote that it was "the essence of culture to *offset natural extremes*, which would otherwise obtain without human intervention." To demonstrate the link between climate control and civilization, Ostwald asked his reader to imagine "the life of the mountain farmer during winter, which still consists in large part of hibernation, as compared to that of the city dweller, which absolutely depends on artificial light and warmth."[3]

Greenhouses (also known in English as glasshouses or hothouses) were an important architectural model for technologies of environmental control. They had existed for centuries, but were rare until glass became relatively cheap to produce in the nineteenth century, when they became widespread in agriculture and beyond. By the mid-nineteenth century greenhouses were built on a scale previously unimaginable, culminating in London's famed Crystal Palace, designed by Joseph Paxton for the Great Exhibition of 1851—a shining symbol of technological dominance over nature, in the guise of their reconciliation. Glass and steel construction subsequently became essential to modern architecture. "It was then," writes Eva Horn, "that arcades, shopping malls, covered amusement parks, and themed baths were born."[4] These were spaces in which the world of commodities was miniaturized and put on view, in turn becoming habitations for people looking to escape the cold, see exotic things, and travel to a modern architectural paradise.

Such spaces promised escape not just from dismal weather, but from the urban environment that industrialization itself had produced. The early phases of industrialization were carried out with little or no regard for the effects on surrounding environments. Due to the concentration of factories in cities, rapid population growth, and a lack of corresponding infrastructure, urban areas were the worst affected by industrial blight. As the environmental historian Frank Uekötter has written, in nineteenth-century cities "the new environmental problems possessed an immediacy that today, at least in central Europe, is only seldom to be experienced."[5] Factories polluted urban water sources with chemical byproducts, poured smog into the air, poisoned the ground, and filled streets and residences with the clamor of industrial production. In 1893, the chemist Theodor Weyl wrote that until the late 1860s, Berlin was so despoiled by waste that the "often nearly black water of the Spree River offered a terrible sight and, in summer, released a disgusting smell that made the inhabitants despair and drove away those out for a stroll."[6] The historian of technology Lewis Mumford called this period the industrial era's "paleotechnic phase," which "was marked throughout the Western World by the widespread perversion and destruction of the environment."[7]

The new technologies and practices of environmental control that developed in the late nineteenth century were thus just as much a response to the environmental effects of industrialization as they were to Europe's insufficiently temperate weather. Mumford considered the greenhouse an exemplary artifact of the "neotechnic phase" of industrialization, one of whose major tasks was "the removal of the blighted paleotechnic environment" and the creation of "life-sustaining conditions within the innermost purlieus of technics itself."[8] Where paleotechnics exploited, extracted, and destroyed, neotechnics bore the promise of a renewed concern with life and the environmental conditions in which it might flourish. The greenhouse modeled this concern as a technology of environmental control that enabled things to grow where they could not grow before.[9]

But what does the climate-controlled architecture of the greenhouse have to do with film? For Mumford, the neotechnic concern for environmental conditions was driven in large part by nineteenth-century developments in biological, physiological, and chemical studies of life, which sought to identify and quantify the material conditions on which living things depended for their existence. "Similarly," Mumford noted, citing the motion studies of Étienne-Jules Marey and Eadweard Muybridge, "the moving picture was in essence a combination of elements derived from the study of living organisms."[10] Technical media such as photography and film were valuable to the science of life because they could fix and preserve its movement, thus insulating it from the passage of time. The greenhouse was likewise a technology of preservation—by housing plants and allowing them to be reproduced and circulated far from their point of origin, greenhouse architecture did for tropical flora what film did for the impression of movement. The winter garden and the moving image, in other words, were both life media, which provided the conditions necessary for (certain forms of) life to be stored, controlled, and reproduced.

What could have seemed a coincidental historical encounter at the turn of the twentieth century—between a winter garden and the beginnings of cinema—evinces a deeper connection that is encapsulated in the word *medium*: while typically referring to technologies of recording, storage, and communication, in biology and medicine the word can designate a substance in which something grows, as in a medium for growing cell cultures. In this sense, a medium is an environmental substrate, the material and energetic surrounding that enables the life and growth of an organism. In this book, I explore various ways in which these two conceptions of media—as life environment and as communication technology—interacted in the film culture of early twentieth-century Germany. In particular, I describe a complex encounter between the apparatus of cinema and the project of managing urban environments in the name of health—a project that often went by the name "hygiene." Cinema entered the world in an age that was obsessed with hygiene, an obsession, I argue, that shaped fundamental aspects of film culture and aesthetics. Cinema at times was even put directly in the service of the hygienic project; at others it was a site of excess and disorder that resisted integration. Before further outlining the contours of this encounter, however, let me provide some context for the rather slippery term *hygiene*.

Hygiene as Environmental Expertise

The project of managing urban industrial blight, as the environmental historian Joachim Radkau writes, "came under such rubrics as 'hygiene,' 'national or public health,' 'urban sanitation,' or 'sanitary movement.'"[11] For reasons that have to do with both its capaciousness and its specificity, I use *hygiene*, a term that came to prominence in the wake of mid-nineteenth-century reform medicine. Doctors and scientists like Rudolf Virchow and Max von Pettenkofer argued against the earlier system of medical policing and advocated for preventive medicine and social reform, drawing attention to the environmental and social determinants of health.[12] As a reaction to the deprivations of urbanization and industrialization, "hygiene" became a discursive space where knowledge from a range of disciplines—medicine, chemistry, biology, architecture, civil engineering, urban planning, social science—could come together in the service of a holistic reform project that was centered around health. According to Eduard Reich's 1870 *System der Hygieine* (sic, *System of Hygiene*), it "comprises far more than was formerly comprehended under dietetics and medical police. Hygiene deals with man as a whole, as an individual and as he manifests himself in the family and in society; it deals with man in all his conditions and relations. Consequently, hygiene comprises the entire physical and moral world, and collaborates with all the sciences whose subject is the study of man and his environment."[13] For Reich, "hygiene" included everything from morality and skin care to the social causes of poverty and the inspection of food and housing.

In the following chapters, the term *hygiene* will primarily refer to the practice of managing health by regulating physical environments, including the way people regulate their bodily presence within an environment. As Reich's definition implies, *hygiene* has a wide range of connotations and associations, not all of which can be encompassed by the way in which I use the word here. The concept has ancient roots, and was taken up by European writers of the Enlightenment. Returning to antique treatises on health by Hippocrates and Galen, seventeenth-century writers like Samuel André Tissot, William Buchan, Bernhard Christoph Faust, and Friedrich Hoffmann authored widely circulated texts about how to avoid sickness and lengthen one's life. Enlightenment hygiene was oriented toward the care of the individual body—indeed, according to Philipp Sarasin, hygiene taught the bourgeois subject what it was to "have" a body in the first place, as something to observe and care for.[14] Pamphlets, treatises, and public lectures on the correct care of the body proliferated, as students of hygiene learned from experts how to regulate the body's relationship to its external environment: what it breathed, ate, and drank; how it was kept clean, fit, and clothed; even what it saw, heard, and felt. Sarasin argues that hygiene thus had both normalizing and individualizing effects. Hygiene was a practice of self-discipline through which one became civilized, while also offering a way

International Hygiene Exhibition Dresden May–October 1911 (Franz von Stuck, 1911). Poster, color lithograph, 89.7 × 70.3 cm. Copyright © bpk Bildagentur / May Voigt / Art Resource, NY.

to understand one's body as particular, one that was different in comparison to others.[15]

By the late nineteenth century, however, hygiene was no longer just an individual matter. From its basis in the study and the statistical normalization of the human body, hygiene in its modern form had expanded to all of practical life. The 1911 International Hygiene Exhibition in Dresden, for instance, offered extensive exhibits on "Air, Earth, Soil, Water," "Settlements and Dwellings," "Nutrition and Food-Stuffs," "Clothing and Care of the Body," "Professions and Trades," "Traffic," and other topics.[16] As an enterprise driven by developing forms of scientific and applied expertise, specialists in a range of disciplines examined the social and material worlds of life under industrial capitalism in light of their effects on health and reproduction among the population as a whole. Doctors, chemists, architects, engineers, city planners, social workers, psychologists, and pedagogical experts worked, sometimes collaboratively, on how to ameliorate the health impacts of industrialization. Different branches of hygienic science developed: urban hygiene, which was concerned with water provision, waste removal, and smoke abatement; social and housing hygiene, which looked at the living conditions of the industrial working class; industrial hygiene, which dealt with pollution, fatigue, and accidents at factories, workshops, and other workplaces and professional contexts; and school hygiene, which was interested in health issues relevant to educational contexts. Hygienic principles were particularly influential in modern architecture and design, where an aesthetic of cleanliness signified a break from the stuffy, stagnant historicism of the nineteenth century.[17]

Whether at the level of the individual, the firm, or the city, these various branches of hygiene shared an interest in the material environment as the enabling condition of health. It is this dimension that I mean to emphasize when using the term. Although "hygiene" overlaps in many ways with what we mean when we speak in English of "public health," this latter term includes various forms of clinical medicine and stresses the public nature of intervention. I prefer *hygiene* precisely because of the concept's preventive methodology and environmental orientation, as well as the way it has historically spanned public, commercial, and private spheres, weaving together the reformation of individual behaviors, homes, workplaces, and public spaces and institutions into a project of populational health.

For those familiar with historical usages of the term, discourses of social, sexual, and racial hygiene also come to mind. In my usage, "hygiene" corresponds to what the historian Alfons Labisch, in order to distinguish it from these other variants, calls "experimental hygiene." "The object of experimental hygiene is the reciprocal interaction between nonliving nature and the bodily condition of every individual and the whole community," he writes, whereas "the object of social hygiene is the reciprocal interaction between the social environment and the bodily condition of select groups or of the total population, and thereby the relationship of society to health, sickness, and death."[18] Sexual and racial hygiene, like social hygiene, moved away from an analysis of the material environment, in this case to foreground individual behaviors and the links between bodily conditions and reproduction. Experimental, social, sexual, and racial hygiene agreed on the aim of using scientific expertise to better the health of the population and often complemented each other theoretically and practically, but could differ starkly as to what constituted effective or ethical means of intervention, the relationships between nature and nurture, what health looked like in practical terms, and who properly belonged to "the population." Thinking through the entangled histories of hygiene and cinema will at times involve discussing social, sexual, and racial hygienic discourses in relation to my central focus on the environmental.

In stressing this dimension of hygiene, I define environments as experimental hygienists did: as physical spaces whose material composition affects human biological processes. In its earlier formulations, hygiene was closely allied to physiology, such that "hygiene became the physiology of the everyday spaces the body occupied," writes Didem Ekici. "The science of hygiene aimed to determine the optimal stimuli in an environment in exact figures for the organism to remain healthy. It quantified and rationalized the relationship between the body and everyday spaces according to health criteria."[19] It examined how environments conditioned health, but also how bodies, in more or less healthy ways, transformed the environments they inhabited. This deeply spatial character can be seen in hygienic reference works, which, instead of being organized by scientific disciplines (such as "the chemistry of hygiene" or "the physics of hygiene"), were frequently divided according to spaces or physical systems: ground and water hygiene, the hygiene of urban waste, domestic hygiene, school hygiene, hospital hygiene, and so on.

As these examples imply, environments could be located at different scales—a kitchen, an apartment, a neighborhood, or a city could all be environments in this sense. The bounds of an environment are always the effect of an observer drawing a relatively arbitrary line in order to define a space or scale of intervention. Hygiene involved drawing lines around environments at different scales in order to regulate them. Moreover, these environments were not discrete or self-sufficient, but overlapping, interpenetrating, and mutually constituting. They were connected by various forms of traffic (people moving through the city, water flowing through pipes, air blowing through windows) and were nested within each other at different scales (the kitchen, which is in the apartment, which is in the building, the neighborhood, the city). Hygienic thinking also involved identifying and regulating the relationships between these different spaces and systems.

For all its shifting between spatial scales, though, hygiene was fundamentally an urban form of environmental practice. It responded to changes driven by the rapid industrialization and population growth of German cities in the period following national unification in 1871. Cities were increasingly significant drivers of Germany's material and economic wealth, but, from the perspective of health experts, they were also sites of contagion, pollution, accident, and degeneration. Crowded and unsanitary housing, punishing factory labor, and inadequate food, waste removal, and care systems threatened to undermine the health of the laboring population upon which industrial society depended. Wage labor, moreover, made people all the more dependent on physical health to survive, at the same time that migration to cities disrupted traditional care networks. With more and more people moving to cities, their hygienic conditions were of concern for the health of the social body as a whole. The health and accident insurance schemes of the 1880s represented a bureaucratic, compensatory strategy for managing the instability of industrial modernity; the project of hygiene reform, meanwhile, was a material strategy that focused on the organization of urban environments.

The historian Dieter Schott has suggested that hygiene can be considered in some respects a "proto-environmental science." Like the environmental sciences of the second half of the twentieth century, hygiene was concerned holistically with the material foundations of life, and functioned as a kind of meta-discipline that brought together knowledge from throughout the natural sciences.[20] Unlike the more recent concern for human society's effects on animal and plant populations, however, hygiene was resolutely anthropocentric and largely amenable to the ongoing march of urbanization and industrialization. In other words, it was a form of environmental knowledge, but was certainly not environmental*ist* as commonly understood today. Nonetheless, as the work of Schott and Radkau suggests, hygiene should be considered an important historical example in any genealogy of environmental or ecological thought. With the rather untimely sound of the word *hygiene*, I hope to retain a sense of this difference, of an environmental discourse that is not always legible in terms more familiar today. This book explores ways that the cinema in Germany was shaped by, articulated, and reacted to this idiosyncratic form of environmental thought and practice.

Apparatuses of Modernity

The Hygienic Apparatus asks how the environmental concerns of hygiene reform in Germany intersected with the then-developing medium of film. How did the ideas and practices of hygiene shape how films were made and exhibited? And what role did film have in the project of hygienic reform? Invented only at the very end of the nineteenth century, film arrived as the hygienic project was already well under way. As I show, this project thus informed how certain parts of German society received and talked about film, and impacted the material forms that film spectatorship and moviegoing took as cinema became an established part of urban life in the 1910s. After World War I, reformers experimented with using film to popularize hygienic ideas, often having to do with personal cleanliness and sexual mores, but also the spaces and environments that people inhabited, worked in, and traveled through. At the same time, material disorder in the environment provided a rich source of inspiration, as filmmakers during the Weimar Republic explored the aesthetic possibilities of film to order and reorder the world apprehended by the camera. And toward the end of the republic, film was a vehicle for exposing the limits of hygienic modernity, which could not resolve political-economic contradictions but only mitigate them.

The "apparatus" of this book's title refers in the first instance to the cinematic *dispositif*, a term introduced to film studies by the French writer and theorist Jean-Louis Baudry in the 1970s. In his essay "Le Dispositif"—translated into English as "The Apparatus"—Baudry went beyond the effects of moving images per se to consider their function within the cinematic situation, the arrangement of elements that conditioned the experience of film spectatorship, such as the darkened theater and the immobility of the viewer.[21] Crucial to Baudry's psychoanalytic notion of the cinematic dispositif is its production of a "cine-subject," who regresses to an earlier stage of psychic development and for whom the film image gives an impression of reality similar to that experienced in dreams. More recent writers who have taken up the term have largely left behind Baudry's psychoanalytic model in favor of rich historical accounts of the various architectures, materials, and practices that have shaped film exhibition and production. Some scholars have asked how the cinematic dispositif has changed over time, while others have sought to decenter cinema, instead viewing it as one of any number of historical "viewing and listening dispositives," as François Albera and Maria Tortajada have termed them.[22]

For my purposes, the term *dispositif* is useful first for its emphasis on acts of spatial ordering and arranging. "In its modern technological usage, a dispositif is an arrangement of devices or apparatuses (*appareil*)," Noam Elcott explains. "In nineteenth-century manuals of photography, science, or magic, for example, a camera might be called an *appareil*, whereas a black screen, photographic darkroom, or theatrical attraction was more likely to be described as a *disposition* or *dispositif*."[23] Attending to ordering practices, and the logics behind them, allows us to make links across areas of film studies discourse that typically remain separate, from exhibition to production to aesthetics. Specifically, it helps us think about the "environmental" dimensions of cinema, insofar as cinema at various levels involves the arranging of spaces that are conducive to particular forms of image production and spectatorship. Secondly, the term connects these material arrangements and their underlying logics to the production of subjectivity. In other words, dispositifs include the human beings who inhabit them and make possible certain modes of action within their bounds.

The other apparatus at the heart of this book is the dispositif of hygiene itself. In referring to hygiene as a dispositif, I invoke a more abstract sense of the term, which Michel Foucault used to refer to a "heterogeneous ensemble consisting of discourses, institutions, architectural forms, regulatory decisions, laws, administrative measures, scientific statements. . . . The apparatus [*dispositif*] itself is the system of relations that can be established between these elements."[24] Hygiene was a dispositif in this sense. It created networks of expertise across scientific disciplines and governmental institutions, and connected expert knowledge to material and administrative interventions. Foucault proposed that a dispositif "has as its major function at a given historical moment that of responding to an *urgent need*. The apparatus thus has a dominant strategic function."[25] This is certainly true of hygienic reform, which responded to particular ways that industrial capitalism was undermining its own ecological and biological foundations. As we will see, it was strategic in that it was largely reactive, working to manage contradictions rather than resolve them. Hygiene was a collection of knowledges and practices assembled to keep the fundamental relations of capitalist modernity in place. Moreover, given its basic orientation toward placing elements in space, hygiene was an apparatus of apparatuses—a "heterogeneous ensemble of discourses" dedicated to judiciously coordinating spatial arrangements and circulations.[26]

Hygiene and cinema met on the messy terrain of urban visuality. By the first decade of the twentieth century, cinema was a significant presence in German cities. Theaters dedicated to the screening of films popped up everywhere, but the cinematic imaginary also infiltrated public space in the form of posters, magazines, and newspaper advertisements. Cinema embodied the modern commercial trade in visual experience, using the film camera to offer up the visible world to paying mass audiences. For its part, hygiene was also intensely interested in producing visibility. For hygienists, urban environmental disorder was also a source of perceptual disorder, a hindrance to visibility, which made the former more difficult to combat. To maintain a healthy environment, one had to be able to identify what was out of place. Additionally, many experts considered perceptual disorder in the environment itself directly unhealthy, in that excessive stimuli could strain the senses. Ordering an environment hygienically thus entailed not only containing harmful materials, but producing a space conducive to acts of visual observation and inspection.[27] The well-known slogan "light and air" encapsulated this double emphasis, in that their presence benefited the body while also enabling hygienic observation.

Hygiene employed a deterministic concept of the environment, akin to what in biology was also called "milieu."[28] At the same time, it was uniquely aware of the dynamic nature of environments, which are constantly perceived, interpreted, and transformed by the living things within them. In this respect, hygiene resonates with the biologist Jakob von Uexküll's notion of *Umwelt*. Formulated around 1900 and often translated as "environment," *Umwelt* attends to the way an organism's sensorimotor capacities construct a perceptual world, which in turn informs the organism's possible modes of action. For Uexküll, different species inhabit qualitatively different *Umwelten*, given that their bodily and sensory abilities differ. Hygiene brought concepts of milieu and *Umwelt* into relation, understanding environments as simultaneously the material foundation of life and as perceptual worlds whose contours implied certain possibilities of interpretation and action. Unlike Uexküll, however, hygiene posited a malleable perceptual world, which could be more or less transparent to the senses depending on how it was constructed and regulated.

And as Inga Pollmann has shown, Uexküll's concept was also generative for early twentieth-century critics who were exploring the effects of film and other technological media on the sensory environment of modernity. For writers like Walter Benjamin, the theory of *Umwelt* broached questions "which were central to film theory in the 1910s and 1920s: the role of perception as the sensible link between body and environment, and world-creation as the active shaping of and engagement with our environment."[29] Hygiene and film shared a concern with how the perceptual world of *Umwelt* interacted with the environment as milieu. Hygiene sought to create a normative relation between the two, reforming the perceptual environment so as to better control the milieu. Film, however, with its unique possibilities of apprehending the world and presenting it to the viewer, could play with the body-environment relation in ways that exceeded the normalizing impulse of hygiene.

Overview

I argue that a complete account of cinema's relation to modernity should include the project of hygiene. This book is thus an inquiry into the ordering and disordering potentials of a medium within a particular cultural context. Film, its exhibition, and its production were rife with the potential for material disorder that could impact health—a fact that made it both highly modern, given cinema's industrial character and mass appeal, as well as, from the perspective of health experts, dangerously primitive. In other words, cinema embodied a uniquely modern atavism of the sort that hygiene was developed to correct. As a result, the institutional sites and aesthetic codes of cinema took shape in dialogue with the logic and practice of modern hygiene. At the same time, film could be used for hygienic ends. It could communicate expert-authorized knowledge to a mass public, but it could also train viewers in hygienic modes of looking and reshape their relationship to the environments they inhabited. In this instance, film functioned as a modernizing force, a *Kulturtechnik* or "cultural technique" that aimed to raise mass audiences from an ostensibly more natural state to a more civilized one.[30] Even as hygiene put film into its proper place, however, filmmakers of the Weimar period reflected on the aesthetic and ideological assumptions underlying hygiene's vision of a stable social order, and engaged cinematic effects that resisted its civilizing mission.

I situate hygiene within the broader effort to manage industrial modernity through the development and application of scientific knowledge. During the Weimar Republic, as Detlev Peukert has shown, this effort was discussed in terms of "rationalization." The Weimar rationalization debates of the mid-1920s, according to Peukert, concerned three main areas of modern social life: industrial production, architecture and urban planning, and lifestyle. With engineering as a model, advocates of rationalization projected "the efficient, scientific-technical organization of production processes . . . onto the objectification of social relations oriented toward the common good."[31] Rationalization promised to calm the sometimes violent dislocations of industrial modernity through the technocratic management of social life. "If Weimar was famously a time of 'great disorder,' " Andreas Killen writes, "it was also one in which Germans were continually exhorted, by doctors, welfare officials, and policy makers, to remake themselves and their society in accordance with new norms and ideals."[32] As the history of hygiene demonstrates, the goal of rationalizing society reached back into the nineteenth century, even if it was not discussed in those terms.

Hygiene can be considered an important precursor to and, subsequently, a component of, Weimar-era rationalization, a lineage reflected in the centrality of health as a common ideal. From the late nineteenth century onward, hygiene experts made far-reaching interventions, with varying levels of success, in each of the areas of rationalization that Peukert identifies. Moreover, by conceiving of health in terms of the population's labor power (*Arbeitskraft*), hygiene helped enable the projection of industrial-capitalist efficiency onto the whole of social life. "Health" in this sense functioned as a flexible and shifting ideal that could both appeal to a lay populace and orient expert knowledge across many disciplines, which could then create guidelines for how to build and run factories, how to direct urban development, and how to live one's day-to-day life—and moreover, in such a way that all of these activities were understood as harmonizing with each other. In this way hygiene had a powerful integrative function, as William Rollins notes, "in an era when Germans were unsettled by rapid economic reversals and riven by growing political fragmentation; across the divides of class and confession, the bottom-line ethic of health, hygiene, and performance increasingly enjoyed widespread and uncritical acceptance."[33] Hygiene was the human facade to rationalization's mechanical heart, that aspect of rationalization concerned with ensuring the well-being of the population. Hygiene, by linking rationalization with human health, provided the former with a rationale, a supposed purpose or benefit one could point to beyond mere efficiency and productivity for their own sake.

In recent books, Killen and Michael Cowan have traced the ways that cinema participated in the administration of social life during the Weimar Republic. Killen's *Homo Cinematicus* traces the entanglement of cinema and the human sciences, particularly psychiatry, as these strove to establish their legitimacy as participants in the project of governing human intercourse. Cowan's book on the filmmaker Walter Ruttmann turns to modernity's disorderly informational landscape, whose accumulation of text, images, and sounds demanded its own technologies of management.[34] In *The Hygienic Apparatus* I hope to complement such histories, enriching our picture of cinema's relationship to the perceived disorder of modernity by attending to the latter's environmental dimensions. Like the historical projects discussed by Killen and Cowan, hygiene strove to produce a kind of order, which in turn was meant to stabilize social life. The order envisioned by hygiene was an environmental or material order, which entailed regulating the circulation of bodies, materials, and energies in smaller-scale environments with discrete social functions (the home, the factory), but also the linkages between these environments into an overall urban system. "The hygienist city," writes Matthew Gandy, "conceived of urban space as an identifiable assemblage of organs: a functional whole that could be shaped and controlled according to a rationalized conception of human will."[35] Hygienic experts were faced with the question of how to integrate the unruly medium of film into the urban organism.

Illuminating the encounter between hygiene and cinema inevitably leads beyond a discussion of mainstream feature films to nonfictional and mixed modes of filmmaking, as well as the material practices involved in film exhibition and production. Consonant with a widening of perspective in film studies beyond the fictional text, *The Hygienic Apparatus* analyzes feature films as well as various kinds of educational films aimed at both popular and specialist audiences. The latter represent the extent to which film during the Weimar Republic was not just an entertainment medium, but was used to communicate expertise and manage social life.[36] Moreover, comparing feature and educational films enables a better grasp of the work each did to intervene in the domain of the visual.

Because hygiene was an eminently practical discipline that was especially interested in modern forms of architecture and technology, this book also deals with film exhibition and production. Chapter 1, "The Hygienic Dispositif," begins with the movie theater. Early critical discourse on movie theaters saw them not just as moral or social threats, but as a material threat to bodily health. Given their architectural novelty and growing presence in the urban landscape, hygienically minded experts scrutinized movie theaters for signs of environmental disorder, and, later, imagined what an ordered theater environment might look like. First, I assess the role that fears of darkness, contamination, and contagion in movie theaters played in early critical discussions of cinema in the 1910s. Concerns about the environmental conditions of movie theaters echoed bourgeois hygienic approaches to the broader "social question," while setting the stage for modernizing impulses during the Weimar Republic. The logic of hygiene also informed fire safety regulations. If social reformers stressed the cinema's similarity to the working-class tenement, municipal regulators zeroed in on its material specificity, as a unique architectural form involving circulations of matter, energy, and bodies. To integrate movie theaters into a broader public safety regime, regulators needed to understand the precise workings of the cinema environment. Finally, I examine film industry discussions in the mid-1920s about movie theater design, which inherited an emphasis on hygienic principles from modernist architecture. Opposing the ostentatious aesthetic of 1920s movie palaces, these hygienists of the cinema wished to produce exhibition spaces that were efficient and therapeutic, spaces of bodily regeneration rather than fatigue. In their own ways, social reform, public safety regulation, and modernist theater design all considered the movie theater a space of potential material disorder in need of hygienic modernization.

The encounter between film and hygiene in early twentieth-century Germany can also be understood as part of a biopolitical history of modern technological media. In recent historiography and cultural analysis, Foucault's concept of a politics of the population that sought to analyze and regulate "propagation, births and mortality, the level of health, life expectancy and longevity, with all the conditions that can cause these to vary" has provided a framework for thinking across the caesuras of modern German history, in which one can find unexpected continuities amid significant differences.[37] Scholars have traced biopolitical ambitions in starkly different political and economic contexts, from Social Darwinism, eugenics, and race science to social welfare programs, cultures of athletics, and struggles over reproductive rights. Media of all sorts have played important roles in biopolitical projects, by producing images of bodies and populations, legitimating expertise, inculcating the value of physical and mental health, transmitting racial ideologies, demonstrating habits of bodily care, and much more.

After World War I, the biopolitical project of reconstructing the body of the German nation employed film as a tool of communication and pedagogy. Medical experts and urban planners imagined a place for cinema within the apparatus of hygiene itself. The war was responsible not only for millions of casualties on the front but significantly higher rates of disease, malnutrition, and death at home. Its final months included outbreaks of a deadly influenza pandemic. This period of death and contagion that haunted Weimar culture in so many ways also made health a national mission.[38] In pursuing this mission, cultural authorities turned to a medium they had previously treated only as an object for regulation and reform. As scholars like Killen and Anja Laukötter have shown, health education films played an important role in propagandizing medical expertise and modern images of the healthy body during the Weimar period.[39] In chapter 2, "Hygienic Modernization," I examine a related set of films that emphasized the relationship between health and the material environment, and promoted the benefits of modern design and urban planning. Some of these films, directed to mass audiences, taught individual viewers their role in producing and maintaining healthy environments, both in and outside the home. They linked hygienic environmental order to a social order defined by norms of gender, age, and ability. Other films, targeted more narrowly at practitioners and bureaucrats, asserted the authority of design and planning experts over the spaces of daily life and framed the ordering of the material environment within a project of hygienic modernization, which promised to reconcile industrialization with the physical wellness of human beings. Film thus served the hygienic project by bolstering the legitimacy of expertise, teaching viewers to see and act hygienically, and showing them how they fit within the broader environmental order of industrial modernity.

Educational films (*Kulturfilme*) like these bear witness to a kind of proto-environmental or ecological reasoning. In the past couple of decades, scholars working in environmental history and the environmental humanities have traced the origins of German environmental politics in Romantic reactions to modernity, the Heimat conservation movement, smoke abatement campaigns, and more.[40] In these genealogies of ecological thought, ideas of nature and landscape play a central role, as that whose destruction motivates attachment, protest, and defense. Films like those discussed in chapter 1 point toward a different mode of environmental imagination, one less invested in preserving nature than in establishing order. Or, rather, the nature which hygiene defends is not that of wilderness, in opposition to civilization, or even that of *Heimat* or cultural landscape (*Kulturlandschaft*). Hygiene's nature is organismic or thermodynamic—it is a material-energetic system or assemblage of organs that reproduces itself in metabolic exchange with an external environment. Fundamentally, it matters little whether such an organism or system is artificial or not, but that it assumes a stable form over time. If it works, self-reproduces, lives, stays healthy—it is natural. In this sense, hygiene was concerned with mastering the nature of industrial modernity, its functioning as a material system.

Hygiene in this modern sense was the practice of health in a thermodynamic world, an age in which energy served as the universal currency of all processes of material transformation. In addition to energy, however, thermodynamics also formulated the law of entropy, the tendency of energy to dissipate over time. This fact of dissipation took concrete form as byproducts of industrial production such as the smoke and dust released by factories, coal-burning stoves, and the grinding of wheels on roads and dirt. These prototypical enemies of hygiene—economically unproductive, difficult to see and contain, often damaging to human health—represented, as Anson Rabinbach writes, "the decrescent order of fatigue, exhaustion, and decline" with which industrial society inevitably contended.[41] They were also aesthetically fascinating. Chapter 3, "Matter Out of Place," analyzes F. W. Murnau's 1926 film *Faust*, whose mise-en-scène is suffused with particulate materials like smoke, dust, and fog. The film crafts a visual language out of the disorderly matter whose environmental presence the project of modern hygiene strove to contain and eliminate. I read Murnau's cinematic visualization of the Faust tale as a rumination on the thermodynamic conundrum of industrialization, which, as it pursues higher forms of order through ever greater expenditures of energy, leaves more and more disorder in its wake. The film also aligns the drifting of particulate matter with both the protagonist's floating attention and the movement of the unchained camera, positing the cinema as a site of subjective dispersion.

Murnau's foggy particulate aesthetics also made unique use of the film studio, an architectural environment more typically devoted to producing visual clarity. As such, *Faust* points to the hygienic principles that informed the dominant practices of studio-based film production. Working at the intersection of film history and the environmental humanities, scholars such as Brian R. Jacobson and Jennifer Fay have examined the material practices of studio film production practice in the context of modernity's conquest of nature.[42] In addition to cinema's imbrication with extractive industry, Jacobson writes, "the film studio embodies . . . cinema's broader worldmaking ambitions—an anthropocentric desire to control and simulate the nonhuman world."[43] In a similar vein, Fay claims provocatively that "insofar as cinema has encouraged the production of artificial worlds and simulated, wholly anthropogenic weather, it is the aesthetic practice of the Anthropocene."[44] My analysis of *Faust* supports these claims, but considering hygiene as an environment-making practice draws attention to ways that film production involved managing the materiality of the human world as well—a conquest of second nature. The film's exceptional use of particulates foregrounds the extent to which the modern film studio usually functioned as a hygienic apparatus, designed to screen out the smoke, dust, and noise of the industrial city. This translated into a dominant aesthetic of environmental transparency in the film image itself, which prized clear distinctions between bodies and their surroundings on screen. In other words, the material practices of studio film production and the images these produced resonated in fundamental ways with the hygienic imaginary.

The hygienic ideal of environmental order was one in which human bodies could carry out the functions necessary for life without hindrance. This ideal inevitably privileged certain bodies over others, for two reasons: hygiene's methodological reliance on statistical norms of the human body, and its equation of health with labor power. Those whose bodies were outside of the norm or were not able to perform the kinds of work dominant in industrial society challenged hygiene's aim of managing environments to optimize health and economic productivity for the population as a whole. Chapter 4, "Bodies Out of Place," examines representations of disability and aging in Weimar-era film that speak to the question of whom the urban environment was actually for. I look at examples of documentary film that portray aging and disabled people as both unfit for modern environments and as themselves sources of material disorder, who make these spaces less efficient, in order to advocate for specialized institutional settings that can accommodate them. Hygiene's ethic of enlightened care for people whom industrialization and urbanization have pushed to the margins was bound up with a logic of containment that segregated in the name of efficiency. Fictional films like Karl Grune's *The Street* (1923) and Murnau's *The Last Laugh* (1924), meanwhile, focus on subjective experiences of environmental marginalization and disorientation. These films reflect how changes in work and the built world produced new exclusions, but also use the camera as a surrogate eye to mimic the experience of being out-of-place vis-à-vis one's environment. They model cinema as an anti-hygienic, intoxicating apparatus that resists integration into the ideals of efficiency, sobriety, and vigilant awareness.

This chapter also points to the link between early twentieth-century environmental discourse and the concerns of eugenics. In addition to valorizing the laboring body, they shared a critique of the modern environment as a source of disability. One strain of argument against the damaging environmental conditions created by industrial modernity focused on how they led not just to premature death but to an increased incidence of disability and long-term illness. For eugenicists, this represented a weakening or "degeneration" of the population, and was therefore a reason to improve hygienic conditions. Although hygiene and eugenics often conflicted, for instance in their conceptions of who properly belonged to "the population," or the extent to which they emphasized environment or inheritance, a conception of industrial modernity as a disabling force was a major point of articulation between the two. A eugenic environmental critique consequently inflected discussions of film and movie theaters as well. Particularly vociferous critics portrayed cinema as a disabling apparatus, whose sensational images presented in darkness could permanently damage the psyches of young viewers.

Eugenics and racial hygiene won influence in public health discourse during the Weimar Republic, especially after the onset of economic crisis at the end of the 1920s. Austerity precipitated a shift away from environmental reform, since this often required significant investment. The state even disinvested from the sort of therapeutic institutions discussed in chapter 4, and instead directed its support toward people considered more (or potentially more) productive. In this climate of scarcity, advocates of sexual and racial hygiene gained discursive authority because these disciplines located pathology in individual bodies, rather than in the material environment or political economy. Chapter 5, "Landscapes of Exploitation," turns to oppositional films made in Weimar's leftist milieu that attempted to reassert the hygienic, environmental critique of urban modernity while also revising and politicizing it. Semi-documentary or newsreel-style films like *Hunger in Waldenburg* (Phil Jutzi, 1929) and *How the Worker Lives* (Slatan Dudow, 1930) borrowed from the visual repertoire of the *Kulturfilm* while using montage editing to place the phenomenon of urban environmental disorder into the context of class exploitation and antagonism. Dudow's film *Kuhle Wampe* (1932), cowritten with Bertolt Brecht, examines the meaning of Berlin's green periphery amid the economic desperation of the late Weimar Republic. Rather than regenerative leisure, as in hygiene's therapeutic conception of green space, *Kuhle Wampe* finds both involuntary migrants living out an empty simulation of their previous lives and political actors imagining a new collective. Together, these films point to the limits of the hygienic apparatus, which could no longer stabilize a contradictory economic system that had eaten away its own foundations. At the same time, they borrow elements of the hygienic imaginary—particularly its emphases on expert authority and bodily fitness—that inject a tension into their emancipatory project.

My thinking about cinema's relation to hygiene has been informed by recent histories of governance, particularly around public health, that trace the interaction of material infrastructures, forms of expertise, and concrete, everyday practices. As Tom Crook writes, modern governance "is a matter of discourse and practice: a combination of cultural-intellectual *and* material-logistical forces."[45] From this perspective, cinema is a fascinating nexus of the discursive, the material, and the practical. It is a form of representation that is uniquely reliant on architecture, infrastructure, and forms of material-logistical expertise, both in its production and exhibition. Throughout the writing of this book, I have tried to articulate how these various levels of meaning, action, and materiality are connected. This has meant reaching beyond my training in German and film studies, which emphasized semiotics and aesthetics over technical systems. If the following chapters reflect a privileging of meaning and aesthetic experience over materiality, they nonetheless demonstrate how cinema contributed to a particularly modern imagination of environmental order, as well as how that imagination shaped the cinema. I hope that this book can spur further thought into the reciprocal relationships between modern media and projects of governance, especially by those with more specialized expertise in technological systems than myself.

This is not a story of how cinema became hygienic. Systems of governance were and are never total. For Crook, the modernity of governance "inheres not in a particular outcome or solution, but in the way in which an administrative problem . . . is posed, practiced, and reformed: or, to put it another way, in open-ended processes of modern order*ing*, rather than the attainment of order as such, or movement toward a particular endpoint or telos."[46] Rather than posit a linear convergence, the following chapters investigate cinema's encounter with a particular form of modern governance: the ordering of the material world that often went by the name "hygiene." Projects like hygiene often generated totalizing visions—such as Benjamin Ward Richardson's sanitary utopia "Hygeia"—but such visions never reflected reality.[47] Experts disagreed among themselves, and often did not have direct access to the political and economic resources to transform visions into reality. Moreover, the range of knowledges and systems involved made their coordination incredibly complex. And ironically, in defining new forms of material order in different domains and at different scales, the developing knowledges that underpinned this new mode of governance generated new possibilities for disorder as well. Perhaps most fundamentally, hygiene was limited by always having to play catch-up to the conditions being created by industrial capitalism, whose functioning it served to maintain and make more efficient. Consequently, cinema's encounter with the hygienic apparatus was multidirectional and multivalent. So, while the book begins by showing how cinema participated in the hygienic project and was in certain ways shaped by it, I increasingly move toward aesthetic, material, and political modes of excess or resistance to it. As much as film could conform to and serve the aims of environmental order, it opened onto uniquely modern forms of dis-ordering as well.

Chapter 1

✦

The Hygienic Dispositif

Health and the Movie Theater Environment

Accounts of early twentieth-century cinema typically foreground the medium's disruptive social and cultural presence. Film enabled new forms of dynamic visual and temporal experience that reverberated throughout the arts, particularly in modernism and the avant-garde. In Germany, it provoked anxiety about the status of theater and literature in national culture. The movies introduced a new domain of social representation in which hierarchies of class, race, gender, and sexuality were reproduced or challenged, and opened new avenues of communication for politicians, scientists, and advertisers. Movie theaters became part of the fabric of urban life and generated new kinds of social encounter.

Film and the crowds it drew, however, also constituted a new material presence. "New cinemas are springing up everywhere, like mushrooms overnight," wrote the cinema reformer Adolf Sellmann in 1912, amid a boom in movie theater construction in Germany. "One can no longer imagine our big cities at night without the brightly lit entrances to the cinemas."[1] Movie theaters were part of a broader transformation of the urban sensory environment, which would be more and more defined by artificial illumination and the distractions of advertising. They also had the potential to change the social and material characteristics of the surrounding locale, as gathering points for large crowds, or, more ominously, as sites of fire danger and urban panic. From a hygienic perspective, movie theaters were thus also a potential source of environmental disorder that could endanger health.

In this chapter I explore how hygienic concepts of environmental order and disorder influenced early German discourse on the movie theater, from the 1910s into the Weimar period. A concern for the link between health and the material environment connected proponents and critics of the cinema, from prewar advocates of cinema reform (*Kinoreform*) to architects and designers of the movie-palace era. Health and safety served as ideals that grounded the claims of various kinds of experts—in housing hygiene, in municipal regulation, in the design of modern consumer environments—to exercise authority over the space of the movie theater and its operation. There were significant differences in how these experts framed the cinema environment and its effects, however, as well as how they proposed to intervene in its functioning. For some it was a space of moral and physical danger, for others a site of replenishment and regeneration. As such, these various expert approaches illuminate different ways in which the movie theater as a viewing dispositif encountered the broader discursive and regulatory apparatus of hygiene in early twentieth-century Germany.

By foregrounding hygiene as a particularly modern practice of environmental ordering, this chapter also complicates the assumed modernity of cinema found in many scholarly accounts. As Annemone Ligensa writes, "despite many factual connections between film and urban life . . . interpreting the new medium as *essentially* sharing the characteristics of modern urbanisation, especially its negative aspects, was itself a particular perception."[2] The modernity of cinema, in other words, was unstable and contested—it was not inherently modern, but had to be made so. Hygienic approaches to the movie theater framed cinema as primitive and proposed to modernize it by adapting its environment to the precepts of health.

Cinema and the Housing Question

Published in 1913, Victor Noack's short book *Der Kino: Etwas über sein Wesen und seine Bedeutung* (*Cinema: On Its Essence and Significance*) begins with a discussion of the "*Kientopp,*" the class of "improvised movie theater . . . that constitutes such a great danger for social ethics and morality as well as for the physical health of the people." He includes a vivid description of the typical interior of these working-class theaters:

> The benches are crammed tightly together and positioned on risers, so that the space between bench and ceiling becomes increasingly narrow. Seating is so tight that there is no space left between bodies: whereby—since, during the film, it's pitch dark between the benches—the sexual attacks on children and women reported in the daily news are made seductively easy. How many children spend their free time after school in the humid atmosphere of *Kientopps* instead of in the fresh air playing healthy games?[3]

Noack's claustrophobic image of the working-class movie theater linked the space's material characteristics to improper bodily proximity and contact. At best, low ceilings, packed seating, and poorly circulated air force moviegoers to violate norms of personal space; at worst, they provide tempting conditions for "sexual attacks" on vulnerable women and children. Noack lamented that such populations might spend their free time in such a dank, dark place, rather than in healthy outdoor air.

Noack's book, along with his other writings on the movies from this time, contributed to the German cinema reform movement that began around 1910. The movement coincided with a boom in urban movie theater construction and represented a middle-class, largely (though not wholly) conservative reaction against the perceived dangers of cinema to social cohesion and established structures of authority. Moral authorities, jurists, and scientific professionals railed against the effects of so-called trash films (*Schundfilme*) on the German population, agitated for a censorship regime, and advocated for the creation of a cinema that was pedagogical and national(ist).[4] Accounts of the German cinema reform movement have typically emphasized its bourgeois moral opposition to what its writers saw as lurid depictions of sex and crime, and the breakdown of social order these were seen to pose.

As Sabine Hake points out, however, depictions of the degraded conditions of working-class theaters were also a mainstay of cinema reform discourse. For Hake, such depictions served a rhetorical purpose for cinema reformers, for whom the unhygienic state of working-class theaters "functioned primarily as a metaphor for the state of the nation," which was "ailing in body and soul."[5] By the same token, focusing on these conditions linked cinema reform's anxieties about the body of the nation to a hygienic discourse possessed of increasing political authority. According to Andreas Killen, the cinema reform movement "became permeated by the hygienic paradigm that was steadily gaining ascendancy in many realms of social policy."[6] In this section, I read cinema reform accounts of the movie theater as one instance of a wider social reform discourse on urban socio-spatial crisis in Germany before World War I, which linked ill health, social antagonism, and moral decline to the environmental disorder of the modern city. For cinema reformers like Noack, movie theaters embodied some of the worst aspects of the urban environment. Below I delineate two central axes of cinema reform's hygienic anxiety—the traffic between bodies, and the traffic between body and movie screen—that reflected concerns among social reformers about the material composition of urban spaces and, specifically, working-class housing. For both cinema reform and the broader reform movement of which it was a part, the idiom of hygiene lent empirical authority to moral objections to modern working-class life; at the same time, it helped transform the material environment of urban modernity (including the cinema) into an object of regulation, a medium through which purportedly vulnerable populations and the social problems with which they were associated could be managed.

Over the course of the nineteenth century, industrialization drew huge numbers of people into cities at an ever-increasing rate. In the last three decades before 1900, the majority of German cities expanded their population between 100 and 200 percent.[7] This rapid population growth was compounded by speculative real estate markets and insufficient planning, all of which led to an acute housing shortage. By the turn of the twentieth century, urban working-class neighborhoods were dominated by tenements, or so-called rental barracks (*Mietskasernen*); these were relatively tall buildings packed into the available real estate, in which the majority of apartments were set back from the street and received little sunlight. Large families crowded into small apartments and often took on lodgers to make up for high rents. These rental barracks, with their lightless courtyard apartments and dank basement apartments, became a major topic in reform discourse around 1900. Applying the logic of hygiene to working-class living conditions, pre-war social reformers identified the material environment of the tenement as the source of a range of social and medical ills, from sexual immorality to mental fatigue and disease. Social critics, reformers, and hygienists decried their conditions and searched for ways to manage what they perceived as a crisis of social reproduction among the urban working class.

For hygienic experts, morbidity and mortality were the paramount concern. For most of the nineteenth century, mortality rates in the cities exceeded those in the country, and medical statistics noted especially higher rates of tuberculosis, which became known as a "proletarian disease."[8] Hygienists like Ferdinand Hueppe, in his contribution to *Weyl's Handbuch der Hygiene* (*Handbook of Hygiene*) on housing and health, blamed overfilled apartments and unsanitary living conditions for contributing to this state of affairs, and concluded that "poor housing conditions matter because they reduce resistance and because they facilitate infection, especially repeated or mass infections."[9] The material disorder of the rental barracks, hygienists claimed, was thus conducive to disease in a number of ways: lack of sunlight and stagnant, moist air allowed potentially harmful bacteria to grow unchecked; close bodily contact offered more opportunities for disease transmission; and, finally, these poor conditions wore down the body's resistance to infection.

The writings of Victor Noack exemplify the hygienic concern with bodily traffic in both movie theaters and other working-class spaces. Noack, who wrote the description of a working-class theater quoted above, clearly considered cinema part of the so-called "housing question." His cinema book was published in the series "Culture and Progress" as one of a group of contributions to the collection "Social Progress: Volumes on Economics, Social Policy, the Question of Women's Rights, Justice and Cultural Interests," which offered brief and affordable texts by experts on any number of modern social questions. The first book of Noack's to appear in the collection was actually *Schlafstelle und Chambre garni* (*Available Bed and Furnished Room*) in 1912, about the problem of working-class families taking on unmarried male lodgers because of high rents. Indeed, most of Noack's work from the 1910s into the 1920s dealt with housing issues, whether in relation to poverty, health, or sexual morality. In *Wohnungsnot und Mieterelend: Ein Erbstück des alten Staates* (*Housing Privation and Tenant Misery: An Inheritance of the Old State*), published in 1918 but written before the war, Noack offered a description of a courtyard apartment that echoed his picture of the working-class movie theater in many respects:

Berlin's courtyard apartments! Out of dark, cramped lodgings crammed full of people and crying children it wells up, taking your breath: cooking fumes, laundry vapors, oven and tobacco smoke, gassy emissions. A mixture of kitchen, living room, and lavatory fumes accumulates between the towering walls, which indeed stand pressed together as if forming a chimney; it pollutes the few square meters in the dark depths, euphemistically called the "courtyard," and eventually squeezes out of the opening way up above at the roof ridge. And yet the windows positioned along this shaft are open like the mouths of asthmatics. The people in the courtyard apartments live in much closer quarters than those in the street-facing flats. Professor Schmoller reported back in 1890 on Berlin's apartment barracks, inhabited by 250 families with 36 apartments on one floor! Here we find droves of tuberculosis, here infant mortality is rampant. Let's look into these so-called apartments, unworthy of the name, unfit to serve as human habitations.[10]

Here, as in the movie theater, a sense of claustrophobia dominates. The space is dark, constrained, and overfilled, not just with people but with noise and smells as well. Linking the social and material environment to illness and death, the author understands the tenement as a pathogenic space. Although the language of hygiene is more explicit here than in Noack's description of the working-class theater—there he only recommended in a footnote that "the 'German Central Committee to Combat Tuberculosis' . . . . [should] take a close look at these 'dens of infection'!"[11]—the similarities suggest he viewed the working-class movie theater a space of disease transmission as well.

Accounts of working-class movie theaters by middle-class commentators frequently mentioned smell, attributed to a lack of proper ventilation. In 1920, a moral reform group in Cologne included numerous olfactory details in their report about local cinemas: "The rooms are usually crowded, the ventilation insufficient, adults and youth smoke unimpeded, everything is shrouded in fumes and smoke mixed with perspiration and dubious aromas."[12] Passages like this use smell as an indicator of disease and echo reformers' accounts of visits to the rental barracks. By 1900, the so-called miasma theory of disease, which posited that disease was spread by way of tainted air, had been strongly contested by bacteriologists and other medical experts, but the link between sickness and smell was a staple of bourgeois hygiene and remained so into the twentieth century. The purportedly overwhelming smell of overcrowded industrial cities was often cited in efforts to build sewer systems and reform the practice of waste removal.[13] Like the dark and dank courtyard and basement apartments of the rental barracks, the odors that offended reformers at the movies indicated unhygienic conditions in need of observation and management.

After the war, which had severely reversed the progress made in the fight against tuberculosis, the social hygienist Friedrich Lorenz worried about public spaces that served as "breeding grounds for the spread of tuberculosis," and specifically "the upholstered seats with their dark interstices that one encounters in trains, theaters, public houses and especially in dark cinemas with their ever-changing mass audiences."[14] In other words, part of the hygienic danger lay in cinema's public, or semi-public, character. Movie theaters were spaces that people inhabited, but only temporarily, leaving traces for others to inadvertently pick up, which made hygienic control difficult. For Noack and other housing reformers, the tenements were similarly problematic. As families shared apartments and rented out rooms, the home, by middle-class standards, was turned into another kind of semi-public space.

If close bodily proximity in crowded movie theaters worried reformers like Noack, the possibility of sexual contact triggered even greater anxiety. Much of the panic, of course, was driven by the desire to uphold bourgeois patriarchy and sexual morality, which were threatened by the specters of extramarital sex, extramarital pregnancy, and prostitution. Discourse on sex in movie theaters had a hygienic dimension as well—or, rather, in the reform imaginary around 1900, hygienic and moral reasoning were inextricable from each other, with each drawing on the cultural legitimacy of the other to stake claims on bodily practices and social life generally. Lack of hygiene, whether attributed to a person, a group, or a space they inhabited, also always signified moral decline. We can note, for instance, that Noack's concern about "sexual attacks" in movie theaters focused on the danger to women and the young, two groups frequently (and paternalistically) identified by hygienic reformers as key to social reproduction and in need of special protection. Noack worried about similar conditions in the overcrowded tenements, particularly when working-class families rented rooms to unwed men. He wrote that the presence of a lodger meant that "the incubatory state is ever present. The soil is fertile for sexual crimes. In the dark of bedrooms shared by the family of the head of the household and 'strangers' (boarders) without the separation of sexes, an incubus always commits his fiendish deeds."[15] Noack's use of the terms "incubation" and "incubus" links bacteriological dangers with a figure of sexual folklore. Like the cinema, the practice of renting rooms to people outside the family created a space that was, for reformers like Noack, simultaneously intimate and public; darkness and the proximity between non-family members provided the environmental conditions for sexual transgression, which Noack analogized to the way unhygienic spaces allow diseases to grow.

While expressing moral outrage in medicalized language, Noack's focus on environment and milieu reflects how hygienic reasoning was also often used to upend a moral logic that would blame sin on individual failings. For reformers concerned with the housing question, for instance, immorality was much more a symptom of unhygienic living conditions than their cause. Echoing arguments among criminologists around 1900 that emphasized the environmental causes of crime, seeing it as a product of inhabiting a disordered social milieu, Noack framed sexual crimes—whether in tenements or movie theaters—as crimes of opportunity, enabled by a combination of social and material factors.[16]

Prostitution was also a common motif in bourgeois descriptions of working-class cinemas. The Cologne report lamented the presence of "obvious streetwalkers, immediately recognizable by their behavior," on the hunt for moviegoing "victims."[17] Bourgeois critics objected to prostitution on moral and medical grounds, connecting sexual transgression with the spread of sexually transmitted disease. According to the bacteriologist Erich Wernicke, prostitution was itself exacerbated by unhygienic housing, insofar as it "flourishes especially well in the dark, the swamp, the whole milieu of unhygienic apartments alongside every possible misery."[18] Sex workers were thus objects of both moral and hygienic opprobrium in reform discourse; they were portrayed simultaneously as victims and perpetrators within the disordered milieu of the urban working class, and were regulated, however ineffectually, by municipal vice squads (*Sittenpolizei*).[19]

The link between prostitution and disease reflected a more general association between moral breakdown, contagion, and spaces of urban sociality. The bacteriologist Wilhelm von Drigalski attributed moviegoing, along with the enjoyment of other urban entertainments, to a lack of parental supervision that was aiding the spread of disease: "The increase in tuberculosis, as well as sexually transmitted diseases in particular, is directly related to the lack of sufficient supervision that in many families, even in 'educated circles,' has become acceptable to an incomprehensible degree," he wrote. "Unbridled addiction to pleasure (cinemas, visits to dubious pubs and dancing) fosters the spread of both infections."[20] Reform discourse cast working-class areas and urban entertainment districts as pathological environments, in which moral laxity and physical degeneration were mutually reinforcing symptoms of social disorder. Cinema reformers linked the space of film exhibition to these broader anxieties about the urban environment and the kinds of social, moral, and hygienic effects it produced, especially among parts of the population they deemed at risk.[21]

Contemporary scholarship has tended to discount hygienic concerns as a pretense for imposing bourgeois morality on an unruly working class. Hygiene certainly functioned to discipline working-class populations, both in the hands of scientific experts as well as moralists who wielded it as a rhetorical cudgel. Nonetheless, hygiene's concern for the material and ecological dimensions of industrial modernity gave the moral panic around cinema a different valence than similar alarm expressed at other popular media and their stigmatized enthusiasts, such as the novel and its female readership in the nineteenth century. This is not to say that hygiene did not buttress traditional forms of authority, gender relations, and class structures; but rather that the material environment played a new role in considerations about how to stabilize and reproduce the established order. The danger of catching tuberculosis at the movies may have been overblown, as even some cinema reformers admitted at the time, but such fears, when articulated in conjunction with class anxiety, also reflected a concern about urban epidemics that had some empirical foundation. Moreover, cinema reformers' initial concern with the material conditions of urban film exhibition framed subsequent discussions of the theater environment in the 1920s, which I outline in the final section of this chapter.

To conclude this section, however, I would like to turn from concerns about dangerous forms of traffic between bodies (whether sexual contact, disease transmission, or both) to a different axis of hygienic concern: the traffic between body and screen. In the movie theater, people not only experienced new forms of sociality, but also engaged in the new visual activity of cinematic spectatorship. From a hygienic perspective, the moving image was part of the theater environment, a material presence whose effects on the viewing body also had to be studied and managed. This also returns us to the question of censorship and film content, a parallel strain of debate among reformers and critics from the early 1910s onward.

For the psychiatrist Eugen Gaupp, the danger of cinema lay in a combination of factors that functioned to break down the psychic autonomy of the viewing subject. Compared to dime novels,

> the cinema, with its temporal concentration of events, has more damaging and nerve-shattering effects. When reading, we can stop as we like, critique the trash novel, and free ourselves from its hold through reflection. With the cinema it is another story. The rapid succession of images intensifies the pleasurable tension to an unbearable level; there is no time for contemplation and thus no time to compensate psychologically. For children and sensitive people alike, the horrific subject matter severely shakes the nervous system without giving us the means by which to defend our psyches against these attacks. When reading, very few people have a vivid enough imagination to perceive a three-dimensional version of the story, but cinema places everything before our eyes in physical form, and the milieu proves favorable to a deep suggestive power: the dark space, the monotone humming noise, and the power of the images all put the critical faculties to sleep. In this way, the drama's content turns into a fateful suggestion, which has its way with the powerless, capitulated psyche of the common man.[22]

In this passage, Gaupp addresses the temporality and photographic nature of the film medium; aspects of film form, such as editing; film content; the sensory environment of the movie theater; and the psychology of children, "sensitive people," and the "common man." The inexorable forward movement of the film strip subjects the viewer to its own temporality, while the quick progression from one image to the next wears down the ability of the viewer to adequately process meaning. Film's "plastic, corporeal view," meanwhile, makes it difficult for the viewer to deny the reality of the image and maintain awareness of the story's status as fiction. These qualities of the medium are only intensified by the "milieu" of the theater itself. Ultimately, the movie theater dispositif enables a dangerously unidirectional traffic from the screen to the viewing subject, whose mental faculties are rendered powerless to defend against the film's "horrific subject matter." A film's content penetrates along a route prepared by the medium in its exhibition context; in hygienic terms, the film infects its audience, whose immune system cannot resist the combined onslaught of the medium's material and formal properties when viewed in the suggestive environment of the theater.[23]

After World War I, the physician Waldemar Schweisheimer likewise worried about the combination of suggestive films with a theater environment that lowered inhibitions—specifically, that certain kinds of films could lead to greater promiscuity, and thus higher rates of sexually transmitted disease. His 1920 book *Die Bedeutung des Films für die soziale Hygiene und Medizin* (*Film's Significance for Social Hygiene and Medicine*) advocated using cinema for the purpose of mass health education, but noted that some film producers have used the rubric of the *Aufklärungsfilm* (sexual enlightenment film) as a cover to trade in sensational depictions of sex. Such films, which Schweisheimer dubs *Animierfilme* (from the verb *animieren*, to "stimulate" or "incite"), "achieve precisely the opposite of worthwhile hygienic goals; they contribute in their effects to the undermining and weakening of public health."[24] He took the prefix *Animier-* from another site of modern, urban hygienic concern, the so-called *Animierbars* which were imagined to encourage sexual promiscuity, "because some young people have their first sexual experiences in bars of this type."[25] Relating a case in which a young girl was seduced by a man sitting next to her after watching a purported *Aufklärungsfilm*, Schweisheimer wrote that these films "entice, arouse by their allure . . . inhibitions fall: the result is the encouragement of indiscriminate promiscuity of the sexes and thus the certain increase in sexually transmitted infections."[26] Given such effects on public health, Schweisheimer argued that the term *Aufklärungsfilm* should be subject to legal regulation and oversight by a central body that included medical experts, so that false ideas about sexual hygiene could be kept out of the public sphere.[27] Indeed, sexual enlightenment films were central objects of discussion as the Reichstag debated what would become the 1920 film censorship law, though most lawmakers were not as careful as Schweisheimer to distinguish between *Aufklärungsfilme* and *Animierfilme*.[28]

Regulation of the theater environment and the regulation of film production through censorship or other means were two parts of the larger question of the social hygienic effects of cinema. Reformers like Noack, Schweisheimer, and Gaupp framed the movie theater as a potentially pathogenic space, alongside other spaces of urban pathology like the tenement or the bar. Cinema differed from these other spaces, however, in that its particular environment served as the framing condition for powerfully suggestive stories of sex and crime, stories that might encourage hygienically dangerous behavior both in the theater itself and beyond. Hygienic concern with the theater environment was thus bound up with anxieties about the circulation of certain kinds of stories and images within a disordered urban milieu, anxieties that the censorship regime established in 1920 aimed in part to address. The reformist impulse thus succeeded in instituting the censorship of films at a national level after World War I, a concrete success that impacted what kinds of moving images could circulate in the public sphere. Though they succeeded in making health a central theme in ongoing discussions of film exhibition and spectatorship, the reform critiques of the 1910s ultimately had little immediate impact on the material conditions of popular film exhibition. In the next section, I examine a different category of potential health risk at the movie theater that directly shaped the theater environment in crucial ways.

Cinema and Public Safety

In the 1914 book *Lichtspieltheater: Eine Sammlung ausgeführter Kinohäuser in Gross-Berlin (Movie Theaters: A Collection of Completed Cinema Houses in Metropolitan Berlin)*, the architect Hans Schliepmann framed his topic with some remarks on the material properties of film:

> The film strip, often several hundred meters long, is made of celluloid, produced from guncotton (trinitrocellulose) and camphor, which means it is extremely flammable. A burning cigar is enough to set off an explosion-like blaze. During projection, the image passes through the beam from the light source very near to the hottest point, and since our lamp also produces substantial heat, every image would burst immediately into flame if it remained still for even a second in front of this hot spot. Here was an extraordinarily great danger that had to be addressed.[29]

Schliepmann's sobering reflection emphasized the risky nature of film projection. By putting a flammable material into close proximity with a heat source, one was asking for trouble; all the more when one invited hundreds, or even thousands, of people to watch it happen. Nonetheless, Schliepmann reassured the reader that "thanks to police interventions, safety in cinemas leaves absolutely *nothing more to be desired*, as they are often inspected for compliance with regulations."[30] Having calmed the reader's fears, Schliepmann began his richly illustrated account of movie theaters, which by World War I were just beginning to be considered seriously by architects and architecture critics. From Schliepmann's perspective as an architectural critic, the dynamic of danger and safety, of risk and containment, framed the entire enterprise of cinema exhibition—the catastrophic risk of fire had to be controlled before the cinematic experience as he understood it could begin. As James Leo Cahill has written, "the specter of disaster haunted the early reception of cinema."[31]

In this section, I examine aspects of the municipal regulatory regime that developed to govern movie theaters in Germany beginning around 1910, which worked to minimize the risks of dangerous phenomena like fire. Although contemporary with the cinema reform movement, and similarly concerned with curbing urban environmental disorder, this discursive formation differed in significant ways and embodied a different strand of hygienic thought and practice. Cinema reform approached the movies from the perspective of the larger social question, and was therefore concerned with their potential long-term effects on social reproduction: from this perspective, the theater's environmental disorder mattered because it made the population sicker, mentally weaker, less morally disciplined, and less able to work. Cinema reformers decried harms that occurred gradually, through repeated visits to the movies. By contrast, movie theater regulations addressed punctual, catastrophic harms, such as fires and stampedes. Moreover, they were agnostic about what occurred outside the theater itself, or rather, beyond the theater's interface with adjacent streets and buildings. Such regulation was meant to produce a kind of traffic safety in and around the movie theater, preventing catastrophic accidents by managing how bodies, materials, and energy circulated within it. We might say that, rather than public health, the regulatory governance of movie theaters addressed matters of public safety—risks of disastrous mass death and injury (keeping in mind that these are matters of health, too). Theater regulation had important consequences for the arrangement of the cinematic dispositif.

Fire had certainly plagued theaters before 1900. In his 1913 chronicle *Die Welt in Flammen* (*The World in Flames*), the Hannover fire commissioner Gustav Effenberger recounted "a history of the great and interesting fires throughout the centuries," divided tellingly into chapters on city fires, church fires, and theater fires. This latter chapter begins with a fitting quotation of a poem by Johann Wolfgang von Goethe:

> "What then is a theater?"
> I know quite precisely
> you cram the most flammable things together
> then it's soon ablaze.[32]

Along with epidemics, fires were an archetypal urban catastrophe, a kind of thermodynamic contagion that could spread quickly in densely built urban spaces. Fire and disease, panic and revolt: battling these pathologies was the project of early modern risk-management practices. Towns in the early modern period, writes Michel Foucault, "posed new and specific economic and political problems of government technique."[33] The town was a "place of revolt" and a "site of miasmas and death," and mechanisms of security—state regulation and policing—arose in response to these potential catastrophes.[34] Theaters had long been objects of such regulatory scrutiny because of the dangers they posed to crowds and the surrounding infrastructure, a scrutiny that carried over to movie theaters when they started popping up in German cities.

As Nitzan Lebovic and Andreas Killen point out, industrial modernity generated new kinds of potential accidents, forms of knowledge to assess risk, and methods for avoiding or mitigating the damage of accidents—all with the aim of fostering health at the level of the population.[35] The material and technological properties of the film medium, however, posed specific risks not found in traditional theaters. Movie theaters, by design, employed highly flammable synthetic material and powerful artificial illumination, products of industrialization that made them, from a regulatory perspective, comparable to factories. In many ways, nineteenth-century scientific hygiene inherited the early modern project of urban risk management, and the branch of occupational or industrial hygiene was particularly attentive to the danger of fire or explosion in factories and other workplaces. While also potentially exposing workers to poisonous substances and harsh temperatures, factory production made use of materials that, if not handled carefully, could combust—that is to say, combust when they were not supposed to, given that industrialization was premised on combustion. In a chapter from the *Handbook of Hygiene* on "Dangers to Workers as a Result of Work and Physical Factors," K. B. Lehmann devoted a significant section to "fire and explosion hazards," noting that "all operations where large quantities of *flammable materials* are amassed—hay, straw, spun yarn fibers, oil, varnish, celluloid, gasoline, benzol, petroleum, spirits, ether, etc.—constitute a considerable fire hazard. Gasoline alone causes a huge number of fires and explosions with numerous deaths annually."[36] Cinemas were simultaneously theaters and industrial image factories that combined old dangers with new ones.

Movie theater fires were initially regulated under existing laws dealing with theater construction, but gradually, the specificities of celluloid, the practice of film exhibition, and the material environment of the movie theater generated a risk mitigation regime that was particular to cinema. A look at the annual administrative reports of the Berlin fire service shows how movie theaters were constituted as a discrete risk category that necessitated specific attention, expert knowledge, and regulation. In the report for the 1908 fiscal year, "cinematographs" (*Kinematographen*) were named for the first time as a specific responsibility of one of the fire service's commissions. Alongside movie theaters, the commission for building safety regulation oversaw warehouses, theaters, circuses, churches, schools, and other gathering places.[37]

The identification of movie theaters as a type of building in need of regulation came in the wake of the first wave of permanent cinemas in Germany, which began around 1905. Before then cinemas had been primarily itinerant, but by 1908 simple storefront cinemas (*Ladenkinos*) serving predominantly urban, working-class audiences were outselling itinerant cinemas by four-to-one.[38] The small addition of cinematographs to the 1908 Berlin fire service report indicates that movie theaters had, for municipal authorities at least, become a recognizable part of the urban environment that they felt was likely to endure.

Because theatrical spectacle often involved fire or other kinds of potentially dangerous artificial illumination, traditional theaters in Germany were often subject to regular observation by municipal fire services.[39] Theater safety was a regular part of the Berlin fire service's administrative reports, which included tables of which theaters were observed and how often, along with accounts of specific fire events. Although cinemas were not listed in the same way and were apparently not subject to the same type of regular observation, beginning in 1909 the reports listed "unusual incidents in cinematograph theaters." The 1909 report described seven movie theater fires, all but one of which occurred in the projection room.[40] Indeed, the list suggests that the fire service was also starting to conceive of the movie theater as the site of a specific category of event: the projector fire. The projector both embodied cinema's industrial character and represented the most crucial pathogenic node of the movie theater environment, the point at which catastrophe might originate and spread.

In Berlin, codified regulation began in January 1912 with the city's first "fire safety measures" dealing specifically with cinemas: one ordinance regulated the placement of advertising placards at entrances to movie theaters, and another addressed the "elimination of motors used in film projection." Until then, movie theaters in Berlin would have been regulated under the 1909 "Police ordinance for the construction, interior furnishing, and operation of theaters, public meeting halls, and circus installations," or, before that, this ordinance's 1889 predecessor. The January 1912 regulations were succeeded by the "Police ordinance of May 6, 1912 regarding safety in cinematograph theaters."[41] This ordinance represented a crucial regulatory step which, in the Berlin context, codified the difference between movie theaters and other types of theaters.

This difference was reinforced by the decision, that same year, to shift responsibility for movie theaters from the building safety commission to the commission for sites of industry (*Betriebsstätten*). Rather than other settings of popular spectacle, the Berlin fire service placed cinemas alongside "factories, lumberyards, combustion plants, chimney sweeping, drugstores, pharmacies, warehouses for liquid oxygen or carbonic acid," and "warehouses for celluloid and explosives."[42] This categorization suggests that the fire service considered movie theaters essentially factories, where potentially dangerous materials were continually stored and used for production, often through intense but controlled exposure to heat and pressure. Whereas traditional theaters or circus performances might be enhanced by industrial technologies, in the cinema, the spectacle was always and necessarily manufactured. Industrial safety also required technical expertise. The section on the *Betriebsstätten* commission's activities during the 1912 fiscal year noted that "innovations in cinematographs, especially fire protection equipment, were inspected and assessed in very large numbers"; and a committee member trained by Messter Film (the company of Oskar Messter, one of Germany's early film pioneers) was setting up a "cinematograph room for experimental purposes at the main fire station," and would train the other committee members once this lab was ready.[43]

Seating and directing the movement of audiences were another important aspect of movie theater regulation. Here, too, cinema ordinances were inspired by their theatrical predecessors. The Prussian theater police ordinances of 1889 and 1909 responded to major theater fires in Nice, Vienna, and Chicago (each of which resulted in hundreds of deaths), and served as models for similar regulations around Germany.[44] These ordinances made architectural and operational prescriptions that could be adapted for cinemas: requiring main entrances and exits on public streets or sufficiently large courtyards; specifying a minimum distance between theaters and neighboring buildings; forbidding living quarters on the premises; specifying the maximum number of seats between aisles, the minimum distance between rows, and the maximum incline of the auditorium; prescribing the width and height of hallways, ceilings, and stairwells; forbidding obstacles in aisles, halls, and exit pathways; requiring marked exits with outward-opening doors; and so on.[45] Such prescriptions were intended to ensure the easy evacuation of the theater in case of fire. Movie theaters were initially governed by theater ordinances like these, and many of their sections regarding entrances, exits, and the auditorium were adapted, if not adopted wholesale, into subsequent ordinances specific to cinemas. As for cinema reformers, the density of bodies in the theater was a problem for safety regulators; where the reformers feared disease and sexual transgression, however, regulators worried about the immediate danger of the audience to itself in moments of panic.

The audience also had to be separated from the projector. Indeed, where later ordinances assume the existence of separate projection rooms in movie theaters, the 1906 "Regulation for the Kingdom of Saxony regarding cinematograph projection" decreed that "the device must be installed in a room that is inaccessible to spectators and fireproof on all sides."[46] In the first decade of cinema, the projector could itself be an attraction, a kind of technological wonder that spectators were interested in seeing along with the images it produced. From the perspective of municipal security, however, it was more akin to a machine in a factory that should be cordoned off from the public and accessible only to trained personnel. The ordinance deemed "xylolite, wooden partitions with asbestos-lined slate siding or sheet iron siding, sheet iron walls and fireproofed tents" to be fireproof. Further, it prescribed that the projection room have a self-closing, fireproof door; that the projection and observation windows into the auditorium remain as small as possible; that its electrical system follow the guidelines of the German Electrical Engineers' Association; that only those films being shown during a screening could be stored in the projection room; and that sand, water, and a fire blanket be readily available in case of fire.[47] The ordinance also, of course, forbade smoking in the projection room. Subsequent ordinances offered further specifications regarding the area and volume of the projection room, its exit pathways, how much and in what way films could be stored there, its heating and ventilation, and more.[48] Such prescriptions worked to control the space surrounding the projector, mitigating the risk of fire, as well as to isolate the projector from the auditorium and the audience, in order to contain any fire that did occur. Separating the technology of projection from the audience mimicked, in miniature, the zoning of industrial areas in cities, which concentrated and segregated industry because of the risks that factories posed to the urban populace.[49]

Regulators also paid great attention to the projector itself. The 1906 Saxony ordinance was relatively sparse in this regard, but contained a few prescriptions about projection lamps and protecting celluloid film from heat that later regulations would elaborate extensively. The 1912 Berlin ordinance, for instance, required that projection lamps have double-walled steel or sheet-iron housing lined with asbestos, with small openings to allow air to circulate; the latter must be covered with wire mesh to prevent sparks from escaping. Furthermore, the heat from the projection lamp should be ventilated to the outside of the building. The ordinance also provided specific guidelines depending on what kind of illumination was being used—acetylene gas, lime light, or electric arc.[50] By 1926, a Prussian ordinance forbade gas, strongly recommended electricity, and made some exceptions for limelight.[51] The movement of film within the projector was also regulated. The 1912 Berlin ordinance stipulated that the film must unroll from one closed spool box and roll up onto another (rather than, say, unrolling from one spool onto the ground), and that the spool boxes themselves must have air holes to prevent overheating. Projectors had to be outfitted with an automatic safety cutoff, a protective shutter that dropped over the light source if the film's movement through the projector fell below a safe speed; and an anti-firing device, which, if the portion of film being projected caught flame, prevented the fire from spreading into the spool boxes. All projectors, finally, needed to be inspected and given a stamp of approval by a representative of the fire service before being operated.[52]

Movie theater regulations increasingly codified the responsibilities of the projectionist. The 1906 Saxony ordinance simply required at least two trained operators to be in the projection room during showtime: one to operate the

projector, and another to observe for fire danger.[53] By 1912, film projection was a certifiable form of technical expertise, with the Berlin ordinance
requiring that projectionists be at least twenty-one years old and possess a
"certificate issued by an accredited examination agency and validated by the
authorities." The projectionist was not allowed to leave the projector while
it was running; at the same time, the ordinance placed limits on the length of
shifts.[54] Such limits echoed concerns within hygiene discourse about mental
and physical fatigue as a cause of industrial accidents.[55] The 1926 Prussian
ordinance went further in specifying the projectionist's responsibility for the
proper use of the projection room, including film storage, the smoking ban,
and keeping untrained personnel out.[56] The increasingly specified role of the
projectionist in movie theater regulations reflected a transition from a popular image of the projector operator as magician or showman, associated with
the period of early cinema, to one defined by technical expertise and machine
labor. The projection room was becoming a space of industrial labor, with the
safety regulation that entailed; the projectionist in turn was a laborer whose
expertise and vigilance were relied on to avoid disaster.

Safety regulations, finally, integrated the movie theater into a broader
regime of municipal permitting and inspection. In 1923, a movie theater fire
in a Prussian city revealed that the *Baupolizei* (local building inspectors) had
issued permits to movie theaters without undertaking inspections to ensure
that they were following safety regulations. In response, the Prussian Ministry
for Public Welfare decreed that all public gathering places must be inspected
by the *Baupolizei* in person at least once a year, as well as whenever the building changed owners.[57] This insistence on regular inspection was codified in
the ministry's 1926 movie theater ordinance, which specified that "the facility
must be inspected prior to initial operations and thereafter annually by an
expert recognized by the district president. The inspection certificate must
be presented to the building inspectors' authority."[58] The regime of safety
regulation thus shaped how movie theaters were constructed and operated,
but also made them objects of regular inspection by municipal authorities.[59]

Looking at movie theater safety regulations opens a perspective on cinema
history that sees it in relation to a broader set of strategies for preventing
and managing catastrophe. In urban contexts, this involved identifying risky
spaces and employing technical experts to devise regulations and monitor
them. To make cinemas safe, regulators drew on expertise in architecture,
engineering, materials science, and fire safety; divided the movie theater into
distinct zones for projecting, viewing, entering, and exiting; prescribed how
celluloid was allowed to circulate within the theater and helped institute a
new class of expert, the projectionist, who was responsible for it; and assimi-
lated the cinema to a regime of municipal inspection.

In Tom Gunning's now-classic formulation, early cinema was a "cinema
of attractions," a mode of film and film experience defined by exhibitionism,
fragmentation, and the direct address of the audience. This early period was

followed by the cinema of "narrative integration," which was illusionist, narrative, and characterized by the separation between the world of the film and that of the spectator.[60] The transition from one to the other involved not just a change in film aesthetics, but in conditions of spectatorship that increasingly disembedded the individual film from the context of its local exhibition, and removed the film projector itself as an object of attraction in the theater. I argue that the logic of public safety played a role in the creation of the cinematic dispositif that followed the cinema of attractions by encouraging the strict separation of film technology from film spectacle and the transformation of the film showman into the projectionist.[61] While not solely determined by it, both of these developments reflected a regime of hygienic regulation that strove to insulate mass publics from industrial technology and instituted various classes of experts responsible for operating those technologies.

The public safety perspective on the movie theater environment perhaps came closest to the reform imaginary discussed earlier in its view of the audience, which echoed widespread late-nineteenth and early twentieth-century discussions of mass psychology that depicted crowds as irrational and dangerously self-destructive. Alongside fire, the audience itself haunted the discourse of movie theater safety, as a second source of potential catastrophe. Numerous writers on movie house architecture and fire safety considered the danger of a panicked crowd equal to that of fire itself. During a fire, Schliepmann wrote, "the audience is gripped by the mass psychosis of panic, and serious accidents and loss of human life are caused by the mindless push to get out."[62] Indeed, for audiences prone to "mass psychosis," the fear of an imagined fire was enough to precipitate a catastrophic event. Such descriptions of audience panic strikingly evoke the spread of fire: it can begin suddenly and spread catastrophically, resulting in mass death. Like fire, the audience was a risk to be managed—primarily by ensuring clear and adequate exits, but also by managing its psychological state. If fear was a potential driver of catastrophe, then the theater had to be made visibly, recognizably safe. According to Schliepmann,

> The spectators must be made aware of [the safety measures and procedures] so that they remain calm in the unlucky event of an incident in the projection room. Not only fire, but a panicking crowd leads to danger. Only those who have themselves experienced panic can conceive what forms of madness the survival instinct assumes in such cases.[63]

Five years later, writing in the periodical *Der Kinematograph*, Walter Thielemann stressed the importance of not only incorporating adequate emergency exits into movie theaters, but of making film audiences conscious of their existence and use: "One can best acclimate the audience to the use of emergency exits when they are opened at the end of the show and the audiences

end up on the street after going through them."[64] In this view, the movie
house was a novel architectural form with unique dangers, whose proper
navigation and use were not obvious; audiences needed to be trained as part
of a broader risk mitigation strategy.

Anxieties about contact, contagion, and uncontrolled circulation were at
the heart of both cinema reform discourse and the public safety regulation of
movie theaters. In the former, the theater was a site of gradual and insidious
harms, such as disease, moral corruption, stunted psychological development,
and sensory fatigue. To use another word found frequently in social hygienic
discourse, the movie theater was a potential space of "degeneration," where
parts of the social body were returned to a more primitive state under conditions of urban modernity. As Robert Heynen argues, bourgeois discussions
about mass audiences at the movies were driven by social hygienic concern
for "at-risk" populations—workers, women, and children—that "drew heavily on racialised conceptions of the Volkskörper that were rooted in ideas of
primitivity."[65] The desire of cinema reform advocates to inculcate hygienic
norms in the audience thus echoed broader reform programs that aimed to
modernize parts of the population who were at risk of degeneration. Safety
regulations, for their part, addressed the theater environment as a site of
potential trauma. In this framework, contagion was sudden and disastrous:
fire and panic could spread quickly if left unchecked by strict regulation of the
theater's technology and built environment. Both degenerative and traumatic
risks had their place within the broader hygienic imaginary: the slow dangers
of working-class living conditions as well as the danger of sudden accidents
found counterparts in attempts to manage the movie theater environment.

Before World War I, however, few critics imagined that the cinema could be
a therapeutic environment. Discourse surrounding the first wave of purpose-
built cinemas in Germany around 1912 frequently emphasized their "festive
atmosphere," but did not connect the leisure they offered to the hygienic ideal
of health. At best, cinemas might be safe, in that they did not pose immediate
risks to the public, but they could not be considered healthy. In the following
section, I turn to a group of Weimar-era architects, technicians, and critics
within the film industry who were influenced by architectural modernism,
in which hygienic principles played a central role. These writers imagined a
theater environment that would be compatible with both bodily health and
the commercial imperatives of film exhibition.

Hygiene and the Modern Movie Palace

World War I prompted a shift in cultural attitudes toward cinema in Germany. While many would never admit film to the pantheon of art, its value
as a vehicle for propaganda and national sentiment became undeniable. As
I will discuss in the next chapter, this recognition would reverberate in the

body of educational films that served the project of postwar reconstruction. It also contributed to the sense that cinema, rather than disrupting the social order, could help stabilize it—to an extent that even outweighed public health concerns in a time of national crisis. During the outbreaks of influenza that swept through Germany in 1918, some cities shut down movie theaters and other entertainment venues where gatherings would allow the disease to spread; many others, however, did not, fearing the effect of such closures on public morale.[66] The idea that cinema could compensate for the miseries of daily life resonated after the war, in the period of hunger and inflation—so much so that by the mid-1920s, architects and designers began to reimagine movie theaters as spaces where spectators could recover from the fatigue of work and domestic responsibilities. Moreover, this hygienic experience could be an attraction in itself. At the opening of the Universum theater in 1928, for instance, architect Erich Mendelsohn rhapsodized not just about its massive screen and auditorium, but its ventilation system as well, which could fully replace the building's air three times an hour.[67]

Once inflation had subsided, Germany experienced a wave of urban cinema construction, spurring discussion among architects, engineers, and critics who were interested in modernizing film exhibition in Germany. According to Andor Kraszna-Krausz, a film critic and editor of the trade journal *Filmtechnik*, movie theaters had evolved somewhat since their beginnings, but there was still much work to be done: "Thirty years ago any sort of venue would do: from carnivalesque magic show booths to tube-shaped shop interiors to chunks of program time in the larger music halls. Thirty years later, it's moving into opulent palaces, at the very least . . . without apparently taking into account the particularities of the films to be presented, as in the olden days."[68] Unlike the bourgeois social reformers before him, Kraszna-Krausz did not direct moral opprobrium at early sites of film exhibition, the circus tents and storefront cinemas; nonetheless, he framed them as a primitive stage of development that should be left in the past. At the same time, however, he rejected the idea that film exhibition should be adapted to existing monumental or historicist architecture. Truly modern movie theater architecture, Kraszna-Krausz suggested, must be derived from the specific qualities of the medium of film and its exhibition.

Kraszna-Krausz's sensibility accorded in many ways with that of modernist architecture of the Weimar period. The discourse of the Neues Bauen (New Building) movement positioned itself against both the working-class tenements, which it regarded as inhumane and therefore irrational, and the bourgeois historicist architecture of the Wilhelmine period, which it saw as material remnants of a past society that needed to be removed in order to bring Germany truly into the present. Hygiene played a crucial role in the imagination of modern architecture, insofar as it provided rational guidelines, legitimized by science, for how spatial design could serve the human organism. In the 1927 manifesto *New Living – New Building*, Adolf Behne demanded "that every architect or builder in every building . . . must always comply with all the demands of hygiene, circulation, aesthetics—in the smallest as in the largest structures."[69] Hygiene was also linked to the architectural functionalization of space, the idea that a given space should be designed for a single purpose within a larger functional plan, like organs in a body. The factory was supposed to be for work, the kitchen for cooking, the park for recreation—and the cinema for watching movies. Hygienic ideals could thus be mobilized in support of a modernist emphasis on medium specificity, at least when it came to the exhibition of film. Designing a hygienic theater was thus part of a project that aimed to distinguish cinema from both fairground entertainment and bourgeois theater.

Kraszna-Krausz's reflection on the state of movie theater architecture appeared in his introduction to a 1926 special issue of *Filmtechnik* on "the modern cinema," in which a number of writers took up the question of how modern architectural and design principles could be applied to film exhibition. These contributions, which were representative of broader discussion within the industry in the 1920s, exemplified a hygienic discourse on cinema that differed from earlier debates on reform and regulation. Where cinema reformers often blamed the poor hygienic conditions in movie theaters (and in working-class neighborhoods generally) on capitalist greed and disregard for human dignity, these writers articulated a vision of hygienic comfort at the movies that accorded with capitalist enterprise. Under the intense economic pressures within the movie business of the 1920s, they imagined ways to commodify the experience of comfort and sell it. They hoped to make the cinema into a therapeutic environment, but as a commercial rather than a moral good—if audiences desired modernity at the movies, hygienic design was a way of making the movie house modern, in a material sense. This discourse on hygienic cinema design found expression in some of the great movie palaces of the Weimar period by architects like Mendelsohn and Fritz Wilms.

This was the time of the movie palace, the large, typically new constructions that could accommodate a thousand (or significantly more) visitors, rather than a couple hundred as in theaters established before the war. While middle-class viewers might have felt that the movie palaces of the 1920s represented a kind of progress, Kraszna-Krausz took aim at their lack of cinematic specificity. These "opulent palaces," he wrote, "[recall] at times historically stylized, at other times modern, haphazard stage spaces or other festive spaces."[70] The new movie palaces may have been luxurious, outfitted with the latest lighting technologies and upholstery, but they still preferred to evoke the cultural legitimacy of theater, thereby undermining the qualities particular to moving image exhibition. Here Kraszna-Krausz echoed a common modernist critique of historicist architecture, whose backward-looking aesthetic was criticized in hygienic terms. For the affiliates of the New Building movement, "nineteenth-century historicism became synonymous with curtain-hung darkness, seclusion, withdrawal into a 'sentimental-romantic half-light,'" writes William Rollins. "Knick-knack-strewn and furniture-choked, the interiors of the preceding generation possessed a 'twilit, patina-layered' atmosphere of clutter that reproduced itself in the heads of the inhabitants and 'lulled to sleep' any spark of the human spirit."[71] Historical styles were dark, nervous, fatiguing; to this, modernism opposed simplicity and brightness, which embodied health and vitality. For modernists like Kraszna-Krausz, the vitality of the moving image could only be unfolded in an architecture that respected the medium's technological and material qualities, which, to his mind, neither pre- nor postwar theaters sufficiently did.

Where Kraszna-Krausz's editorial introduction named the inadequacies of film exhibition in Germany, further articles in the special issue articulated a positive vision. This positive vision is perhaps best evoked by the word *Verkehr* (traffic or circulation), which connoted both a sense of booming capitalist enterprise as well as the metabolism of a healthy organism. Taking up the mantle of the chemist and pioneering hygienic scientist Max von Pettenkofer's analysis of the "physiology of the house" in the nineteenth century, the contributors to the *Filmtechnik* special issue concerned themselves with the physiology of the movie theater, devoting special attention to the circulation of bodies, air, and sensory impressions in the space of the cinema.[72] In the most immediate sense, *Verkehr* meant foot traffic, the movement of people through the theater. Fire safety ordinances, of course, had long since made this an object of regulation, in both traditional and film theaters, but the increased scale of the new movie palaces raised this problem anew. "During short intervals the theater must be emptied of spectators and then filled again. With several thousand seats, the architect is faced with a serious problem," wrote Leo Witlin in his contribution, "Design Principles for Large Cinemas."[73] Furthermore, for those in the film industry, traffic in the theater was not just a matter of safety but of profit—the smoother the flow of traffic, the more seats could be sold. For the engineer and set designer Witlin, whose articles on a wide range of technical problems relating to the film industry appeared frequently in *Filmtechnik* and other trade journals, "the problem of such a cinema can be considered solved when, with thousands of seats at full capacity, people circulate absolutely smoothly and comfortably."[74] Witlin envisioned a movie house architecture that was comfortable and efficient, for the visitor but also for the owner, who would profit from this efficiency. As it was for the movie theater regulators discussed above—and, as we will see in the next chapter, for the hygienic imaginary more broadly—*traffic* was a central term in the modernist vision of a hygienic theater.

The architect Hanns Jakob, in his contribution "Form and Hygiene of Movie Theater Construction," stated paradigmatically: "A space offering rest, pleasant to the senses in every respect after the work and worries of the day, should warmly envelop the visitor and put him in a festive, happy mood."[75] Modernizing film exhibition, from this perspective, meant creating theaters that were therapeutic, in contrast to the fatigue produced by daily labor.

Implicitly, movie theaters past and present too often reproduced the fatiguing mental and material disorder of urban daily life. Instead, Jakob proposed harnessing the physiological effects of light and sound in order to create a therapeutic space. First discussing the visual and auditory dimensions of the viewer's experience in the movie theater, Jakob stressed the importance of avoiding strong or sudden contrasts between light and dark. Darkly colored walls in the auditorium that contrasted too strongly with the illuminated screen were uncomfortable and difficult for the eyes to adjust to, resulting in "the rapid onset of fatigue and exhaustion" in the viewer.[76] Jakob recommended light walls that reflected some of the screen's light and mitigated the contrast between screen and surrounding environment. He also warned against keeping the auditorium too dark during intermissions or between screenings. Adequate light in the auditorium let viewers read the program without strain and more easily adjust to the brightness of the screen when the film began.

Dr. K. Retlow's article "The Projection Screen" addressed the screen's role in the movie theater environment and its potential to cause the spectator discomfort. Retlow outlined best practices for screen size and placement, warning against placing it too high ("those in the first row shouldn't strain their necks") or too close to the front rows of the auditorium, making them into "torture chairs." An excessively large screen could also be uncomfortable for those in the front rows, whose eyes "must tirelessly dart arrow-like back and forth across a too-large screen in order to catch all the details. This produces serious eyestrain, and the spectators never come back again."[77] Jakob and Retlow's concern with eyestrain resonated with contemporary medical interest in the physiological effects of film-viewing on the eyes, as well as hygienic discourse about the benefits of proper illumination in the home, at school, and at work.[78]

Jakob likewise wanted to protect moviegoers from loud noise, lamenting that "the brittle shattering of sounds on concrete and iron structures kills the effects of the best, most costly orchestra."[79] There were similar worries about the auditory environment of urban modernity, which hygienic experts feared would not only damage the ears but produce widespread nervousness. Loud noises from factories, we read in August Gärtner's *Leitfaden der Hygiene* (*Guide to Hygiene*), can create an "anticipatory affect," a "state of agitation, triggered by the expectation of a familiar or repeated noise," which "has a detrimental effect on the nervous system," and thereby pose a health risk to the public.[80] For Jakob, controlling the visual and auditory environment according to hygienic principles could make the movie theater into a therapeutic space, in which viewers were sheltered from the fatiguing extremes experienced outside.

In addition to the eyes and ears, Jakob was also interested in the "effect of the movie theater on the tactile and olfactory senses via heat, cold, drafts, and fresh airflow."[81] As Gärtner wrote in his hygienic guidebook, "the air in living

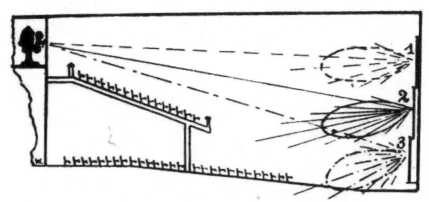

Abb. 7. Schnitt durch ein Lichtspieltheater.
1. Wand zu hoch. 2. Wand richtig. 3. Wand zu tief.

"1. Screen too high. 2. Screen just right. 3. Screen too low." Illustration from K. Retlow, "Die Projektionswand," *Filmtechnik* 2, no. 26 (December 25, 1926): 522.

spaces worsens with human presence, circulation, and activity."[82] Writers saw this as a particularly acute problem for movie theaters given that they operated more frequently than traditional theaters. Uncomfortable heat had long been a problem in enclosed theaters. Discussing ventilation in the *Handbook of Hygiene*, Theodor Weyl noted that "biological processes in humans, as in all organisms, create heat," some of which is transferred back into the surrounding environment, which explained why "rooms hosting large groups of people, one after the other, over a long period of time, gradually heat up. In full theaters, temperatures up to 30 degrees have been recorded."[83] The question of how to properly ventilate and cool public spaces like train stations, churches, and theaters was much discussed among hygienists, architects, and engineers. Jakob urged cinema architects to think holistically and take ventilation, heating, and cooling into account from the beginning when designing a theater.

Georg Otto Stindt, a frequent commentator on film technology in trade journals and the author of a treatise on film aesthetics, explored the topic in more detail in his contribution to the *Filmtechnik* special issue, "Air in the Cinema."[84] Stindt depicted the movie theater as a kind of organism whose air should circulate properly: good air should come in, bad air should go out, and a moderate temperature should be maintained. Echoing Pettenkofer's air circulation experiments, Stindt offered his estimate of the correct conditions for a movie theater:

> Take a galleried theater with around 1200 seats, with, at best, 10,000 cubic meters of air space. The technician with his ventilation system

must strive to change the air often enough to renew these 10,000 cubic meters every 15–20 minutes! Since a typical German cinema today has two showings, in this period of time all the air has to be completely replaced with new, fresh air about 16 times.[85]

Stindt then summarized what he saw as the new consensus among ventilation engineers. Before entering the auditorium, outside air should be rinsed with a water misting device, in order to remove dust and particles. From there, circulation should happen differently depending on the season—in winter, warm air should enter the theater from below, rise, and exit the top of the theater with the aid of fans; in summer, cool air should enter the auditorium from above. Stindt provided detailed diagrams of both cases. Retlow, in his article on projection screens, noted that dust and moisture in the air also affected the screen's reflectivity, depending on its material. "Matte white plaster or oil-painted screens [become] darker in a short period of time due to dust," he warned, while "aluminized screens usually change color very quickly, aided by humidity. Glass-beaded screens soon get dusty and become darker; cleaning them is hardly possible."[86] Air quality thus also affected image quality, which in turn could affect the eye's ability to view the image comfortably.

Ventilation and cooling technologies were a hallmark of hygienic modern design—and none more so than refrigeration. Air conditioning by refrigeration had been developed in the 1910s in the United States, and by the 1920s was being installed in U.S. movie palaces and advertised with great fanfare to audiences looking to escape warm summer temperatures.[87] Aware of this development across the Atlantic, Stindt regretfully noted that "American systems reportedly costing up to 200,000 dollars are of course out of the question for German budgets."[88] Although the German economy had recovered somewhat since the postwar inflation, German theaters still could not afford to install refrigeration technology, and would have to remain, in this regard at least, behind the cutting edge. Instead, Stindt recommended a "cooling tunnel" "of stonework or concrete" that could be filled with ice during the hottest weeks of summer.

In another *Filmtechnik* article from 1927, Stindt extended his hygienic consideration of temperature in the movie theater to the domain of interior decor, by linking the affective qualities of color to the subjective feeling of warmth or coolness. "People say: this or that color, for example, red, is warm, or pale yellow is cool."[89] Colored decor should therefore be employed with an awareness of this effect. "The moviegoer looking to find a cool place in the theater in summer would certainly feel uncomfortably warm in a red or orange environment," Stindt wrote, but would "in winter, on the other hand, perceive green walls and decorations as cold and unwelcoming. Generally one can say that a reddish orange is the best, most pleasant color for a theater."[90] Stindt suggested employing mobile walls if possible, so that the decor could be reconfigured according to seasonal changes. As Sarah Street and

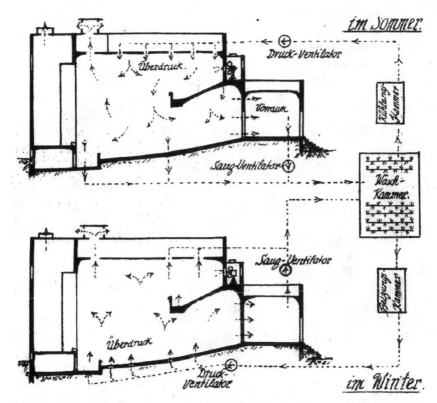

Diagrams for ideal air circulation in summer and winter. Illustration from Stindt, "Die Luft im Kino," *Filmtechnik* 2, no. 26 (December 25, 1926): 514.

Josh Yumibe write, color—especially interior color lighting—was an important part of the movie palace experience: "Cinema exhibition culture of the 1920s was imbued with a desire to move spectators with a totalized ambient chromatic experience that began as soon as they entered the theater."[91] Stindt's considerations here linked this color consciousness to a hygienic logic, using principles of moderation and comfort to offer guidance in the use of color in the movie theater. Where the modernist architectural imagination typically preferred the cleanliness of white over decorative color, Stindt's article suggests a role for color in hygienic architecture as well.[92]

For Alfred Wedemeyer, the cinemas designed by the architect Fritz Wilms embodied the modernist vision of the hygienic movie house. In the mid-1920s, Wilms designed more than half a dozen theaters in Berlin alone.[93] In his introduction to a 1928 collection of Wilms's preliminary sketches and photographs of his theaters, Wedemeyer recapitulated the modernist assessment of earlier exhibition sites as merely improvisatory and primitive. After the period of fairground and storefront cinemas, however, specially constructed cinemas were built in which, due to the "rapid development of large cities," it was "necessary to take into account fire safety, hygiene (through heating and proper ventilation), and especially speedy evacuation routes."[94] In such theaters a "festive atmosphere" is required "for the leisure hours and as a distraction after the work and worries of the day, for the greatest number of all social classes, both the intellectual and the working class."[95] Like the contributors to *Filmtechnik*, Wedemeyer imagined the modern theater as a therapeutic space, which not only offered a mental and physical respite to individual moviegoers, but cumulatively helped ease social tensions as well. Wedemeyer identified Fritz Wilms as a "specialist in this field in Germany"[96] and went on to discuss a number of his Berlin theaters, which bore the hallmarks of hygienic modernism: the "elegant comfort" of the Turmstrasse Ufa-Theater's auditorium, generated by indirect colored lighting which could be "gradually adjusted lighter or darker";[97] the "warm and festive atmosphere" of the auditorium in the Rote Mühle theater at Halensee; and the emergency lighting and circulating air system for heating and cooling in the Mercedes-Palast in Neukölln. Writing about the Mercedes-Palast for *Filmtechnik*, Leo Witlin (mentioned earlier as a contributor to the special issue on the modern movie theater) praised its "cutting-edge air supply system."[98]

For Witlin, the theater was also remarkable in that it made the experience of hygienic comfort accessible to a working-class audience. The Mercedes-Palast was built in the working-class neighborhood of Neukölln, a fact Witlin interpreted as part of a trend in cinema construction moving away from the central entertainment districts to outer-lying areas of Berlin. "The builders have the welcome intention," Witlin wrote, "of giving the residents of less economically advantaged neighborhoods a chance to enjoy themselves for a few hours at an affordable price in pleasant surroundings."[99] The massive scale of the theater—with 2,600 seats, it was one of the largest movie theaters in Europe—allowed the operators to charge relatively low entrance prices. Witlin's description, of course, flattered the builders, who primarily intended to make a profit, depicting them as beneficent social reformers. Nonetheless, theaters like the Mercedes-Palast offered an experience of hygienic lighting and HVAC technologies to many working-class Germans for whom these were inaccessible in daily life; since workers had increased means for leisure in the second half of the 1920s, there was money to be made selling them the comfortable environments they were otherwise denied.[100]

In recent years, film and media scholars have returned to the notion of the cinematic apparatus or dispositif, or what Noam Elcott has referred to as the "judicious coordination" of elements that produce the experience of cinema.[101] Attempting to go beyond Jean-Louis Baudry's ideological account of the apparatus, critics have drawn attention to the historical variety of concrete material arrangements and practices that have been involved in film exhibition, with regard to theater architecture, lighting, interior design, upholstery, food and drink, and more.[102] Typically, and not unreasonably, these accounts are oriented around spectatorship, thinking about how the material environment of the theater creates the conditions for a particular (dis)embodied form of visual experience. Film spectatorship is taken to be the telos of movie theater design and exhibition practice.

This is certainly true—to an extent. Thinking about hygienic practices in movie theaters makes us aware of the multiple ordering logics that shaped the theater environment, not all of which were organized around spectatorship per se, though they certainly affected the cinematic experience. In other words, the goal of creating a collective viewing environment determined the fundamental contours of the theater environment, but a hygienic dispositif—a network of discourses and practices linked by the aim of optimizing the health of the population—shaped the experience of cinema as well. As I have shown in this chapter, the hygienic apparatus intersected with the movie theater environment in different ways and at different historical moments: first from without at the height of the German social reform movement, which was concerned with managing what it perceived as the environmental disorder that led to working-class social disorder; and later, during the Weimar Republic, from within the film industry itself, as it tapped into a broader enthusiasm for health as part of a modern lifestyle. Meanwhile, the movie theater as a novel phenomenon was also integrated into a municipal regulatory apparatus that maintained urban environmental order, in ways that concretely shaped its design and operation. In their own ways, all three discourses functioned as vectors of modernization, whereby the site of moviegoing was subjected to new forms of expertise and rationalization according to the principle of health.

Sometimes the cinematic and hygienic dispositifs reinforced each other, while in other ways they conflicted. The tendency toward an absorptive mode of spectatorship that accompanied the development of narrative cinema encouraged the removal of the film projector from the auditorium into a segregated space of its own—as did municipal fire safety regulations. These same regulations, however, meant that auditorium exits would remain visible during exhibition, which introduced a small but perceptible moment of resistance to full absorption into the world on screen. At the same time, the darkness that still dominated in the auditorium continued to irk hygienically minded moral reformers, who decried the opportunities for sexual transgression it offered.[103] In this way, the movie theater would never fully embody the ideal of hygienic architecture, for which illumination was paramount. It would continue to function as a space of at least partial obscurity, where the cleansing eye of hygiene could not see.

Nonetheless, by the beginning of the Weimar Republic, political elites and scientific experts increasingly recognized cinema's value as a propaganda tool. Before the war, German elites had treated film in many ways as a degenerative influence, a working-class entertainment to be contained. The explosion of propaganda during World War I, however, made film's potential as a vehicle for mass communication impossible to overlook. Though the auditorium remained dark, film was put to use as a medium of enlightenment. Whereas this chapter was concerned with the physiology of the movie house, chapter 2 examines film as a vehicle for visualizing the physiology of other environments at different scales. Cinema thus also became a site where experts in design, architecture, traffic, and urban planning articulated a narrative of hygienic modernization and demonstrated hygienic ways of thinking about, perceiving, and acting in the spaces of everyday life.

Chapter 2

✦

Hygienic Modernization

Visions of Environmental Order
in the Weimar *Kulturfilm*

In the first postwar issue of the journal *Öffentliche Gesundheitspflege* (*Public Health*), editor Rudolf Abel expressed hope that the arrival of a social democratic welfare state would be favorable to hygienic goals, and implored the state to understand, despite its dire economic situation, "that combatting internal enemies—that is, factors that endanger the health of the *Volk*—is no less important than arming oneself against external opponents."[1] According to Abel, disease, malnutrition, and housing shortages presented the most immediate dangers to health. He worried that demobilization would bring diseases prevalent on the front back to Germany, particularly typhus, dysentery, and sexually transmitted infections. Statistics would later show that the rate of tuberculosis in 1918 had not been seen in Germany since 1894. (Abel makes no mention of the 1918 flu pandemic.) Blockades and food rationing caused widespread malnutrition that would be difficult to overcome, even with blockades lifted and humanitarian assistance from former enemy countries. Lack of housing and poor living conditions would also continue to plague a country without sufficient building materials or the money to purchase them. In the longer term, Abel wrote, "the whole of our thoughts and aims must be directed toward the rebuilding of the German *Volk*."[2] In other words, Germany also had to recover from the significant population loss incurred during the war, which killed approximately two million on the front, as well as 800,000 at home from disease and malnutrition.[3] Health experts thus conceived of the war and its aftermath in terms of its effects on the size and overall health of the German population.

This situation spurred projects throughout the 1920s that aimed to educate the populace about how and why they should stay healthy. Health was to become everyone's responsibility, an injunction that demanded efforts on a mass scale. Exhibitions were a popular format. The "Health, Social Care, and Bodily Exercise" ("Gesundheit, soziale Fürsorge und Leibesübungen," or Gesolei) exhibition in Düsseldorf, for instance, attracted nearly eight million visitors in 1926.[4] Health experts also turned to film, a medium that German cultural elites had earlier treated with skepticism, but whose propaganda potential had been demonstrated during the war. Films dealing with health topics—most often, individual and reproductive health—comprised a significant part of cultural education films (*Kulturfilme*) produced during the Weimar Republic. As I show in this chapter, however, visions of hygienic modernity in postwar Germany also involved producing—or, at least, imagining—an ordered material environment. Where prewar health experts had been interested in the potential scientific uses of film technology, they had by and large considered the mass cultural phenomenon of cinema to be a source of environmental and perceptual disorder. Afterward, they asked to what extent cinema could be made part of the apparatus of hygiene. Could film be integrated into the broader ensemble of hygienic institutions and practices? In what ways could film serve the project of ordering the urban environment?

This chapter examines Weimar *Kulturfilme* that were addressed to different audiences and which dealt with different environmental scales—the kitchen, the apartment, the street, and the city. In terms of production context, these films ranged from municipal public health initiatives to modernist architectural reform projects. Despite their differences, these films employed consonant visual rhetorics of urban order and disorder, and made the case for modernization through hygiene. They depicted their respective environments as dispositifs in the more concrete sense of the term: arrangements of built space, bodies, and various forms of material traffic that created particular conditions of perceptibility and forms of subjectivity. They promoted ways of hygienically optimizing these environments, and, depending on their intended audience, taught viewers how to participate in the hygienic project by properly inhabiting or navigating them. In other words, they encouraged viewers to think of themselves as hygienic subjects whose ways of seeing, attending, and acting in relation to their environment influenced their own health and that of those around them. Moreover, images of environmental order doubled as visions of social order in a time of great upheaval and perceived disorder. By situating the social within material environments, these films naturalized it and posited a world more easily controlled by expert knowledge and intervention. They showed how bodies could relate harmoniously to the environments they inhabited, but also what kinds of bodies belonged where.

Before discussing these films in detail, I turn to the broader context of film and health education after the war. The confluence of mass health education efforts with film constituted a para-cinematic dispositif—now in the more abstract sense—involving forms of funding, production, distribution, and exhibition that existed to a certain extent alongside the apparatus of commercial cinema.

Health Education and German Film after World War I

In 1922, Dr. Curt Thomalla claimed that "there is no more effective way of fighting pseudo-occultist bunk, lay superstition against mental institutions, alcoholism, and many other social ills than the movies—and no simpler way of spreading healthy body culture, rational population policy, and so on."[5] Writing in the Zeitschrift für Medizinalbeamte (*Journal for Medical Officials*), Thomalla argued that film could promote health through knowledge, employing a rhetoric of enlightenment that aligned with broader discourse around Kulturfilme. Made properly in collaboration with experts, health education films could dispel old superstitions and provide a mass audience with scientifically legitimate advice.[6] To stress the urgency of this task, Thomalla reminded his readers that "talk of 'reconstruction' has already become a buzzword. But here there is a way toward effective cooperation, which ultimately can play a not insignificant role in the reconstruction we've longed for."[7] Postwar reconstruction, in other words, meant healing the social body, and Thomalla hoped that film could contribute to this task.

Thomalla, a neurologist who had served at a military hospital during the war, took on the directorship of Ufa's Medical Film Archive in 1919 and played an important role in producing hygiene films in the early postwar period.[8] With support from the German Welfare Ministry and other state agencies, Thomalla began by producing training films for medical students, but soon turned to films for mass audiences. By the time of his 1922 article on "Hygiene and Social Medicine in the Popular Education Film," the Ufa Medical Film Archive had released *Die Geschlechtskrankheiten und ihre Folgen* (*Venereal Diseases and Their Consequences*, 1920), *Säuglingspflege* (*The Care of Infants*, 1920), *Die Wirkung der Hungerblockade auf die Volksgesundheit* (*The Effects of the Hunger Blockade on Public Health*, 1921), *Krüppelnot und Krüppelhilfe* (*The Plight and Care of the Disabled*, 1920), *Die Pocken, ihre Gefahren und deren Bekämpfung* (*The Threat of Smallpox and How to Fight It*, 1920), *Die weisse Seuche* (*The White Plague*, 1921), a film about tuberculosis, and *Wie bleibe ich gesund?* (*How Do I Stay Healthy?* 1922), a two-part film that provided instruction on healthy practices for everyday life.[9]

Such films were shown in a variety of contexts, and their exhibition usually differed from that of standard commercial fare. In addition to public screenings in commercial movie houses, Thomalla wrote that closed screenings had been organized by industrial sickness funds, unions, and professional organizations. Some teachers, he claimed, even used the archive's films for classroom instruction, though this was probably rare, given the expense and labor involved.[10] In the first few years of *Kulturfilm* production, a lecturer would accompany the film live at the theater, explaining what was being shown on screen and providing context. This practice was common in cinemas even for narrative films before 1910, but *Kulturfilme* also had strong affinities with popular illustrated lectures, which had a long pre-cinematic tradition.[11] Thomalla's Medical Film Archive provided texts for lecturers at their films, which the lecturers could adapt according to the exhibition context and audience. By 1922, Thomalla was producing films designed to be shown without a lecturer, but *Kulturfilme* would continue to mimic the lecture form in various ways, such as including a diegetic lecturer in the film itself. This reflects what Klaus Kreimeier identifies as the logocentrism of the genre's films, which, in spite of—or perhaps because of—their confidence in the power of images, subordinated image to text.[12]

Because of their often sensitive topics and the variety of contexts in which they would be shown, health education films had to be adaptable. A film lecturer could go some way toward tailoring the film experience for the audience, but there were other methods as well. Thomalla produced two versions of his film depicting a vasectomy, *Der Steinach-Film* (*The Steinach Film*), in 1922: first as a "scientific lecture film" and a second "looser treatment of the topic for a general audience."[13] Health education films were often available in multiple versions, for expert audiences on the one hand, and lay audiences on the other. Versions could be gendered as well. In 1920, the Medical Film Archive released one version of *Venereal Diseases and Their Consequences* for a male audience and another for a female audience, to be shown in separate, gender-specific screenings.[14] For the film *The Care of Infants*, in addition to adapting the lecture to specific audiences—"according to whether one was speaking in the city or the country, in front of teenaged girls or experienced women, in front of nurses or female factory workers"—Thomalla recommended stopping the film between sections to allow for questions, or repeating sections so that the material could sink in.[15] Health education films were not necessarily meant to be screened as coherent, self-sufficient works, but as pedagogical tools to be implemented within specific contexts.

Thomalla claimed that although the Medical Film Archive's productions had been successful in commercial cinemas, "unions and sickness funds have been the best and most appreciative customers for pedagogical hygiene films."[16] This remark demonstrates the extent to which the insurance schemes of the late nineteenth century created a market for hygienic knowledge in institutions that had been incentivized to care about the health of working people.[17] Working people, obviously, had a direct material interest in hygiene, since their ability to work depended upon bodily health, but this alone did not necessarily translate into the exhibition of health education films meant for popular audiences. Unions and insurance agencies that wished to encourage their members to care for their bodies provided the capital necessary for renting films and organizing screenings. In other words, despite popular hygiene's bourgeois origins, middle-class moviegoers were not the only audience for health education films. At the same time, their reception among working-class audiences was not due only to a spontaneous popular desire for them, or a unidirectional imposition of bourgeois values, but arose out of a negotiation between state authorities, scientific experts, and institutional representatives of working-class interests.

Health education films took the body and sexuality as central objects, as earlier scholarship has emphasized. "As part of population-political considerations, sexuality would fall under state control and serve to produce healthy offspring," writes Ulf Schmidt. "In the attempt to exert influence [over the population], films were accorded a special role due to their suggestive power."[18] So-called *Aufklärungsfilme* (sexual enlightenment films) about human reproduction and sexually transmitted disease combined fictional and documentary episodes, medicalized images of human anatomy, microscopic photography, and animations to impart hygienic knowledge of sexuality to mass audiences. They emphasized the authority of medical experts and the social duty of practicing sexual hygiene. As Anja Laukötter argues, the visual techniques on display in these films also transmitted new ways of seeing and knowing the body.[19] X-ray images and animations—for example, of bacteria entering the skin, circulating in the bloodstream, and spreading to internal organs— displayed the otherwise invisible interior space of the body and produced an abstract visual body against which the viewer could measure their own.

Most health films focused on the body not necessarily because individual behavioral choices were the main determinant of health (rather than social or environmental factors), but because they were what individual viewers could control. Hygiene did not stop with the body, however. Hygienic discourses were just as concerned with the material environments in which modern life increasingly took place. How did health education films address this dimension of the hygienic project? How did they provide new ways of imagining environments and how they functioned, as they had done for the human body?

In the next section, I discuss films that dealt with hygiene in the home, an environment over which health experts presumed that most viewers had some control. Beyond the home, however, we have to expand our notion of "health education" in order to see the logic of hygiene at work in a wider range of urban environments. The subsequent section examines the street safety film *Im Strudel des Verkehrs* (*In the Vortex of Traffic*), which focuses on a category of event not usually thought of as a matter of hygiene: the traffic accident. While viewers may not have been able to design the spaces and forms of transit they used daily, here individual behaviors could nonetheless determine the difference between life and death. In considering filmic visions of healthy environments, finally, we can also turn to films not necessarily meant for mass audiences. The last section analyzes the urban planning film *Die Stadt von Morgen: Ein Film vom Städtebau* (*The City of Tomorrow: An Urban Planning Film*), which was primarily meant for other architects, planners, and bureaucrats. Here we see how film could envision the engineering of health at a much larger scale than the kitchen or the street. *The City of Tomorrow* also shows how film, along with being a medium of communication with the masses, facilitated communication across different classes of experts as well. This reflected the constitutive interdisciplinarity of hygiene, which brought together different forms of knowledge toward the goal of governing the environments that comprised industrial modernity.

Healthy Homes and Modern Kitchens

In early 1922, the Ufa Cultural Division released the two-part film *Wie bleibe ich gesund?* (*How Do I Stay Healthy?*) whose production had been overseen by Thomalla and Dr. Nicholas Kaufmann, Thomalla's main collaborator at the Cultural Division's Medical Film Archive. The film consisted of two fifteen-minute parts, *Hygiene des häuslichen Lebens* (*Hygiene of Domestic Life*) and *Hygiene der Feierstunden* (*Hygiene after Work*), thus comprising the entirety of one's daily life not spent at work.[20] The first part, *Hygiene of Domestic Life*, is structured around a typical weekday for a typical family, presumed to consist of a working husband, one or two children, and a wife whose primary responsibilities are in the home. A series of quick scenes depict waking, washing, dressing, cooking, eating, shopping, playing, homework, and bedtime from a hygienic perspective, often cutting between behaviors that should and should not be emulated. Ideally, the film was meant to be accompanied by a lecture, which the producers also wrote.[21] In Thomalla's words, the film advocated "rational systems of work and domestic life, and above all healthy sport," and was "made with the assistance of Dr. Tugendreich and the social welfare doctors of the City of Berlin."[22] Gustav Tugendreich led the social hygiene division at Berlin's municipal health office for a brief period after World War I, and his participation indicates that the film was targeted at an urban audience.

The film reflects the long-standing status of the home in hygiene discourse, which saw dwellings as a crucial factor in the health of the population. Working-class tenements constructed in the period after Germany's 1871 unification were notoriously overcrowded, dark, damp, and poorly venti-lated. As discussed in chapter 1, reformers attributed what they saw as moral, social, and physical disorder to this environment, whose material disorder posed a threat to social reproduction. With regard to the nation's physical health, the home was viewed as a crucial site of disease transmission. In the volume of *Weyl's Handbook of Hygiene* devoted to *Bau- und Wohnungshy-giene* (*Hygiene of Buildings and Homes*), Adolf Rath wrote that "whoever wishes to trace the causes of epidemic disease will always return to the place where people eat, drink, and sleep, where they reproduce family life—their dwellings, in their homes."[23] Consequently, hygienists studied the mate-rial environment of the home in great detail, and conceived of dwellings as organisms whose health was defined in terms of their ability to carry out a range of hygienic functions, such as air circulation, temperature regulation, waste removal, and access to sunlight and clean water. Household activities like cooking, eating, sleeping, and bathing should take place in separate spaces, like physiological functions localized in discrete organs. In the late nineteenth century, dwellings were subjected to mathematical norms. "While physicians meticulously measured bodies," writes Didem Ekici, "hygienists measured dwellings to determine the optimal height and distance between each apartment, cubic air volume, window area, ceiling height in each room, and so on for the body to remain healthy. They converted their findings into statistical data to arrive at universal norms for the healthy house."[24] Hygiene studied homes as organism-like subsystems within a larger urban ecosystem.

But who was responsible for maintaining the home's environmental order, as defined by the prescriptions of hygiene? A healthy home depended in large part on how it was inhabited, not just how it was constructed. Concerns about the hygienic conditions of domestic spaces in Germany were reflected in the increasingly widespread practice of *Wohnungsaufsicht*, or "housing inspection." Implemented at the municipal level beginning around 1900, housing inspection allowed state health authorities to monitor the living conditions of the population—particularly the working-class population—on an ongoing and systematic basis. Housing inspectors would check for properly maintained floors and windows, adequate air volume and ventilation, functioning toilet and waste disposal, low humidity, and general cleanliness. Beyond these environmental conditions, according to Rath, inspectors would also make sure homes were not overcrowded (a difficult problem due to chronic urban housing shortages) and that sleeping areas for non-married adolescents and adults were separated by sex (purportedly to prevent the spread of venereal diseases).[25] Incentivized by the new health insurance schemes and the need to maintain the labor force, housing inspection opened the ostensibly private sphere of social reproduction to a hygienic regime guided by experts and sanctioned by the state.

Monitoring the material environment of the home could only do so much, however. Hygienic modernization also meant educating the populace about how to dwell hygienically. In this section, I examine two postwar films about hygienic dwelling: *Hygiene of Domestic Life*, described briefly above, and *Die Frankfurter Küche* (*The Frankfurt Kitchen*), a short film depicting a modernist model kitchen. These films employed a comparison structure, a common *Kulturfilm* technique, which juxtaposed proper and improper home use and allowed the viewer to quickly recognize examples of good or bad behavior. In other words, these films taught one to see the home through a hygienic gaze, and made the viewer—specifically, the female viewer—responsible for producing hygiene at home, thereby establishing the housewife as the household's local hygienic authority. This feature was common to other films discussed in this chapter as well: to combat the potential for urban material disorder, they posited a figure of hygienic authority that was accountable for a given environment. These films conveyed practical knowledge and trained viewers to see hygienically, but just as importantly, they worked to establish a chain of authority based on expertise that stretched from scientific hygiene to those in charge of enforcing order in everyday environments. Moreover, who was allowed to wield this authority, and in what spaces, was ultimately bound up with a patriarchal conception of social order.

The first sequence of *Hygiene of Domestic Life* cuts between two couples waking up in their respective bedrooms. "What a sense of well-being upon awakening, what a feeling of crisp energy and swelling joy for life," declares a prefatory intertitle, "when you've slept refreshingly in a clean room with an open window, under light covers." The sequence exemplifies how this and other health-related films depict interior space hygienically. The well-rested couple rises quickly from bed in a well-lit bedroom, in which no artificial light source can be seen, suggesting the presence of sunlight. The bright walls are free of decor and reflect the sunlight. In combination with the happy, energetic inhabitants, the room's lighting and mise-en-scène create a sense of freedom and vitality. Not so in the contrasting bedroom: "But here? Fear of fresh air, overheating under thick feather blankets, resulting in fitful sleep, agitating dreams, and waking up in a bad mood, lack of invigoration even after a long period of rest." The "bad" couple is awakened by an alarm clock, shown in close-up with animated streaks representing its startling wake-up call. The bedroom is dark until the husband turns on a light, which reveals a claustrophobic space covered in curtains, blankets, and busily patterned wallpaper. The couple has difficulty waking up, ostentatiously yawning, stretching, and rubbing their eyes. The artificial lighting implies the lack of sunlight and closed windows: "The poor, spent air fills the space like a veil of fog, day and night." The two bedrooms instantiate the visual-spatial coding of hygiene common to films like this (as well as in architectural modernism, as we will see shortly). Unhygienic space is dark, stagnant, overrun by unnecessary material and visual elements; hygienic space is bright, minimally decorated, and ideally sunlit, suggesting a kind of naturalness and harmony between material form and organic function (in this case, sleep).

Of course, environmental order requires maintenance, and *Hygiene of Domestic Life* assigns this task to the housewife. Once husband and child have left for work and school—after a proper breakfast for the whole family—the "good" wife is shown opening windows, airing out the bedding, and cleaning with a bucket and mop. (A feather duster is unhygienic since it just puts dust back into the air, and, as the film informs us, "the room's dust contains germs.") The kitchen is given special attention: "The hygienic kitchen. Waste is to be disposed of in securely sealed containers, which must be emptied into the dumpster daily." We are shown a clean kitchen as a woman puts food scraps into a specially labeled receptacle. The film also exhorts the viewer to prevent hairs from falling into the meal and to keep dogs out of the kitchen, and we then see a disorganized kitchen in which a hungry dog has its fill of table scraps that have ended up on the floor. The film singles out the pantry as a potential source of disease, since unhygienic conditions can allow bacteria to flourish. "The typical unhygienic pantry. Housewives, who among you is not without sin?" An insert shot depicts "the proliferation of bacteria, which a single fly left on a Petri dish after walking on it with its dirty feet." This and other medicalized images, like anatomical diagrams and close-ups of hands and feet showing the effects of improper posture and clothing, inject the voice of scientific authority into the routines of daily life. The kitchen scene, specifically addressed to the housewife, scolds her for her laxity and encourages her to take up scientifically tested hygienic prescriptions, making her into a kind of nurse for the home who carries out the doctor's orders. The housewife is given a modicum of authority within the home that comes with expertise, but this authority depends on and defers to the true experts. In a fashion typical of hygienic modernization, housekeeping becomes rationalized while maintaining a strict gendering of labor and domestic space.

Labor is divided according to both gender and age. For the wife and mother, the home is a space of work, in which her unwaged labor reproduces the male worker and produces the next generation of workers; for the working husband, the home is a space of regeneration, in which he recovers from the strain of waged or salaried labor. The child also labors without pay, but in a different way than the housewife. As a potential worker or housewife, the child performs the labor of self-production, both physical (bodily development) and mental (education). *Hygiene of Domestic Life* points to the responsibilities of the parents and the effects of the material environments of daily life in this process. Proper food, washing, and clothing are necessary for healthy physical growth, but outdoor play is necessary as well, and not just anywhere: "The dusty streets with their musty air are a poor substitute for playing in the open air." (As we will see in the traffic-safety film discussed in the next section, the street is a decidedly unhygienic environment for play.) Education happens primarily at school, but this labor continues at home in the form of homework, which must be balanced with the need for physical activity. "Schoolwork should be finished early enough so that children can still play in the fresh air by daylight for a few hours." The home should also provide an ergonomically sound environment for schoolwork. The film recommends having a "school desk" (*Schülerschreibtisch*) at home to encourage proper posture, and emphasizes the importance of adequate illumination for reading and writing. Here the film takes another opportunity to scold mothers, with a scene of a woman who takes the reading lamp for herself while her child does homework. "It's sad when mother reads novels, while daughter ruins her eyes." At the end of the film, the wife tries to read in bed while her husband sleeps, but is again rebuffed, as the annoyed husband turns out the light: "Books in bed are poison for the nerves." In its depiction of the hygienic home, the film cannot envision a space for female recreation, which seems always to infringe upon the regeneration and self-production of husband and child.

Hygiene of Domestic Life thus simultaneously naturalized and modernized the patriarchal nuclear family in a period of social crisis. Its vision of environmental order was tightly linked with a desire for social order, at a time when war and economic calamity had eroded the ideological and material foundations of the bourgeois family. *Hygiene of Domestic Life* took the family as a given, but also gave it a modern rationale—health. The family is rationalized as an efficient and necessary organ of healthy social reproduction, as is the woman's place as caretaker of the domestic environment. In this way, the film instantiated central features of the hygienic imagination more broadly: it grounded the social order in material environments and updated preexisting forms of social hierarchy for the modern age by positing health as their telos. In *Hygiene of Domestic Life* the family became another kind of hygienic architecture, an ordering structure that guided the population toward healthy living.

In this the film reflected a rationalized and productivist conception of the home: the home as a factory of social reproduction. The 1927 film *The Frankfurt Kitchen*, which depicted a model home kitchen designed by the Austrian architect Margarete Schütte-Lihotzky, further developed the factory-like vision of the kitchen found in domestic hygiene discourse. Lihotzky's design emphasized efficiency above all and was marketed as a way to significantly reduce the daily labor of wives and mothers. Architects like Lihotzky and Bruno Taut, in his book *The New Dwelling*, drew inspiration from the work of Christine Frederick in the United States, whose books *Household Engineering* and *The New Housekeeping* advanced a notion of rationalized home labor that would improve domestic life and liberate women from unnecessary toil.[26] Echoing Frederick, Lihotzky herself stressed the link between efficiency and health, writing that women of the day "are so overburdened that, in time, their overwork will not be without consequence for national health as a whole."[27] In other words, for Lihotzky, rationalization and hygiene were of a piece. Considered in aggregate, even small inefficiencies in the home could add up to significant effects on the health of large populations. Modern architects saw design as a vehicle for the rationalization of everyday life that could improve both the productivity and health of society as a whole.

Lihotzky's kitchen was part of a model dwelling exhibited at Frankfurt's 1927 Industrial Exhibition by the New Frankfurt urban planning project under Ernst May. May was Frankfurt's head urban planner from 1925 to 1930, a period of relative economic stability in Germany during which some large cities were able to pursue more ambitious programs, especially with regard to housing. May proposed a rationalized model of social housing that valued functionality, efficiency, standardization, and hygiene. Over the course of his tenure, May's office constructed thousands of new homes and apartments, but multimedia public relations work, including film, was also an integral part of the New Frankfurt project.[28] In 1927 and 1928, the photographer and filmmaker Paul Wolff directed a series of short films on the

New Frankfurt architecture that served as an advertisement for the project. The series, "Modern Architecture in Frankfurt am Main" ("Neues Bauen in Frankfurt am Main"), included sections on the home construction factory, which rationalized and industrialized home-building in new ways; the "minimum dwelling," an apartment designed for maximum functionality and comfort within a relatively small area; and a film on the Frankfurt Kitchen. These films were primarily intended to demonstrate the New Frankfurt projects to other architects and urban planners at exhibitions, conferences, and private screenings. *The Frankfurt Kitchen* appealed to an audience with expertise and cultural authority, and therefore emphasized the hygienic benefits of the kitchen's design rather than providing practical advice to those who would actually be using it.

Wolff's film about the Frankfurt Kitchen demonstrates its benefits using the now-familiar comparison structure. Here, though, the film's ire is not directed at the housewife per se but at the inefficiency and hygienic inadequacy of previous designs. The first sequence depicts a woman in a traditional kitchen laboriously chopping kindling, taking paper tinder from a drawer, and starting a fire before she can even put a pot on the stove. We then see the transition from the old to the modern kitchen. Here, surfaces, containers, and appliances are arranged both to separate cooking processes (to prevent contamination) and to minimize the distance traveled. The latter improvement is visualized by way of two animated overhead diagrams: one of the distance the housewife travels to cook a meal in the traditional kitchen (about 90 meters) and a corresponding image of the Frankfurt Kitchen (8 meters). In the first diagram, a line crisscrosses the space, retracing some paths multiple times; in the second, the line elegantly proceeds from one station to the next as on an assembly line.[29] Indeed, as one of the final intertitles explains, "as with factory and office work, the aim is to enable the housewife to achieve optimal performance with minimal effort." *The Frankfurt Kitchen* offers a harmonious picture of rationalized domestic labor that promises not only to increase a housewife's productivity but to ensure her health (by preventing fatigue) as well as that of her family.

Although not directly addressed to its potential user, the film nonetheless offers a step-by-step depiction of the new kitchen's proper use: the cook gets a shiny pot from the cabinet, sits on the rotating chair, chops cabbage, swipes the scraps into a conveniently located waste drawer, moves the pot from the stove to the directly adjacent haybox, pours ingredients from standardized aluminum containers, empties the waste drawer into a garbage chute, washes dishes, and irons clothes on a board that folds out from the wall. By depicting this process, the film echoes the architecture critic Adolf Behne's claim that the "new architecture presupposes a new mode of habitation . . . a new mode of habitation, however, presupposes a new human being."[30] *The Frankfurt Kitchen* both demonstrates "a new mode of habitation" and literally replaces the occupant of the old kitchen with a new person: the traditional

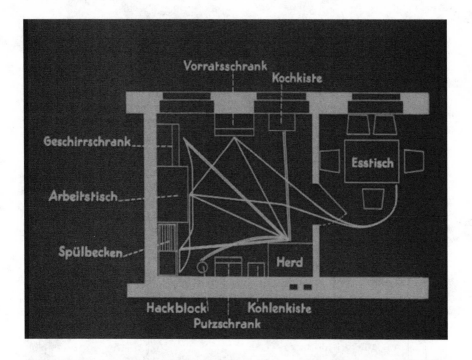

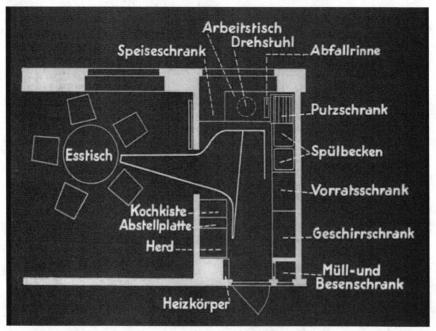

Typical path traversed in a traditional kitchen (90 meters) vs. a modern one (8 meters). Stills from *The Frankfurt Kitchen* (dir. Paul Wolff, 1927).

kitchen was occupied by a woman in middle age, wearing an apron, while the cook in the Frankfurt Kitchen is a markedly younger woman dressed in short sleeves and a skirt, with a modern bobbed hairstyle (or *Bubikopf*). The film thus links its vision of domestic rationalization to the much-discussed image of Weimar's New Woman. As Christiane Keim argues, while the film's new woman still occupies the domestic sphere, she appears as an agent of modern, industrial efficiency, rather than the loving, selfless housewife of old.[31] As in *Hygiene of Domestic Life*, *The Frankfurt Kitchen* modernizes woman's position in the patriarchal family, making her the image and guarantor of social health. Rationalization, in this context, commonly means the application of the principle of efficiency to daily life; here we see how it takes on an additional meaning, as the justification of social hierarchy through an appeal to the principle of health. In other words, health serves as a modern rationale for pre-existing divisions of labor whose legitimacy was under threat.

The film's explicit pitch stresses the new kitchen's efficiency. As Lihotzky's comments cited above suggest, efficiency and health were bound together in discussions of domestic rationalization, and were inseparable in hygiene discourse. Subtly but insistently, the film visually underscores the Frankfurt Kitchen's hygienic benefits. Hygiene interpreted beauty as health; by replacing the older occupant of the traditional kitchen, whose strain and fatigue are repeatedly emphasized in intertitles, with a younger one, the film links household efficiency to a normative image of the healthy body.[32] Moreover, the shots of the Frankfurt Kitchen emphasize its brightness. Multiple images prominently feature the large window at the chopping station, whose semi-transparent curtain diffuses the bright sunlight outside, creating a warmly illuminated working area. Access to sunlight was the hallmark of hygienic architecture. In addition to sunlight, a vase of flowers helps refute typical complaints about the coldness and artificiality of modern design. Reflective metal surfaces, like those of the steel pots and aluminum containers, anticipate what Adrian Forty has called the "aesthetic of cleanliness," which "in the decades since the 1930s . . . has become the norm in the domestic landscape."[33] In contrast to the relatively dull light of the traditional kitchen, whose ornamented containers trap dust and dirt, the visual code of Wolff's *The Frankfurt Kitchen* conveys not only the space's efficiency but its hygienic quality.

Both motion and cleanliness were key to early twentieth-century visions of environmental order. Motion—controlled motion—was just as important as the surface appearance of cleanliness. *Hygiene of Domestic Life* and *The Frankfurt Kitchen* familiarized viewers with visual markers of cleanliness, but in emphasizing activity and movement they also gave cinematic form to a particularly modern understanding of the home as not just a space but an environment, a material system that sustained life. In so doing, they implied that the home was not a space apart, a static respite from the ceaseless activity of modern life outside, but was itself crisscrossed by various forms of interacting material and social traffic in need of regulation. Discussing Lihotzky's kitchen, William Rollins notes a broader dynamic of hygienic rationalization, which promised to make people freer by reducing necessary labor, but which "also tends to direct and confine the people under its sway, imposing upon them what Jünger called 'traffic discipline' (*Verkehrsdisziplin*): a rigid set of schedules, limits, and other technically determined requirements."[34] In so doing, the project of hygiene participated in the Taylorization of daily life, moving the principle of efficiency from the factory to the home, a domain of social reproduction where women traditionally had more autonomy, and subordinating it to a regime of expertise.

Life and Death in the Street

As one might guess, traffic discipline was applied to public spaces as well. During the Weimar period, images of urban streets and their crisscrossing lines of traffic came to symbolize the disorder, contingency, and complexity of modernity more than perhaps anything else. At the same time, street traffic was a phenomenon of real, material complexity, whose ongoing technological evolution demanded regulatory systems and behavioral adaptation on the part of those who wished to navigate it. Keeping pedestrians, playful children, bicyclists, carriages, buses, streetcars, and automobiles in their proper places as they all—ideally—weaved around each other, was no simple task. The 1925 traffic safety film *Im Strudel des Verkehrs* (*In the Vortex of Traffic*), written by Willy Rath and directed by Leo Peukert for Ufa's *Kulturfilm* division, provides practical advice on how to navigate city traffic safely, and thereby contribute to the hygienic orderliness of the urban environment more broadly. Subtitled "a film for everyone," *In the Vortex of Traffic* is framed as a pedagogical lecture directly addressed to the audience and consists of short scenes, by turns comic and tragic, which demonstrate both proper street conduct as well as the consequences of disregarding the rules of the road. The film shows how urban order must be kept in balance through myriad acts of individual self-discipline, and, failing that, police enforcement.

The film's concern with traffic accidents placed it in the realm of hygiene discourse, though this may not have been obvious to its contemporary viewers. While hygiene experts had successfully raised public awareness of epidemic diseases and how to prevent them from spreading, some warned that accidents had not received nearly enough attention. In an article arguing for the use of film to promote accident prevention, Dr. Curt Thomalla noted that

> Berlin's governments, public utility organisations of every kind, technical and professional associations and the schools regard it as their duty to cooperate in safeguarding public health and in spreading the necessary doctrines throughout the length and breadth of the land.

The same, however, does not apply to the prevention of accidents. The mass of the people are unfamiliar even with the use of the term; it has no exact meaning for them.[35]

This was the case despite the fact that "the totality of accidents claim more victims and result in a larger number of deaths than the gravest epidemics."[36] By the late 1920s, Thomalla understood accidents as part of the larger project of hygienic reform, and he served as the organizational director of the 1928 National Accident Prevention Week (Reichs-Unfallverhütungswoche) in Hamburg. Thomalla gathered thirty films for the event that addressed the problem of accidents in the workplace, at home, and on the street.[37] He cited *In the Vortex of Traffic* as a forerunner of the traffic-themed films shown at Accident Prevention Week.

Following a brief introduction by an internal narrator, the film begins with a comic depiction of motorization's effect on the urban environment. "In hardly twenty-five years, the world-conquering motor ushered in the Age of Traffic," the narrator announces. We see a street from the year 1900, in which pedestrians wonder at the appearance of an automobile; the film then flashes forward to the present, where cars surround a bewildered old man like sharks circling prey in the water. This dystopian image, however comic, is reinforced by the image that follows. "On his way around the globe, the traffic monster [*Moloch Verkehr*]," an intertitle states, "came to us, too." A monstrous incarnation of traffic—a giant robotic figure composed of automobiles and train cars, animated in stop-motion—invades a busy metropolitan square and collapses, halting the flow of vehicles and pedestrians. This introduces the film's central concern: "The untamed giant shows us, by the day and by the hour, his terrifying form: the accident!"

In 1924, the psychologist Karl Tramm argued that film and other visual propaganda could prevent accidents and save lives if they answered the following questions "in an attention-grabbing and generally understandable manner": "(1) How do accidents happen, (2) what causes them, and (3) how can they be avoided through deliberate thought and action?"[38] Inspired by campaigns in the United States and England, Tramm suggested numerous strategies for raising and maintaining awareness of the dangers of accidents, from standardized warning symbols and simple slogans (like "safety first") to emotional appeals and comic exaggeration (particularly for youth). *In the Vortex of Traffic* employs all of these, addressing the variety of ways one might put oneself or others at risk on the road, whether as a pedestrian, a driver, or a passenger. The film cautions children against playing in the street; urges pedestrians to use sidewalks and crosswalks; warns drivers not to speed or consume alcohol; and admonishes train and streetcar passengers for trying to board or exit vehicles while they are still moving. The tone careens wildly from comic vignettes of distraction or carelessness—such as when someone discards a banana peel on the street, causing a man to slip and nearly be run over—to scenes of tragic recklessness, including a woman who commits vehicular manslaughter and subsequently ends her own life. In the course of the film, we learn the standardized gestures used by the traffic police (*Schutz-polizei*, or *Schupos*) to direct traffic, as well as handy rhyming mnemonics for pedestrians. By imparting rules and techniques for preventing accidents in specific situations, *In the Vortex of Traffic* aims to provide knowledge that is both authorized by expertise and directly useful to viewers.

At the same time, the film labors to convince the audience of the efficacy of hygienic intervention guided by expert knowledge—in the first place, by establishing the legitimacy of film itself as a pedagogical tool. For educated German audiences, film was still of dubious pedagogical (if not hygienic) value, with many believing that its emphasis of image over speech and its lack of interactivity were antithetical to learning. If the producers of *In the Vortex of Traffic* wanted the film to be shown to children, they had to convince teachers and traffic police, who might organize special screenings, that such a film could be effective. Like Tramm in his plea for safety awareness campaigns, the film first highlights the apparent efficacy of traffic safety propaganda in the United States. Following the traffic monster sequence, an intertitle informs us that "effective propaganda, which for example in New York . . . is to thank for the drop in child mortality from 30 to 16 per month, is now used to also teach German schoolchildren." A "specially assigned police officer" then presents a traffic safety film to a class of schoolchildren, providing commentary as it plays in the role of the *Kulturfilm* lecturer. In this scene, the presence of the police officer assuages anxiety over the filmic medium's dangerously suggestive influence, ensuring that the pupils will avoid rather than imitate the bad behavior they witness on screen. The scene also functions as a kind of suggestion for potential customers, about how the film could be presented in a classroom. The mediating role of the film lecturer is also mimicked in the film itself, by an internal narrator who declares at the beginning: "From Berlin's police headquarters, I have been given the honorable task of delivering a lecture to you." This internal narrator assures us that the material presented in the film has been approved by traffic experts, and frames the scenes that follow as lessons rather than entertaining fictions.

Bolstering trust in experts and those responsible for producing and maintaining order was a central feature of hygiene education, and the management of traffic was no different. At the end of the classroom scene, the children rush to the podium to shake the police officer's hand. In addition to promoting the use of film as a tool for urban hygiene pedagogy, the film assures us of the competency and goodwill of traffic police. One of *In the Vortex of Traffic*'s longer sequences depicts the training and testing of prospective traffic policemen. We see one recruit at a tachistoscope as a training officer tests his speed at recognizing signals; another officer explaining one-way streets to a group of recruits in front of a massive scale model of the center of Berlin; recruits practicing gestures to guide traffic; and finally, training on a mock

A traffic safety film being screened in a classroom. Still from *In the Vortex of Traffic* (dir. Leo Peukert, 1925).

intersection with real pedestrians, carriages, and cars. These scenes aim to increase confidence in the authority of the police and the rules of the road, which constitute a regulating superego with regard to the otherwise natural disorder of the street. The Dortmund police, which had edited their own copy of *In the Vortex of Traffic* for use in schools, saw traffic safety education as an opportunity to improve the image of police generally in the eyes of children. After an outdoor safety lesson near a police station, the class would be invited to tour the premises. "The reason for this invitation," the head of the Dortmund *Schutzpolizei* explained, "is to bring the police and young people closer together. Youth should get some insight into what modern policing means. They should also recognize that the police station isn't the lion's den, but that the uniformed officers who work there can be counted among their best friends."[39] *In the Vortex of Traffic* likewise pursues the double strategy of offering lessons in traffic safety while also legitimizing the authority of those imparting it. Indeed, the familiarity of the film medium and the authority of the police are each used to reinforce the cultural legitimacy of the other. Using a popular entertainment medium, the police can present themselves to mass audiences as beneficent protectors, while their preexisting authority reassures those who might doubt the medium's pedagogical value.

After learning about how traffic police are trained, we see them in action, in two scenes that stage traffic control as an assertion of culture over nature. The film cuts from the police training field to shots of cats and dogs fighting: "this is how they get along: pedestrians and drivers." This is followed by two scenes of traffic conflict resolved by police. In the first, presumably set in the nineteenth century, two women converse in the street and block the path of a horse-drawn carriage. The two parties argue until "Herr Watchman" arrives to sort things out. We then witness an identical scene set in the present, in which the carriage is now an automobile and the watchman is a modern traffic cop. By framing the sequence with fighting animals, traffic is portrayed as a site of natural aggression, in which the egoistic pursuit of self-interest leads to conflict. At the same time, as domestic animals, dogs and cats can potentially be tamed by an external authority. The traffic cop thus functions to ensure the smooth flow of traffic by taming the selfish, animalistic impulses of pedestrians and drivers. The policeman is an agent of hygienic modernization who mediates between conflicting interests, enforcing lawfulness against the threat of descent into a Darwinian struggle for life. On the ground, as in this sequence, *In the Vortex of Traffic* portrays traffic accidents as the expression of a sometimes brutal war of all against all that characterizes urban life, but which can be tamed by the introduction of a cultural superego. Seen at a distance, as in the film's opening, traffic appears as a force of nature whose risks can only be managed, not eliminated. The film's view of the street as a kind of natural environment in need of regulation reflected hygienic discourse more broadly, which treated the modern city as a space in which nature constantly threatened to break through the constraints of civilization, whether in the form of human aggression or other dangers like fire or contagious disease.

In these two vignettes, the dynamics of traffic regulation are gendered. Both depict women disturbing traffic by engaging in activities more suited to the domestic sphere: in the first, gossiping; in the second, applying makeup. Urban authority, by contrast, is embodied by male figures. As in the films discussed in the previous section, hygiene discourse simultaneously naturalized and modernized the space of the street, reinforcing and codifying preexisting notions of who belonged where in the urban landscape. Furthermore, the sequence points to the way women were constructed as the paradigmatic students of hygienic education, at home and in public. Women were the subjects most in need of modernization, both with regard to newly rationalized practices of domestic labor as well as the navigation of the modern city, with which they were presumed to have little experience. *In the Vortex of Traffic* implies that the transition from nature to culture on the urban street involved internalizing a hygienic gaze coded as masculine.

Ultimately the film wishes to inculcate such a gaze in its viewer, first by modeling ways that pedestrians can (literally) watch out for others, and then by encouraging self-critique. In an early scene, a man catches a woman as she falls out of a passing streetcar, and teaches her a rhyme that explains the correct way to disembark. However, the man is infatuated to the point of distraction, and must in turn be rescued by a young boy, who teaches the man how to properly cross the street. This scene and others like it display ordinary pedestrians acting as traffic cops, watching out, helping in moments of need, and educating others. Furthermore, the man's watchfulness in one moment and distraction in the next emphasize the need for constant self-monitoring and the repression of instinct. Later, an extended comic sequence depicts a man from the country unsuccessfully attempting to navigate Potsdamer Platz, engaging in one risky gambit after another. We are encouraged to laugh at this rube, whose knowledge of modern traffic is obviously inferior to ours. The sequence ends, however, with a clever reversal of the gaze, when the lecturer says: "Sure, ladies and gentlemen, you laugh at this bumbling man from the country. But hand to heart—haven't you sometimes acted just as recklessly?" Andreas Killen's summary of the Weimar-era response to the problem of workplace accidents applies equally to traffic, and this film in particular: "Accident safety meant internalizing a new gaze, one that was, first and foremost, directed inward."[40] By adopting such a gaze, the film implies, culture can discipline nature both at the individual level and with regard to traffic as a whole.

At the same time, the film implies that self-discipline and vigilance are what will integrate society into a balanced and harmonious whole—in other words, they will help produce the city as a functioning organism, rather than a field of conflicting interests. As Dietmar Fack writes, quoting traffic safety evangelist Wilhelm Vonolfen, "the community spirit, the ability to socially integrate the individual personality, is the basic prerequisite of successful traffic education. The education of the individual was seen as the means for realizing the common interest in an 'organic orderliness and usefulness.'"[41] The film's final image stresses the individual's integration into society as a whole. As if to test our skills of visual apprehension like the traffic police undergoing psychotechnic training earlier in the film, the internal narrator commands: "And now to conclude—give me once again your most rapt attention for the following words." We then see a composite shot. A traffic cop stands in the center, stretching the entire height of the frame, while smaller scenes of traffic are superimposed on each side of him; the superimposed scenes sometimes overlap, but no collision interrupts the smooth flow of pedestrians, cars, carts, streetcars, and trains. All the while, to the policeman's right, as if looming behind him, the faint image of a skeleton plays a violin. Text fades in around the policeman, summarizing the film's message: "We can't do it alone! Do your part through prudence and attention—then there will be no more accidents." These final words emphasize traffic safety as a collective endeavor, while the surrounding traffic montage offers an image of the city as a well-functioning (if complex) organism. The authority and expertise of the traffic police work together with the specter of death to mediate conflicting interests and ensure the orderliness of urban space.

"Do your part through prudence and attention." Still from *In the Vortex of Traffic*.

The prominence of police in a film about bodily safety points to how Weimar-era discourse about social disorder in urban public space intersected with hygienic concern for health and order in the material environment. As Sara Hall has documented, after the war, many city-dwelling Germans interpreted political violence and street crime as signs of an increasingly disordered public space in need of control, exacerbated by a sense of mistrust between police and the populace. The police consequently engaged in public relations campaigns to improve their image, while also encouraging people to join the effort to control urban space by becoming more aware of their surroundings. Policing during the Weimar Republic thus moved "away from old-fashioned repressive, spectacular law enforcement towards distinctly modern techniques of power at work through more superficially visible, but less forceful, networks of productive social discipline."[42] This describes the type of seeing advocated by *In the Vortex of Traffic* and anti-accident propaganda generally. Just as in the modernization of policing, part of the hygienic project involved delegating some responsibility to citizens themselves to monitor their environment for disorder, whether at home, in the street, or at work. Films like *Hygiene of Domestic Life* and *In the Vortex of Traffic* promoted cooperation between hygienic experts and laypeople by modeling this type of self-surveillance.

Unlike *Hygiene of Domestic Life*, however, *In the Vortex of Traffic* posits not air or dirt but people themselves as sources of environmental disorder. The film's vision of orderliness is thus simultaneously environmental and social, a picture of how the street can be rationalized in order to reduce injury and death, but also of whom the street is for: primarily men of working age, while women and children are prone to interrupt traffic by taking domestic activities into the street. Older people, too, are excluded, such as in a scene portraying an older man bewildered by modern Potsdamer Platz. These exclusions indicate some of the ways that hygienic environmental order was articulated with normative conceptions of gender and bodily ability. In chapter 4, I explore the topic of disability and aging in relation to hygienic visions of urban space; in the following section I show how urban planners proposed to deal with the problem of modernity's environmental disorder.

Cities of Today and Tomorrow

Images of street-level disorder in Weimar culture often functioned as a synecdoche for urban modernity as such. Moving from the street to the larger scale of the city as a whole, we can find the ordering logic of hygiene at work in early twentieth-century urban planning discourse as well. The 1930 film *Die Stadt von Morgen: Ein Film vom Städtebau* (*The City of Tomorrow: An Urban Planning Film*) rises above the hustle and bustle of the street to give cinematic form to a higher-level urban order, and in doing so it demonstrates the extent to which hygienic order was envisioned as analogous to that of a biological organism. Directed by a pair of architects, Maximilian von Goldbeck and Erich Kotzer, the film introduces modern concepts of regional and city planning. It is structured simply, with the first half dedicated to a critical summary of urbanization since the nineteenth century, while the second half envisions an ideal city as it could develop if planned properly. The film historian Thomas Elsaesser ascribes *The City of Tomorrow* to a loose subgenre of *Kulturfilme* associated with the modern architectural movements of the 1920s, in which "the documentation of social conditions, the demonstration of technical processes, and the advocacy of architectural solutions were linked with one another in an exemplary way."[43] The film's ending, which praises the healthiness of the rationally planned city, clarifies the hygienic benefits of an ordered urban environment whose growth mimicked that of a natural organism. *The City of Tomorrow* was funded by a collection of state, regional, and municipal groups and was addressed primarily to planners and other city officials who might influence policy.[44] Consequently, the film is not concerned with imparting advice for daily life, and instead outlines the hygienic imaginary's broader vision of modernization. It encourages its viewers to think of the city's different spaces as linked in a system, which can be orderly or disorderly depending on how it is organized.

The City of Tomorrow also puts hygiene's strategic rhetorical use of nature on full display. When it came to hygiene's imagination of society, nature functioned as both foil and ideal. On one hand, hygiene represented social conflict as a reflection of nature's irrational, unchecked aggression, and promised to impose the order of culture. On the other, it was a form of social engineering in the sense elaborated by historian Thomas Etzemüller: a "transnational and interdisciplinary project of recreating through artificial means a lost natural order of society."[45] While opposed to nature as conflict, hygiene thus also posited itself as a corrective to civilization, a moderating force that would realign an excessively artificial society with the purportedly natural social and bodily needs of the human being. In this way, hygiene could appeal simultaneously to pro- and anti-modern sentiments, rejecting "nature" when it referred to social conflict and embracing it when it entailed the maintenance of social order. As with depictions of the family discussed earlier in the chapter, *The City of Tomorrow* imagines hygienic modernization as an ordering of the material environment that nonetheless keeps fundamental (that is, "natural") social relations in place. The film thus deploys nature as a flexible and ideologically convenient term in service of its vision of a future in which hygienic expertise has disciplined modernity's social and material disorder.

The first sequence of *The City of Tomorrow* begins by showing "how our towns and especially the cities grew and became what they are: seas of houses, full of noise and smoke, without sun and air." *The City of Tomorrow* initially frames its intervention within a narrative of modernity alienated from nature. The film's first images are of a panorama of rolling farmland, a cattle-drawn hay wagon, and a picturesque village, along with the intertitle: "The town lay quiet and peaceful." The subsequent urbanization is depicted with a mix of animated aerial views of an exemplary city, population statistics, and illustrative documentary inserts, which serve as visual evidence of what has gone wrong. Typical of landscape preservation and urban reform discourse of the period, these images show crowded train platforms, landscapes despoiled by coal mining, smokestacks and tenements, and children playing in streets and tenement courtyards. The aerial animations, meanwhile, depict runaway development that crowds out urban green spaces and covers the city in a layer of soot. An intertitle proclaims: "This city makes healthy living impossible! Removes the people's connection to nature! Lets the body and soul of generations wither!" Here, nature means green nature, the outdoors, which the first generation of green urban planners saw as vital to the maintenance of human health and sought to restore to industrial cities in various ways.[46]

Alongside this depiction of the city's artificiality in opposition to green nature, however, the film also depicts the process of urbanization itself as altogether too natural. The animations and intertitles suggest that the problem is not urban development as such—the film is subtitled "A Film about Urban Planning"—but development without a plan (*systemlose Entwicklung*). In

The overgrown city. Still from *The City of Tomorrow* (dir. Maximilian von Goldbeck and Erich Kotzer, 1930).

the animations, buildings pop up like weeds, colonizing whatever available space is most convenient in the moment. The wild, unchecked growth of the city is driven by unthinking self-interest: economic considerations lead industries to crowd around natural resources, workers to crowd around factories, developers to build on former green spaces, train tracks to be laid on the most direct paths, and so on. This critique of urbanization echoed that of a number of important regional and urban planners, such as Robert Schmidt, who helped pioneer regional planning in the Ruhr area. For such planners, writes Ariane Leendertz, nineteenth-century urbanization had led to cities that were characterized by "a loss of form, the individual elements in space had begun to 'disturb' one another,' 'order' and 'conformity' were missing."[47] One senses an implicit rejection of liberal economics in this critique, but one couched in functional-biological language that avoids direct reference to political economy and maintains the scientific authority of the expert planner.

In depicting historical urbanization as both destructive of nature and itself excessively natural, *The City of Tomorrow* introduces its audience to an ecological perspective that is ultimately concerned less with distinguishing between nature and culture than with producing a stable system. The city is viewed as the result of a confluence of geographic conditions, natural

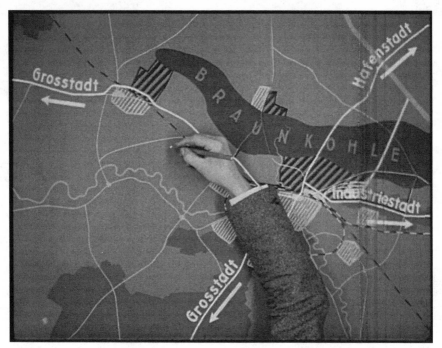

The planner's hand. Still from *The City of Tomorrow*.

resources, transport technologies, human modification of the environment, the pursuit of material gain, and other forces. The question is whether these forces are ordered or disordered, whether they cohere into a form that allows sustainable growth, or are constellated such that they undermine the city's own reproduction.

The second half of the film imagines a process of ordered growth: "how conscious creative will [*bewusster Gestaltungswille*] can direct city development." We first see the overhead map of the small city whose development went awry the last time around, returned to its original form. Then, however, an iris transitions to an even larger map of the entire surrounding area, including neighboring cities and the various waterways, railways, and roads that connect them. Before a plan can be made, the planner requires a holistic knowledge of the geographic, economic, and even geologic characteristics of the region. The planner's exhaustive research is represented by a montage of maps revealing different aspects of the terrain, and statistical tables of economic and demographic data. Returning to the comprehensive map, a hand enters the frame and draws the new urban plan, designating areas for industry, residential development, roads, railways, a freight depot, an airport, recreational green spaces, agriculture, and forestry. Each of these has its role to play in the functioning of the whole.

Thus far, the film has provided the viewer with a holistic view of urban development and encouraged confidence in the experts who should be tasked with guiding it. According to Leendertz, producing order meant that urban planners first had to create an image of the whole; quoting Robert Schmidt, she writes, "the state and its administrative bodies had to conform to the new, modern times, had to leave behind the 'age of the frog's-eye view' [*Froschperspektive*] and embrace the 'age of the airship and the bird's-eye view' [*Vogelperspektive*]."[48] In the spirit of social engineering's desire for rational transparency, *The City of Tomorrow* translates the planner's statistical and cartographic image of the city into cinematic terms. It is tempting to call the film's use of large-scale animated maps an attempt to offer a literal bird's-eye view, but they possess a stability, exemplarity, and legibility that aerial photography could not achieve. Instead of indexical authenticity, the animated maps reduce the city to an abstract image of the interlocking systems that determine its life and growth, like an anatomical illustration. The city is presented as knowable and therefore manageable, for those with the proper maps and statistics. At the same time, the film only shows each map or table partially, and cuts quickly from one to the next, suggesting that a detailed understanding of the urban organism is beyond the capacity of the average viewer. We are meant to leave planning to the planners, with an awareness that their work is based on extensive empirical data.

Following all of this work, "well-planned, the city now develops." Housing and industry develop separately and within limits; recreational green spaces and surrounding nature preserves are easily accessible; public transportation connects homes with factories, while industrial and express traffic is routed to avoid passing through residential and business zones. Allotted its proper place within the whole, each of the urban organism's subsystems performs its work without interfering with the others. An intertitle declares: "Conscious design, no longer 'the free play of forces,' creates an organic urban landscape [*organisches Stadtgebilde*]." The urban planner's design guarantees the orderliness of life in the city, as a now-absent God once guaranteed the order of nature. The "organic urban landscape" is an artificial organism, ordered in its spatial form and growth in time.

The way *The City of Tomorrow* compresses time to demonstrate this growth is crucial to its depiction of the city as an organism. In speeding up relatively slow processes to make them visible, the film's animations resemble time-lapse photography, which was often used in educational films to show processes of organic growth. In an article on slow-motion and time-lapse photography in an anthology of texts by *Kulturfilm* producers, K. Krüger noted that the effect provided "a good total view of very slowly developing phenomena" and had been used to produce images "of the growth of crystals, of the blooming of flowers . . . recently even the development of living creatures in eggs, the proliferation of cancerous cells, of chemical reactions, of the action of white blood cells, the growth of new tissue."[49] Time-lapse images of plant growth were especially popular, such that the 1925 film *Das Blumen-wunder* (*The Miracle of Flowers*) built a feature-length story around them.[50] Analogous to the regional maps shown earlier, which allowed the viewer to grasp the city as a coherent geographical whole, *The City of Tomorrow*'s time-compressed sequences of urbanization lend these processes an appearance of orderliness. By adapting a technique associated with organic growth, the film depicts planned urban development as both natural and controlled.

The City of Tomorrow's imagined urban organism stands in implicit opposition to a sense, shared across lines of political division, that industrial cities were profoundly disordered. This sense is crystallized in the film's ironic invocation of "the free play of forces," a phrase originally associated with critiques of liberal free-market economics, but which by 1900 was also deployed to signal the purported meaninglessness and disorder implied by a Darwinian worldview.[51] For the anti-liberal Right, unregulated capital upset divinely ordained—and therefore natural—hierarchies in human society, while Darwin threatened to undo the very notion of a natural order planned by God. From this perspective, the "organic urban landscape" proposed in *The City of Tomorrow* could appeal as a way to maintain social hierarchies within a pseudo-natural order modeled on the organism. On the Left, some accused Darwin of projecting a liberal economic ideology onto nature in positing a universal "struggle for life" between individuals, providing scientific cover for structures of exploitation that were in no way natural. In this light, the promise of urban hygiene lay in its call to subordinate profit to the biological necessities of those living in the city: their need for housing, sunlight, clean air and water, and green spaces for recreation. At the same time, the organic model offered an image of naturalness rooted, at least potentially, in cooperation and solidarity rather than competition. Ultimately, though, there is something fundamentally conservative in the way the film de-politicizes social conflict and exploitation. More directly than the other films discussed in this chapter, *The City of Tomorrow* shows how the logic of hygiene translated the political and economic contradictions of industrial capitalism into material terms, treating them as problems of spatial and environmental organization.

The City of Tomorrow's final minute shows the results of urban planning in human terms. We leave the animated map behind in favor of images of people in idealized urban surroundings: "Here, the human being can lead a healthy life in sunny and airy homes, in direct contact with nature." In every shot, the built environment contains elements of (green) nature—people stroll along a tree-lined street, a couple tends to chickens being raised in a courtyard, families relax in gardens and grassy yards. Images of young children and babies recur insistently. The final five shots of the film consist of a toddler on a blanket, a baby playing in a large outdoor crib, two shots of a group of babies playing on a blanket in the grass, and a baby in a carriage in front of a row of flowering bushes. These images link the environmental order imagined in the rest of the film to the biopolitical aim of growing the population and its labor power. Given the previously unthinkable numbers of young men killed and injured in World War I, malnutrition due to rationing and food shortages, and deadly epidemics at home and on the front, health and population became central to discussions of Germany's postwar recovery. If Germany's economic (and, implicitly, military) power relied on the strength of its laboring population, hygiene proposed to strengthen the nation through rational planning.

This program accorded with a eugenic conception of populations that had broad currency in public health discourse, which viewed populations in terms of "quality" as well as quantity. The film's final images of children resonate against a background of eugenic thought that prized white, European bodies and aimed to reduce disabilities in the populace. While explicit racial hygiene was quite controversial throughout the 1920s, and was rejected outright by many experts working in other hygienic disciplines, forms of "passive" or "positive" eugenics can be seen operating in countless health initiatives of the time. As Michael Hau has shown, for instance, the widespread promotion of sport and physical fitness during the Weimar Republic was part of the "'care for the hereditary endowment' (*Anlagenpflege*) which tried to make sure that people could realize their full hereditary potential without being stunted by an adverse environment."[52] Such efforts did not see nature and nurture in opposition to each other, but as two complementary dimensions of populational health. The end of *The City of Tomorrow* reveals how modernist planning utopias, concerned first with producing an ordered and harmonious urban environment, could be allied with eugenic visions of health.

This eugenic dimension of the film could accommodate a range of political orientations. On one hand, the film heralds an industrial city in which everyone, regardless of class, might have access to living conditions adequate to their biological needs and enjoy the type of healthy life promoted in hygiene discourse. On the other hand, the film's shots of healthy, happy, white children could also be understood within the broader racialization of hygiene in the late 1920s and into the 1930s. Racial hygiene, which responded to anxieties about degeneration among the working class as an effect of urban living conditions, alcoholism, malnutrition, sexually transmitted disease, and other characteristically modern ills, had long been part of hygiene discourse, but gained prominence toward the end of the Weimar Republic.[53] Within this framework, *The City of Tomorrow*'s concluding emphasis on reproduction could be read according to a narrative of racial regeneration. Though the film does not itself deploy the language of racial hygiene, the period's racial imaginary would certainly have inflected how some viewers understood its vision of an organic, healthy city.

As Michael Cowan writes, Weimar-era filmmakers like Walter Ruttmann and Svend Noldan, who produced *The City of Tomorrow*, used "film itself as a medium of biopolitical intervention," making films that sought to improve the health of the population by spreading hygienic knowledge.[54] This goal is more readily apparent in films that offered viewers advice about how to conduct their everyday lives, with regard to household cleanliness, sexual health, or accident prevention. *The City of Tomorrow* does not provide hygiene advice of this kind, and, although the directors made overtures to a mass public, Jeanpaul Goergen notes that the film was mainly shown to audiences with a professional interest in urban planning.[55] From a hygienic perspective, it was more important that the average viewer wash their hands than conceive of themselves as part of an urban organism (though this might help them understand why hand-washing is good); the intended audience was more plausibly the educated and political classes that would have the power, directly or indirectly, to help produce an organically functioning city if they viewed it as such. Even so, the film instantiates a hierarchy of expertise that we see in films for popular audiences as well. Though it imparts a modest knowledge of urban planning to the viewer, it does so only to the extent that the viewer understands the purposes to which this expertise is being put. The audience is not meant to wield this knowledge critically, but merely to subscribe to the goal of producing a healthy urban organism and fulfill their respective roles accordingly.

Across different scales, from the domestic kitchen to the urban system as a whole, visions of environmental order in the Weimar *Kulturfilme* were tied to a fantasy of social order in a time of economic and political upheaval. They most immediately responded to the environmental and health effects of urbanization, industrialization, and the war, but they also drew energy from a broader sense of social disorder. Films like the ones discussed in this chapter translated the disorder of capitalist modernity into spatial and environmental terms, and promised that a technocratic arrangement of things, people, and spaces would lead to an organically functioning community. Rather than question class and gender hierarchies, they put them to use within a hygienic logic that delegated a kind of environmental authority while at the same time suggesting what kinds of people belonged where within the urban system.

In their more practical form, like *Hygiene of Domestic Life* or *In the Vortex of Traffic*, such films modeled a visual environmental awareness, which was itself a component of the hygienic subjectivity they ultimately wished to encourage. This visuality followed what the historian Chris Otter calls an oligoptic, rather than panoptic, visual logic. Analyzing transformations of urban space in Victorian England, Otter argues that behavior was not regulated by a panoptic architecture that tightly circumscribed the individual's movements and behavior, monitored by an all-seeing, centralized gaze. Urban space, rather, was "oligoptic," defined by a relative freedom of movement under conditions of reciprocal observation and self-observation. Oligoptic space is "an arena within which a small group of people observe each other: it is a place in which mutual oversight takes place," and in which "looks, gazes, and glimpses are distributed relatively symmetrically."[56] Oligoptic visual relations are exemplified in a film like *In the Vortex of Traffic*, which teaches viewers to monitor themselves and others around them, since no official authority could possibly surveil everything that happens on a city's streets. Even where authorities do monitor public space, "these supervisors or superintendents had a privileged, but humble, verifiable, and certainly not omniscient, point of perception."[57] The traffic cop, for instance, does not simply make a decree, but listens to the various parties involved in an accident—his function is to mediate, rather than impose.

Otter also emphasizes that unlike the panopticon, oligoptic relations allow for spheres of privacy. This is true in the sense that authorities were not (always) allowed to monitor all domestic spaces, but hygiene still encouraged making the home into a space of mutual oversight. In *Hygiene of Domestic Life*, parents monitor their children and each other. Even films like *The City of Tomorrow* and *The Frankfurt Kitchen*, which foreground god's-eye views of the city and the kitchen, don't do so in order to surveil individual behaviors, but rather to create the conditions under which free movement and hygienic vision can occur. The films examined in this chapter thus worked to bolster an oligoptic visual regime by teaching viewers both how to see hygienically and why they should do so. By giving mass audiences the knowledge necessary to become effective monitors, the work of seeing could be harnessed in the service of health.

As Tom Crook argues, the modernity of public health beginning in the mid-nineteenth century consisted in its systematic quality, whereby different administrative and technical apparatuses at different scales became linked. According to Crook, the distinction between "public" and "private" hygiene belies the way modern public health involved an intensification of the links between the two: "personal cleanliness," he writes, "was profoundly social."[58] This is most apparent in *In the Vortex of Traffic*, in which individual choices are seen to have immediate social effects, for good or ill. Whether or not the films explicitly linked the personal and the social, however, their emphasis on a systematic and scalar mode of thinking was an important aspect of their modernity. The viewer may not need to see how traffic police are trained, for instance, but understanding the different systems at play in material life was crucial to the kind of modern hygienic subjectivity these films encouraged.

Non-photographic inserts and sequences served a crucial purpose in this regard, by investing concrete visual experience with a knowledge of phenomena that were not directly visible. The diagrams depicting the housewife's patterns of movement in *The Frankfurt Kitchen* condense space and time, allowing the viewer to see individual actions as part of a cumulative, more or less efficient process that is dependent on spatial design. *The City of Tomorrow*'s maps and animations of urbanization place its images of streets and smokestacks within a larger system of environmental order or disorder, which in turn reflects historical processes. Both examples use shifts in temporal and spatial scale to change the meaning of everyday, more easily photographed sights and actions.[59]

In other words, the *Kulturfilme* of the Weimar period did not convey the hygienic only through their images of healthy bodies and clean surfaces, or in training vision (though they did do these things). They also modeled a way of thinking, which attempted to comprehend how the material environments that comprised modern life were constituted, as well as the rationality that legitimated them. To do so, they made use of film's unique potentials, to jump between spaces and scales; to manipulate time, by halting it, eliding it, or speeding it up; to combine text and image, so as to guide the viewer's interpretation of the latter; and to incorporate different forms of visual representation, from photographs to abstract animations. All of these techniques combined in films like *In the Vortex of Traffic* or *The City of Tomorrow* to spur the viewer to construct a cognitive map of the traffic system and the urban system, and of what it meant for things to be in or out of place in each. Viewers learned how to think in terms of environmental order and disorder and grasp the links between different material systems.

Hygiene was more than the aesthetic of cleanliness associated with certain forms of modernist architecture and design, characterized by the circulation of light and air and the predominance of the color white.[60] It was a logic of environmental order, authorized by expertise, but which could be wielded by experts and laypeople alike. Teaching the underlying logic of hygienic order could also provide mass audiences with a sense of agency over their lives, insofar as health was an important precondition for maintaining one's livelihood under capitalism. At the same time, hygiene offered a rationale for the status quo by eliding the distinction between material arrangements and political-economic relations, between environmental and social order. In these films the environmental order of hygiene represents itself, *pars pro toto*, as evidence of the rationality (or possible rationality) of the social order as a whole. Such a rationality was all the more important after World War I, when political order was no longer supposed to be founded on irrational forms of authority. Hygiene's modernity consisted not just in its aesthetic expression, but in its drive to coordinate material systems into a dispositif and impose rational order.

Hygiene was also modern in its recognition that order demanded constant work to maintain. In this regard, it incorporated the thermodynamic insight that physical systems tend toward disorder and require new inputs of energy in order to keep running. Weimar-era *Kulturfilme* like the ones discussed in this chapter thematized the labor of thermodynamic maintenance and envisioned a modernity that was clean, healthy, and efficient. Film, however, as a medium based on photographic indexicality, was also uniquely capable of representing contingency and disorder—everything that the labor of hygiene worked to repress. The next chapter examines how hygiene's entropic underside returned to haunt the cinematic image in F. W. Murnau's 1926 film *Faust*.

Chapter 3

✦

Matter Out of Place

Pollution and Distraction in F. W. Murnau's *Faust*

Faust emerges from a fog. Following the credit sequence of Murnau's 1926 film, an intertitle commands the viewer: "Behold! The gates of hell are opened and the horrors of the masses plague the earth . . ." The first shot then throws us into a turbulent brew of smoke and vapor that completely fills the frame. A light seems to emanate from the background, but the intervening fog obscures any sense of spatial extension or scale. Through a dissolve, this primordial haze gives way to an image of the Horsemen of the Apocalypse, whose steeds rise and fall rhythmically as they are buffeted and nearly enveloped in roiling clouds. Then a light appears—the sun, rendered with special effects, rises to pierce the haze. Flashing pillars of light overtake the frame, blinding our view of the riders, until the glowing eyes (and glinting fingernails) of Mephisto, played by Emil Jannings, peek out of the darkness. Now, in place of the sun, an archangel steps forth, sword raised, and demands that Mephisto stop torturing humanity, to which he replies, thick smoke rising behind him: "The earth is mine!"

Forms of particulate matter like those on display in this scene, such as smoke, dust, vapor, and fog, were especially troublesome for modern hygiene. Given hygiene's focus on disease prevention, early interest in particulate matter was spurred by the emerging science of bacteriology, whose epochal discoveries in the nineteenth century disproved long-standing miasma theories of contagion and pointed to the possibility that particles in the air could transmit disease. Dust, as historian Anselm Wagner notes, thus attracted "the attention of biopolitical hygienic measures that aimed to contain, remove, and destroy it, and warn the population of its dangers through broad-based educational campaigns. Removing dust was thereby no longer simply about creating order, but was raised to a form of disease and plague prevention."[1] Not just the concern of scientists, particulates like smoke and dust were an immediately perceptible effect of urban environmental degradation, apparent to the eyes, the nose, and the skin. As Frank Uekötter writes, "smoke was the most severe air pollution problem of the late nineteenth and early twentieth centuries. Wherever coal was used in major quantities, smoke and soot, the typical by-products of incomplete combustion, infested the local atmosphere, provoking countless complaints and attempts at abatement."[2] While it was understood that particulates did not cause disease in the way that something like cholera did, it was increasingly clear that they posed health threats of their own, when they came into contact with skin or were inhaled. Hygienists put particulate matter under the microscope and, like cells, bacteria, or microorganisms, classified it according to its different forms and physical behaviors. In practical terms, William Rollins writes, "dust avoidance took on the status of a categorical imperative."[3] Turn-of-the-century hygiene manuals and journals contained numerous analyses of particulates in the home, the street, the factory, and other places, and guidelines about how to combat or control them.

More fundamentally, particulates represented the threat—or, rather, the fact—of entropy. Smoke and steam were important objects of research in the nineteenth-century science of thermodynamics, which sought to understand the physical transformations of energy in order to increase the efficiency of engines.[4] Smoke was a material index of the tendency of physical systems toward disorder, of the thermodynamic principle that in any transfer or transformation of energy, some of that energy dissipates, rendering it unusable. Coal could be used to generate heat and electricity, but in the process, some of it also became smoke—a highly disordered particulate material that could not be made into much of anything, and was consequently released into the environment. Industrialization promised that great quantities of energy would be used for the advance of civilization, and thermodynamics aided this process, but it also recognized, given the inevitable increase of entropy, that the ultimate end point of any physical system was dissipation, decay, heat death. Seen from this perspective, the project of hygiene was one of managing entropy. It was a post-thermodynamic project that acknowledged the disordering material effects of industrial modernity, but strove to insulate the human population from them and shore up the integrity and laboring ability of the human body. Hygiene aimed to prevent the great disordering power of combustion from being directed back at the human population, instead channeling it elsewhere through ventilation, vacuuming, filtering, urban planning, and other means.

In this chapter I read the particulate aesthetics of Murnau's *Faust* in relation to the hygienic fight against entropy. The film's narrative can be read as a melancholic story of industrialization as a pact with the devil, whose combustive power has despoiled a previously harmonious world. At the level of the image, however, the film is unique in its embrace of the particulate and its defiance of the hygienic. I argue that *Faust* uses particulate matter to insist on the dissipatory possibilities of cinema, using film to obscure bodies and disperse its spectator. *Faust*'s unhygienic images, moreover, point to the ways in which the film's production itself flouted the hygienic norms common to studio filmmaking. As both process and product, then, *Faust* reveled in the entropic, taking the bad air of the city and turning it into a medium of aesthetic experimentation. The film demonstrates hygiene's intimate relationship with studio cinema, as a form of cultural production that both depended upon the maintenance of environmental order and made environmental disorder a form of aesthetic practice. Moreover, *Faust* suggests that dispersion, simultaneously material and subjective, is at the heart of the cinematic experience. Such an understanding of cinema, which embraced the dissolution of boundaries between self and world, sets it fundamentally at odds with the project of modern hygiene, which sought to order the environment so that the human subject could maintain the fiction of its self-sufficiency and coherence.

Particulates, Industrial Hygiene, and the Film Studio

In her 1964 book on Murnau, Lotte Eisner described *Faust*'s opening and concluding scenes as "fugues of light, orchestrated with incomparable mastery." Eisner's assessment heralded *Faust*'s current status as a high point of Expressionist *Lichtregie* ("lighting direction" or "lighting design"). Anne Hoormann subsequently included *Faust* in her book on the poetics of light in early twentieth-century German cultural production,[5] while Frances Guerin discusses the film in her more recent book on lighting technology in German films of the silent era.[6] Anticipating such readings, Eisner wrote, "light and movement: all Murnau's experiments and discoveries . . . came to full fruition in *Faust*."[7] This focus on light, however, suggests a visual clarity that belies the film's literal fogginess. Andor Krazsna-Krausz's contemporary review in *Filmtechnik* better captured this aspect of the film: "Smoke, pregnant with mystical dangers, links and frames his images, in which blinding whites flare up and the deepest blacks are seen. He projects striking beams of light into the viewer's eyes, only to blind them with soot, smoke, and steam in the next scene."[8] From the prologue to the stake-burning that ends the film, forms of particulate matter pervade the imagery of *Faust*. As Kurt Pinthus joked in his review of the film, "every time that Faust (or the director) doesn't know what to do, we see him sitting on an outcropping surrounded by fog, giving the impression that he takes a steam bath whenever he's grumpy."[9] As much as it is a fugue of light, *Faust* is a fugue of fog. Its lightscapes are suffused with particulates that rise, hang, blow, billow, stream, condense, and dissipate.

The sheer ubiquity and variety of particulate matter in Murnau's film exceeds its use as a mere special effect. It resonates with the industrial world of smokestacks and steam engines, a world driven by fuels whose combustion had immediately palpable environmental effects. For Mark Cioc, the dominance of fossil fuels such as coal signaled the "beginning point of modern

environmental history," which was characterized by "a shift from an economy based (at least potentially) on a sustainable yield (*Nachhaltigkeit*) to one
based on the utilisation of a non-renewable resource (*Raubwirtschaft*)."[10] By
1900, according to the environmental historian John R. McNeill, the industrial and household use of coal accounted for the major part of air pollution,
"filling the skies with smoke, soot, sulfur dioxide, and various other unsavory
substances."[11] The Rhine river valley, which offered numerous advantages
for industrial production, suffered from aerosol pollution severe enough to
warrant mention in more than one global environmental history.[12] Around
this time scientists began to study the consequences of airborne pollution for
vegetation and human health, isolating substances released by factories and
tracing their effects.[13] By 1910, industrial particulates were the subject of
their own scientific journal, *Rauch und Staub: Zeitschrift für ihre Bekämpfung* (*Smoke and Dust: Journal for Combatting Them*). Engineers developed
new technologies, such as the electrostatic filter, to control particulate emissions, though these were only used to the extent that profits were not unduly
affected. Larger political efforts at controlling the "plague of smoke" (*Rauch-
plage*) remained haphazard and at best locally effective throughout the 1920s
and beyond.[14]

Specifying how particulates affected human health was just the beginning.
In their contribution on the "Prevention of Smoke and Soot in Cities" to
Weyl's Handbook of Hygiene, Louis Ascher and Ernst Kobbert (a doctor
and factory director, respectively, whose collaboration points to the larger
confluence of medicine and engineering in modern hygiene) identified four
areas of ill-effect: damage to climate, buildings, plants, and people. Based
on a statistical analysis, Ascher found "a significantly higher mortality rate
from non-tuberculitic acute lung diseases in the areas . . . and industries with
the most smoke and soot, which cannot be explained by climatic, social, or
infectious influences."[15] In tracing the spread and effects of particulate matter, hygienists were forced to consider the entire ecology of the city: its flora
and fauna, their interactions with each other and their material environment,
and how these interactions affected their biological functioning. The ecology
of dust in urban homes, streets, and factories was also studied intensely. At
the annual meeting of the German Association for Public Health in 1907, a
Prof. Dr. Heim from Erlangen spoke of the dangers of particulate matter in
the home, which consisted "of street dust carried in by shoes, clothes and
wind, dust produced by domestic activities, and dust from the skin and hair
of people and pets."[16]

Industrial hygienists were especially concerned with particulate matter. K. B. Lehmann, for example, devoted a chapter to dust in his treatise
Arbeits- und Gewerbehygiene (*Labor and Industrial Hygiene*) of 1919. Dust,
he declared, "may not be tolerated in factories. Its prevention or removal is of
the utmost importance."[17] Particulate matter posed a range of problems for
factory work. In factories, large masses of material underwent physical and

chemical transformation, in the process often generating particulates. Factory workers were exposed to these particles in much higher concentrations than those outside, and the potential effects of exposure, from damage to the skin, respiratory system, and eyes to poisoning and death, could vary widely depending on the material in question. Moreover, certain kinds of aerosols (such as airborne flour in bakeries) could be flammable, leading to massive explosions should they be set alight. Any number of chemicals thus needed to be evaluated scientifically, while sprays, vacuums, and filters were developed to manage particulates in factory spaces. Beyond human health, loose particulates in some cases also damaged the bottom line. In a 1918 lecture on "Fog, Smoke, and Dust," the German chemist Volkmar Kohlschütter noted that particulate by-products represented a loss of potentially valuable raw material. Because natural resources were not infinite, he argued, it would be prudent "to ensure control" over this nebulous material which "all too often escaped productive use."[18] In factories, where modernity was forged, dust remained a persistent concern—a material reminder of the force of entropy that could never be completely overcome.

The battle against particulates took place in film studios as well, which in many ways operated like factories and adopted the precepts of industrial hygiene. As it was in the movie theater, the danger of fire was a major concern that haunted the filmmaking process. Particulates, and the flammable materials sometimes used to produce them on set, posed considerable risks to workers and the material capital of the studio—its film stocks, lights, sets, wardrobes, prop collections, and buildings. More generally, the flammability of celluloid and set construction materials caused particular worry. By 1924, the Babelsberg studio where *Faust* was filmed had an extensive underground film storage facility whose layout, ventilation, and lighting were designed with fire prevention in mind, as well as an on-site squad of firefighters. "Two fire hoses and all the necessary first-aid implements serve these efforts," reported Alex Kossowsky for the *Film-Kurier*.[19] These were particularly necessary because, while fire and explosions were dangerous for the industrial production of movies, they were also cinematic attractions in and of themselves. Film studios thus had to be able to respond not only to accidental fires, but to fires set on purpose as part of the routine process of filmmaking— sometimes even using leftover celluloid stock as fuel. In 1928, the pioneering film technician Guido Seeber hoped it would soon be possible "to make a truly useable, non-toxic material that produces smoke quickly and in any amount, and that can be easily (quickly) scattered, dispersed, or stabilized as needed."[20] As Brian R. Jacobson writes, "light- and sound-isolating worlds were also dangerous studio hotboxes."[21] Like other sites of industrial production, film studios had to negotiate risky thermodynamic processes that could spiral out of control.

The practice of industrial hygiene was meant to keep the studio's capital, both human and material, safe and able to produce day in and day out.

Studios also practiced a form of hygiene oriented toward the moving image itself and the visual world it created. The visual environment of the film image, or at least the kind of visual environment preferred by the dominant mode of narrative film, had to be ordered in particular ways that could not be taken for granted. By the 1910s, film studios began to be erected on the edges (rather than in the middle) of cities, one advantage of which was the clearer air. In his filmmaking manual *Der Film: Seine Mittel—seine Ziele* (*Film: Its Means and Goals*), the director Urban Gad, one of the first to utilize the studio at Babelsberg, wrote that "for photographic reasons, the film studio must have plenty of sunlight, and cannot therefore be located in the middle of a smoky and dusty city. It must be housed out in a suburb, where there aren't any smokestacks."[22] Writing in *Der Film* in 1925, Felix Pfitzner called dust "the camera operator's greatest enemy. Besides quiet, the first requirement of the modern studio is clear air, as free of dust as possible; the highly sensitive film negative must absolutely be prevented from producing 'gray pictures' [*graue Aufnahmen*]." Pfitzner listed the range of current methods by which dust was cleared from the studio, from large-scale ventilation systems to handheld dusters and spray bottles.[23] Particulates were an object of concern for film producers for general reasons of industrial hygiene, but they also had specific material effects on film images.

"Film studios and studio films should be seen as quintessential human-built worlds," Jacobson argues in *Studios before the System*. "In their new studios, filmmakers produced not simply films, but artificial worlds that were on par with the synthetic spaces of the modern built environment."[24] Of particular importance is the extent to which these artificial worlds reproduced a hygienic logic that privileged an environment where vision could function unimpeded and easily separate figure from ground. It may seem unremarkable that filmmakers wanted images undisturbed by dust, but the unusual particulate-filled frames of Murnau's *Faust* help us reflect on this assumption. The preference for dust-free images over "gray" ones is an indication of how the aesthetics of studio-produced films resonated with a hygienic imagination of environmental disorder, which was seen as a threat to the autonomy of the human subject. The "environmental and spatial control" possible in the studio was used to articulate this logic in the film image itself.[25] Environmental transparency could not be taken for granted. The studio dispositif, an elaborate coordination of architecture, engineering, lighting, set design, lenses, and more, generated the conditions for fabricating legible images, characterized by objects and figures that could be clearly distinguished from each other and their surroundings. For Gad, clarity was the ultimate aim of filmmaking. "The foremost task of film," he wrote, "is and remains to illuminate human faces and forms clearly, in a psychological as well as physical sense."[26] This fundamental aesthetic operation of studio filmmaking—creating an environment in which human characters could emerge out of the chaos of the visible world—depended on the complex environmental order of the film studio.

For hygienists as for filmmakers, particulates threatened easy distinctions between bodies and environments. In hygienic terms, smoke and dust insinuated themselves everywhere—from one part of a city to another, from streets through windows, and from the air onto the body, where they could be absorbed by skin, eyes, and lungs. The fight against the smoke and dust plague was thus an attempt to artificially produce and maintain a distinction between the body and its environment that industrialization was making ever more precarious (and that, otherwise, science was revealing as illusory). Studio filmmaking embodied an aesthetic corollary to this project. By distancing itself from the city, making itself independent of the sun through artificial light, filtering particulates, and other means, the studio provided conditions under which human bodies could appear whole and discrete—that is, as bodies, rather than as thermodynamic systems subject to entropy and the dispersive force of industrial modernity.

Anti-Hygiene

With *Faust*, however, the studio functioned not as a filter but as a container, which the filmmakers filled with particulate matter, in effect turning the studio's hygienic separation from the dust and smoke of the city against itself. *Faust* offers an aesthetic analogue to the hygienists' fascination with particulates by staging seemingly endless permutations of light, air, and dispersed matter, through which we observe their physical behaviors and refractory qualities. In the opening sequence alone, we see fog whip around the horsemen of the apocalypse and dissipate behind them; the gently rolling haze below the emerging sun; the dark soot surrounding Mephisto that undulates with menacing, explosive force; the blown steam behind the angel that intersects with outwardly radiating beams of light, making them appear to ripple; the expanding and condensing steam that serves as a transition to our first view of Faust; the vaporous interior of Faust's experimental orb, illuminated by flashes of light and emanating individuated puffs of steam; and strands of steam lit from below that wisp in front of Faust's face, before a strobing cloud swallows him. A later plague scene extends this combinatorics, with altostratus clouds hanging over the village as smoke from wood fires below rises peacefully; the spreading darkness of the smoke-plague; street dust lifted by wind; hooded men with smoke-belching censers escorting the bodies of victims out of the city; the lonely emission of Faust's candle as he reads the Bible; shadows of smoke painted onto the walls of the city by burning fires that signal a descent into apocalyptic frenzy; dust spit out by old books against whose uselessness Faust rages—and so on. Like a hygienist cataloging the devilishly vast range of particulate substances and their behavior under changing environmental conditions, Murnau's film obsessively pursues the cinematic possibilities of particulate matter.

Faust was not the first spectacle to employ the aesthetic effects of particulates. The film can be considered part of a genealogy of techniques of artificial darkness, which Noam Elcott has traced from phantasmagoria and Wagnerian opera to photographic darkrooms and darkened movie theaters.[27] By attending to these techniques, in which smoke and other particulates often figured as tools of obscurity, Elcott exposes a dimension of modern visuality that goes unnoticed in accounts that focus on technologies of vision and illumination. Jannings's Mephisto, for instance, directly invokes the phantasmagoria, a popular visual entertainment of the late eighteenth and nineteenth centuries.[28] These shows, named by their most famous practitioner, Etienne-Gaspard Robertson, involved rear-projecting images of ghosts, skeletons, and other ghoulish figures with a magic lantern onto a semi-transparent screen. By moving the lantern farther away from the screen, Robertson's ghosts would grow larger, seeming to approach the audience.[29] Murnau adapted this effect for *Faust*, which occurs twice in the scene in Faust's study. After Faust accepts his offer of restored youth, Mephisto covers Faust with the magic cape. In the next shot, Mephisto is superimposed onto an image of the study, with Faust covered in the background and his pile of burning books in the foreground. Mephisto blows on the flames, and as they get bigger so does he, until his ghostly figure occupies nearly the entire frame. Following the transformation, Mephisto conjures the image of a semi-naked woman above Faust as he awakens. Faust jumps to his feet, and once he sees the image it grows larger, seeming to approach him, before vanishing into thin air. The film thus translates classic phantasmagoric effects by means of superimposition, a specifically cinematic technique that mimics the appearance of diaphanous and ghostly forms.

Smoke plays an important role in Mephisto's repertoire of visual tricks. After the prologue, Mephisto releases a plague in the form of dark smoke, which disperses the town's festival grounds and clears the way for his own appearance before Faust. When summoned by the desperate scholar, Mephisto arrives in a smoky conflagration. For the visual magician, the ability to obscure is just as important as the power to make appear. Smoke constitutes an evanescent veil, whose dispersive quality marks the visual obscurity it produces with impermanence and a promise of revelation.

Moreover, smoke could itself serve as an illuminated surface, revealing the light passing through and blurring the distinction between presence and absence. In his phantasmagoria, Robertson would sometimes project images onto smoke. In his book *The Wonders of Optics* (1869), the French popular science writer Camille Flammarion reprinted an account of a performance in post-revolutionary France:

> Robertson . . . threw upon a brasier containing lighted coals, two glasses of blood, a bottle of vitriol, a few drops of aquafortis, and two numbers of the *Journal des Hommes Libres*, and there instantly

Mephisto's plague of smoke. Still from *Faust* (dir. F. W. Murnau, 1926).

> appeared in the midst of the smoke caused by the burning of these
> substances, a hideous livid phantom armed with a dagger and wear-
> ing a red cap of liberty. The man at whose wish the phantom had been
> evoked seemed to recognise Marat, and rushed forward to embrace
> the vision, but the ghost made a frightful grimace and disappeared.[30]

In the transformation scene, Mephisto likewise appears on a screen of smoke,
produced by the burning books. As the cameraman Seeber pointed out in
1928, cinema had quickly adopted the use of fog and smoke from the magic
theater of the nineteenth century.[31] In *The Black Imp* (1905), for instance,
the early filmmaker Georges Méliès used smoke to mask the appearance and
disappearance of the mischievous title character. As in illusionist stage performances, the film employs smoke to obscure the spectator's view and mask
the technique behind the trick. In trick films such as those of Méliès, magi-
cal disappearance depends on an "invisible" edit, in which time is elided by
stopping and restarting the camera—hopefully without the viewer noticing.
Smoke aided the invisible edit, insofar as a sudden change in form was less
jarring in the case of an amorphous cloud. Also, the burst of smoke, typically
produced by lighting a small amount of lycopodium powder, would draw

attention away from other elements of the image that might have changed from one shot to the next.

Richard Wagner integrated these kinds of phantasmagoric effects into his stagings. According to the music historian Gundela Kreuzer, steam played a major role in productions of Wagner's *Ring* cycle in the 1870s, introducing "the international operagoing public to a visually alluring element that transcended the painted scenery and practicable structures then commonly used for illusionist stage design."[32] Productions at Bayreuth and elsewhere made use of industrial technologies, such as locomotive boilers, to pump steam onto the stage. Kreuzer notes that for Wagner, steam was crucially linked to moments of transformation, both poetically and practically. In Wagner's stage directions for the *Ring*, steam signaled transitions from one location to the next by their changes in color or quality, from the infernal Nibelheim to the misty Rhine; and marked bodily transformations, such as when Alberich dons the Tarnhelm. Onstage, Kreuzer writes, steam was "a malleable Tarnhelm for the stage itself,"[33] serving to obscure complicated changes in scenery that would otherwise break the spell of the performance.

Aerosols serve similar poetic functions in Murnau's *Faust*. They suffuse nearly all the locations in the film's first half, but their varying qualities mark changes in scene. The blowing vapors in the prologue give way to the blustery black smoke of the plague, which is succeeded in turn by the relatively peaceful dustiness of Faust's study, the eerie dust of the crossroads, the gentle clouds of the magic cloak sequence, and so on. Aerosols link these different spaces as parts of the same diegetic universe, but separate them according to their movements, darkness, and weight. Akin to the Wagnerian practice of obscuring the stage while scenery is switched out, fog occasionally fills the frame between scene changes in *Faust* as well, for instance after the angel commands Mephisto to observe Faust in the world below. A completely clouded frame dissipates to reveal Faust, a use of fog that parallels the cinematic iris or dissolve. Finally, as in the *Ring*, smoke appears in scenes of corporeal change, such as in Mephisto's appearance at the crossroad and the restoration of Faust's youth.

Kreuzer notes, however, that Wagnerian performance never completely mastered the use of steam onstage. For some critics, steam called forth images of industrial production and the mundane world of capitalism to which Wagner's spectacles were meant to provide an alternative. It had a tendency to sink too quickly, revealing technical operations that were supposed to be hidden, or to settle in the "mystical abyss," damaging musical instruments. And the production of steam offstage could be noisy, introducing a jarring aural element into the performance. For Kreuzer, "steam revealed that both the operation and effects of such a complex multimedial endeavor would always escape total control."[34] Filtered through the movie camera, however, the aerosols in Murnau's film are utterly mastered. While monumental films such as *Faust* were multimedial during the production process, involving actors, painters, lighting technicians, and so on, the photographic lens flattened the *Gesamtkunstwerk* into a discrete image and any unruly fog was simply discarded at the editing table. Moreover, as I will discuss later, *Faust*'s particulates deliberately evoke industrialization, foregrounding at the level of content the technicity that Wagner's productions strove to mask.

From the standpoint of industrial hygiene, the production of *Faust* was a risky undertaking, both for the people involved and for the studio's material infrastructure. The film's set designer (and steam technician) Robert Herlth reported that two of the film's stars, Jannings and Camilla Horn, complained of the shoot's extreme conditions. The final burning scene put particular strain on Horn, who Herlth said spent "hours tied to the stake, with flames leaping round her from twenty lyk[o]podium burners" and whose eyes became "red and sore from winds of dust or salt." Jannings faced similar difficulties when filming the scene in which Mephisto appears above the city to release the plague. In a heavy suit, Jannings was buffeted by wind from huge fans and surrounded by the soot used to represent the plague: "in the end not only was the actor cursing and swearing, but everyone else felt like going on strike too."[35] Arno Richter, Herlth's assistant, wrote that during the production of *Faust* "the studio would be full of stifling smoke: old film was being burnt in the doorway in order to create a denser atmosphere, and without the slightest concern about fire!"[36] Richter also noted that Murnau closed the set of *Faust* to anyone not directly involved in the filmmaking, including Ufa studio head Erich Pommer.[37] While Richter did not explicitly link the closed set to the extensive use of smoke, one can surmise that Ufa would have frowned upon Murnau's indifference to industrial hygiene.

Faust, from production to end product, flew in the face of the hygienic imperative. Rather than evacuate the studio of particulates, Murnau filled it with them; instead of producing visual distinctions, he dispersed them. In the fog of *Faust*, bodies emerge and dissipate, spaces and scenes dissolve into one another, earth and heaven mingle. "Gray pictures," as Pfitzner called them, were the point. The conditions of the film's production certainly risked the health of those on the set; at the same time, however, the film reimagined the apparatus of studio filmmaking. If the dominant mode of film production was consonant with the aims of modern hygiene—to shore up the integrity of the human body, and thereby the human subject, in the face of entropy—*Faust* embodied a cinema that embraced the inevitable decay to which both the image and viewer are subject.

Pollution and Entropy

After nineteenth-century thermodynamics, matter could no longer be conceived of as stable in any meaningful sense. "In his later lectures," as Anson Rabinbach writes, the physicist Hermann von Helmholtz "observed that the second law of thermodynamics indicated that all energy ultimately 'dissipated'—its flow was essentially irreversible and tended toward inertia. This view gave rise, especially after 1860, to predictions of the 'heat death of the universe,' the great cosmological exhaustion implicit in the teleology of nature."[38] Once an energetic equilibrium had been reached, remarked Helmholtz in 1854, "the universe from that time forward would be condemned to a state of eternal rest."[39] Not matter but energy—unstable, transforming, and transformative—was the common currency of the physical world, and wherever it was concentrated it tended to dissipate. In this section, I trace how *Faust* engaged with some of the implications of a thermodynamic worldview.

Mephisto's first appearance on earth presents him as a menacing agent of dispersion. Having wagered that he can tempt Faust to sign over his soul, Mephisto breaks the barrier between the natural and supernatural by initiating a plague, which Murnau renders as an emission of smoke. In one of the film's most famous images, Jannings's Mephisto looms over the town while a thick, black smoke seeps out from below his massive wings and demonic regalia. The plague arrives during a public festival. In a celebration of communal urban life, costumed acrobats and shadow players perform on makeshift stages for crowds that fill the streets. One performer collapses, signaling the presence of the plague, and the densely packed crowd disperses amid a relentless, death-bringing, dusty wind.

Murnau's visualization of the plague as blowing smoke brings to mind theories of miasma, according to which disease was spread by way of "bad air." By the 1920s, of course, the miasma theory had been disproven by bacteriologists such as Robert Koch, but it continued to have popular currency long afterward. Staging a plague in an early modern city, *Faust* recalls the urban disease outbreaks to which the practice of quarantine and, later, the hygienic reform movement itself responded, seeking to control such outbreaks through sanitary infrastructure, inspection, and public health institutions. The plague also had a specific meaning in the context of the Weimar Republic, alluding to the context of mass death that framed hygienic reform during the period—specifically, the influenza pandemic of 1918–19, as well as the death wrought by the First World War.[40] In the immediate aftermath of the war, health experts stressed that the project of national recovery was confronted not just with losses caused by the war itself, but with the postwar population's ongoing vulnerability to disease, due to malnutrition, medicine shortages, and other factors.

As I have suggested above, however, the smoke in *Faust* also brings to mind the problem of urban air pollution. Scientists and medical professionals spoke of a "plague of smoke" in industrial cities, a term that *Faust*'s scriptwriter Hans Kyser evoked in his description of Mephisto's plague as an "exhalation of pestilence" (*Pestatem*).[41] The smoke problem embodied the thermodynamic conundrum of industrialization, in which new technologies generated ever more pulverized rock and incinerated coal, which demanded in turn incredible feats of dusting, vacuuming, and filtering. The proliferation of particulate matter was symptomatic of how industrial capitalism consistently valorized the productive potential of thermodynamic science while obscuring or ignoring its entropic implications—a contradiction that the project of hygiene tried to mediate. In Murnau's film, particulates unite these two dimensions of thermodynamics: they index the presence of fire in all its productive power; at the same time, they embody dispersion and threaten to eventually consume everything.[42]

In narrative terms, *Faust* presents the industrial smoke plague as a devil's bargain. Equating the scientific pursuit of mastery over nature with the supernatural, the film associates both with particulate matter. Begun in the smoke- and fog-saturated prologue, this link finds its culmination in Faust's first encounter with Mephisto. Despairing over his inability to fight the devastating plague, Faust tosses his books into a fire in his study. In the fire, however, he notices a book that has opened to a page; he pulls the book out and reads the singed pages through the smoke, finding instructions for summoning the "Prince of Darkness." Faust goes to the crossroad, draws a circle in the dusty ground, and raises the book to the sky three times, invoking the devil's name as fog fills in over the full moon. Flame and smoke rise from the circle on the road, wind creates a vortex of fog around Faust, lightning flashes, and a ball of flame falls from above, landing in a burst of fire. A robed figure with glowing eyes remains calmly sitting on a rock. Terrified, Faust flees through the fog-soaked landscape, but the eerie devil reappears in every shot, finally appearing seated in the scholar's study, where he playfully doffs his cap in greeting. "You have summoned me. Here I am!" Mephisto holds a massive sheet of parchment, upon which an oath writes itself—the letters emerge onto the paper from right to left, smoking, as if written in gunpowder and lit: "I renounce God and his heavenly hosts. For this I shall receive all power and glory in the world." With a promise that he will be able to help his plague-stricken town, Mephisto convinces Faust to agree to the oath for a trial period of one day, and Faust signs in blood.

This scene cements the link between the visual presence of particulate matter, the power of scientific knowledge, and Promethean transgression. Mephisto is a creature of smoke; Faust first glimpses his name in the ashen pages of a burning book, and he arrives as the smoking residue of a fireball from the sky. Written in ash, the text of Mephisto's oath similarly emerges from an act of combustion. Moreover, Mephisto's appearance in Faust's world has the structure of a scientific—or, at least, alchemical—process. Faust reproduces experimentally what had been recorded in the burning book; the experiment successful, Faust discovers new possibilities of worldly power. The film stages scientific progress as transgressing a metaphysical division between the natural and the supernatural, which results in a turbulent storm of residue.

Mephisto also appears here as a figure of condensation. He is the product of an alchemical reaction, the incorporation of swirling, dispersed forces given form through Faust's incantation. In turn, he promises to allow Faust to concentrate the disparate powers of nature—"all power and glory in the world"—in his person and subject them to his will. And in a sense, Mephisto follows through on his promise. True, Faust does not fight the plague, since the townspeople threaten to stone him to death after he cowers at the sight of a cross. He despairs and returns to his study, ready to end his life with poison. Mephisto refuses to let him off so easily, since the trial period of one day is not yet over, and tempts Faust with the possibility of restored youth, conjuring an image of the young Faust upon the surface of his dish of poison elixir. "Your life was only dust and decay! Pleasure is everything!" Faust agrees. Mephisto throws his coat over Faust and lights it, along with the room full of dusty books, aflame. Mephisto gleefully removes the coat, revealing the young Faust. The transformation is staged as a repetition of Mephisto's own arrival—Faust's renewed youth is the product of a conflagration. Moreover, it is fueled by Faust's own books, which Mephisto likens to particulate dust, a kind of leftover of the past which must be collected and combusted to fight entropy and reverse time. Here too, Mephisto condenses and concentrates. In his aged form, Faust himself seemed on the verge of dissolution, his soft white hair providing a gauzy transition between himself and his visual environment. The young Faust is brightly illuminated in contrast to his surroundings; the film gives him stark definition. The dust of time has seemingly been wiped away, entropy overcome. Of course, this will not last. Associated with both dissipation and concentration, Mephisto embodies the thermodynamic interplay whereby order can be temporarily produced or maintained in one system only at the cost of more disorder elsewhere.

Consequently, Faust leaves disorder in his wake. Later, bored with the pleasures offered by Mephisto, he seeks a place whose uncorrupted beauty might provide him with a spiritual regeneration to match his newly youthful external form. Contemplating his next undertaking on a foggy mountain perch, Faust's desire is reawakened by a vision of home—which he calls *Heimat*, or "homeland"—which appears over the mountain fog like a phantasmagoric image. While a desire for home makes sense psychologically, since Faust has become unmoored from his past through his association with Mephisto, the word *Heimat* of course had a broader resonance, especially in discussions of the effects of industrialization on natural landscapes, and became a central term in late nineteenth- and early twentieth-century German conservationism. Institutions such as Prussia's Staatliche Stelle für Naturdenkmalpflege (State Office for the Conservation of Natural Monuments) and the nongovernmental group Deutscher Bund Heimatschutz (German Heimat Protection League), both founded in 1904, worked to protect the German landscape from the encroachments of industry. According to Thomas Lekan, these bourgeois conservation efforts saw "a causal link between an aesthetically pleasing environment and an individual's proper moral and physiological development, as well as a close connection between environmental health,

national character, and social stability."[43] After the war, such efforts resonated with the project of national health, with rural landscapes serving as
a regenerative counterpart to the disordered and unhealthy environment of
the industrial city. Along similar lines, Faust looks for salvation in a place
untainted by the dramas and desires of his earlier life. Having dissolved into
air, Faust wishes to be grounded again, to literally and metaphorically return
to the earth.

This is what he seems to find. Faust's *Heimat* bears little resemblance to
the dark, smoke-filled city of the film's first scenes. Everything is bright and
crisp, illuminated but without the disturbing presence of particulates that
render illumination itself palpable. Moreover, the town is depicted in relative
harmony with nature. The scene at Marthe Schwerdtlein's, which ends in
Faust's seduction of Gretchen, is especially bucolic, with stone architecture
blending seamlessly with grasses and budding trees. Mephisto and Faust spy
Gretchen as she plays with a group of children in Marthe's garden, a number
of whom wear flower wreaths on their heads. Faust sneaks up on Gretchen
after the children scatter, who return a moment later to encircle the pair
and join them in mock matrimony. The children leave once again, and Faust
chases Gretchen around a tree, catching her for a kiss.

This seduction triggers the corruption of *Heimat*, however, as smoke returns
to cloud the images of the film. At night, Faust secretly enters Gretchen's bedroom, while, unbeknownst to him, Mephisto tips off Gretchen's mother and
brother Valentin, who discover them in the act. Faust and Valentin fight, and
Mephisto intervenes further, fatally stabbing Valentin and alerting the towns-
folk to the murder. Faust and Mephisto flee, taking to the clouds, after which
we see the funeral of Gretchen's brother and mother, who has apparently
died of shock. In the cathedral filled with drifting censer smoke, we realize
that Faust himself has become an agent of dissolution, playing for Gretchen
the role that Mephisto had played for him. In the next scene, Gretchen has
been cast out. She carries her child through a wintry landscape, and in images
reminiscent of Mephisto's earlier plague, harsh winds blow clouds of snow
around her, until she collapses. The swirling particles threaten to erase her
completely. Faust's attempt to return to a prelapsarian *Heimat* thus fails
utterly; instead, he has caused this idyllic, presumably ahistorical space to be
ripped violently into the thermodynamic age. Clear skies and crisp light are
clouded by censer smoke and blasting snow—Faust has brought the plague
of smoke to the very place where he sought spiritual renewal. Ultimately, the
film implies, return is impossible; entropy directs the arrow of time.[44]

All that is left is further dissipation, or, as Murnau stages it, a kind of
sublimation. Extending the film's visual link between particulates and phantasmagoria, Gretchen now hallucinates, seeing a gently rocking crib for the
baby against the falling snow. A group of men discover her unconscious, half-
buried in the snow, her child dead. She cries out to Faust for aid, which the
film visualizes with Gretchen's face superimposed over blowing clouds and a

landscape that unfurls below us, arriving finally at Faust on his cloudy, rocky perch. Faust and Mephisto ride to save her from being burned at the stake, but Mephisto returns Faust to old age just as he is about to intervene. Faust throws himself on the stake just as it catches fire. Gretchen recognizes Faust and we see him young again. They kiss, and are consumed in smoke. Following Faust and Gretchen's final kiss, we see the conflagration at a distance. Suddenly, however, an orb of light is superimposed over the flames and the lovers appear in its center. They ascend up, out of the frame, as if transmuted into a gaseous state. In the logic of the narrative, it seems they have found a kind of thermodynamic loophole: energy cannot be destroyed, only transformed. Instead of dissolving into ash, the lovers are raised to a higher plane.

Billowing fog and smoke overtake the image, and we are back in the nebulous realm where we first saw Mephisto's confrontation with the angel. The angel is back, who halts Mephisto's persecution of Faust by invoking "one word" that renders the pact null and void: "Love." As envisioned by Murnau, the glowing word unites the two aspects of the nineteenth-century thermodynamic imagination: on the one hand, it shoots off spears of artificial light and approaches the screen like a steam train, evoking a vision of productivity and progress; on the other, it sheds copious fog in its wake, signaling transience and dissipation. In thermodynamic terms, "love" seems to be energy itself—according to the angel it is "the eternal word," the only thing that persists and that ultimately dissolves all pacts. Not even the devil can fight it.

For Michel Serres, the painter J. M. W. Turner was the first to translate a thermodynamic understanding of the universe into pictorial terms. In rendering clearly defined forms, painters of an earlier era had reflected Newtonian physics and its world of solid, discrete objects that moved and interacted in predictable ways. In the searing hazes of Turner's canvases, however, one saw "line abandoned in favor of random matter, without definition, statistically grouped in parcels. On the one hand clouds of ice, on the other clouds of incandescence. . . . Turner understood and revealed the new world, the new matter. The perception of the stochastic replaces the art of drawing the form."[45] Fascinated with the instability and unpredictability of particulate matter, Murnau's *Faust* brought the thermo-dynamism of Turner into the cinema—or, rather, back into the cinema. In her reflection on the links between film and thermodynamics, the theorist Mary Ann Doane notes that a similar fascination characterized the work of some early filmmakers like Méliès and Lumière, for whom the camera's function was "to register contingency, to transform it into a representational system while maintaining both its threat and its allure."[46] According to Doane, however, classical narrative cinema chose a path analogous to that of statistics, which developed as a strategy for managing the inherent unpredictability of the material world as recognized by thermodynamics. In light of Doane's account, we can see how *Faust*'s invocation of an earlier cinematic tradition, in the figure of Mephisto, for instance, goes hand in hand with its rejection of the dominant practice of studio hygiene, as well as its emphasis on the contingent movements of particulate matter.

By linking the problem of industrial air pollution to the thematics of entropy, *Faust* also makes clear that the hygienic project of quelling environmental disorder was as much concerned with time as it was with space. "Thermodynamics is about the inevitability of loss, of dissipation," Doane writes, but "it is also accompanied by the desire to minimize loss, to manage inevitability, and therefore to manage time."[47] Hygiene in factories, markets, schools, streets, and homes aimed to beat back the process of material decay so that society could reproduce itself and history could advance unimpeded.

Dissipation and Distraction

This dynamic, whereby modernity upsets some equilibrium or unity that hygienic measures are developed to restore, played out at the level of human subjectivity and perception as well. "It is possible to see one crucial aspect of modernity as an ongoing crisis of attentiveness," writes Jonathan Crary, "in which the changing configurations of capitalism continually push attention and distraction to new limits and thresholds, with an endless sequence of new products, sources of stimulation, and streams of information, and then respond with new methods of managing and regulating perception."[48] In this section, I link *Faust*'s interest in material disorder to anxieties about the fragmentation of experience and subjectivity. In this reading, the film becomes a parable of modern spectatorship, and the particulate matter that surrounds the protagonist comes to figure the drifting, dissolving quality of his attention and striving. The entropy that defines the thermodynamic universe turns out to include the observer of that universe as well, whose subjective decoherence is accelerated by modernity's combustive force.

Faust is thus also a film about *Zerstreuung*. In English, *Zerstreuung* is most often translated as "distraction," and has become a key term in critical writing about modernity. The word entered contemporary academic discourse in the 1980s, when English readers (primarily in film studies) were introduced to Siegfried Kracauer and Walter Benjamin, whose cultural criticism of the interwar period served as a crucial guide for those seeking to understand the condition of modernity.[49] In the cinematic context, *Zerstreuung* (alongside cognate terms like *Ablenkung* and *Unterhaltung*) primarily refers to an attitude of distracted spectatorship, which Benjamin famously called "reception in distraction" (*Rezeption in der Zerstreuung*).[50] The plot of Murnau's *Faust* hinges on this kind of looking, as Mephisto more than once seduces the easily distracted protagonist by spectacular means.

Decades before its appearance in German discussions of cinema, however, the word *Zerstreuung* had entered the language of physics as a translation of William Thomson's concept of the "dissipation of energy"—in other words,

Zerstreuung was a way of describing entropy, or the tendency of energy to become unusable for performing work.[51] Indeed, to a certain extent, nineteenth-century psychology conceived of attention in ways that resonated with the insights of thermodynamics. In his account of the discourse on attention in the human sciences, Crary argues that attention and distraction were not opposites. Building on his earlier history of the nineteenth-century science of vision, in which he demonstrated the gradual replacement of a stable, transcendental subject of knowledge with an unstable, corporeal observer, Crary shows how attention, almost from the moment of its articulation as a physiological concept, could not be understood as an ideal capacity whose otherwise autonomous functioning was only disturbed or impinged upon by the body.[52] Instead, attention came to be defined by its corporeal character, and like the thermodynamic concept of energy, it was something that inherently drifted and dissipated.[53] In *Faust*, the protagonist's attentive faculties and the drifting particulates that suffuse the image allegorize each other in their dispersion; and both reflect a thermodynamic universe tending toward disorder. The protagonist and the particulates that surround him become ciphers for each other, with subjective and material dissipation bound together.

The film's prologue juxtaposes two images of Faust, the first offered by the angel and the second by Mephisto. The angel declares: "Man is good: His spirit strives for truth!" We see Faust in his role as teacher, heavy book in hand, lecturing to a group of rapt students whose faces are illuminated by a glowing astrolabe in the lower half of the frame. Faust praises the human freedom to choose between good and evil as the greatest of all miracles. Mephisto, meanwhile, accuses Faust of hypocrisy and greed—while praising truth, Faust in fact seeks wealth. Next, we see Faust performing an experiment. He observes a spherical glass container, filled with steam and pulsing light, into which he pours a liquid. Steam explodes from the sphere and fills the frame, before clearing to reveal Faust's disappointed face. Together, these contrasting images echo the changing configurations of vision, knowledge, and subjectivity outlined by Crary. In the first, Faust occupies a stable position with regard to the glowing orb, which serves as an emblem of truth; although the orb is present in the scene, Faust does not look directly at it, but stands above it. If anything, his gaze would turn first toward the book he holds, which mediates truth for the subject. Likewise, his pious students look not at the orb, but at their teacher. Faust here models the transcendental subject of knowledge whose spirit observes the physical world as if from without. In Mephisto's image, however, Faust is drawn in. The second glowing orb enraptures him. He does not simply observe the experiment, he attends to it corporeally, moving around it, hovering over it, and, above all, looking at it, opening his eyes so wide as to furrow his brow. The angel and Mephisto present Faust in turn as detached, serene, in command of vision and truth; and as embodied, distracted, in pursuit of an elusive gratification. Faust's dilemma, the conflict between spirit and body, knowledge and pleasure, is framed as visual—light illuminates, providing the precondition for human freedom, but it also attracts, subjecting the viewer to its pull.

The theme of visual attraction persists throughout the film. The town fair offers a range of spectacles to the delighted crowds: fools dance, acrobats perform, a man wrestles a bear, a shadow play unfolds on a cloth screen. When Mephisto interrupts the fair by releasing a plague, he demonstrates his status as a master of the visual, with the power to both conjure and dissolve images. It is this power that he turns against Faust, by disguising himself, tempting Faust with erotic visions, changing Faust's appearance, and so on. Both the carnivalesque entertainments of the fair and the figure of Mephisto evoke the attractions of early cinema, in which exhibitionistic spectacle prevailed and cinematograph magicians like George Méliès combined the tradition of stage magic with experiments in filmic special effects. Thus, although presumably taking place centuries before, Murnau's *Faust* speaks to the "ongoing crisis of attentiveness" described by Crary that emerged in the nineteenth century and whose most extreme embodiment, for many in the early twentieth century, was the moving image. Many cultural critics considered cinema a threat to a normative subjectivity characterized by the autonomy of the mind and its mastery over the body.[54]

Murnau's film takes up uses of smoke familiar from phantasmagoria and early cinema and aligns them in particular with two cinematic techniques that had come into use since the time of Méliès: the fade (or dissolve) and the "unchained" camera. A fade begins with darkness and gradually brightens to reveal a new scene (fade-in) or gradually darkens to mark the end of a scene (fade-out). As an editing technique, the fade was useful for providing softer and clearer transitions between scenes than the more typical hard cut. In this way, fades took on some functions of the iris, an earlier technique used to mark scene transitions; as *Faust* implies, however, the fade had antecedents in the use of smoke and fog in theatrical illusions and early cinema, to facilitate gradual, rather than sudden, appearances and disappearances.[55] In the prologue, the spatial (or even ontological) discontinuity between Faust, on the one hand, and the angel and Mephisto, on the other, is smoothed over by fog transitions. The angel orders Mephisto to "look down there!" and the intertitle is followed by a shot of drifting smoke or vapor. It seems to occupy no space in particular and functions purely as a transition. After a second, the shot of Faust as teacher appears, over which the transitional vapor is now superimposed; the vapor then both dissipates and fades out, combining the two techniques of revelation in a single shot. By aligning particulate matter with the editing device of the fade, Murnau's film encourages a gaze that is both dispersed or *zerstreut* (drifting seamlessly from one space to the next) and phantasmagoric (unable to distinguish sharply between reality and illusion).

The dispersion of the gaze is radicalized in one of the film's most famous scenes, the ride on Mephisto's magic cloak, in which the camera itself mimics the motion of fog or clouds. Mephisto lays down his cape, beckoning Faust: "Step on my cloak . . . and the earth revolves around you!" The window to the study suddenly breaks, and the pair take off into the air. For the next shot, cameraman Carl Hoffmann placed the camera on an undulating track over a model city and landscapes, so that we as viewers experience the ride for ourselves.[56] We begin looking down while passing over rows of pitched-roof houses. Still in motion, the camera pans up, tracing the spire of a Gothic cathedral as we ascend further. A pair of shots depict Mephisto and Faust in the clouds before returning to a point-of-view shot from the cape. We now glide over a foggy landscape of trees and mountains, endless clouds above and rising steam below, with a veiled sun in the background. Gradually sublime nature is replaced by Romanesque architecture as we arrive in Parma for the Duchess's wedding. The scene stages the camera as enabling a kind of cloud vision as we drift along on currents of air, unhindered by oceans or mountains.

In a chapter written for Eisner's book on Murnau, the set designer Herlth related an anecdote about the invention of the "unchained camera" employed so spectacularly in *Faust* and *The Last Laugh*, on which Herlth also worked. While filming a scene involving cigar smoke in *The Last Laugh*, Murnau was dissatisfied with the camera's relative stasis. "We need something more intense," Murnau said, "if only we could fly with the smoke." Herlth explains:

> We didn't realize that we were already assuming the existence of a mobile camera; for us it was the stairs that presented the difficulty. We had made the first step without knowing it. Someone was sent for a ladder, the camera was fixed at the top, and the not insubstantial [cameraman Karl] Freund took up his position. We removed half the set and moved the ladder slowly towards the stairs; the camera followed the smoke, rising with it up the stairs as the ladder was wound upwards.
>
> "We've got it!" cried Murnau.[57]

Herlth's anecdote links the birth of the mobile camera with the movements of particulate matter; the previously stable gaze could now melt into air. In 1924, Murnau described the new possibilities of the mobile camera: "Progression and collapse, the becoming and passing away of an existence never before imagined, the symphony of bodily melody and spatial rhythm, the play of pure, streaming movement, shot through with vitality. It can be created with this mechanical, de-materializing apparatus."[58] In Murnau's language, the mobile camera is somehow both embodied and immaterial, in this way evoking the liminal materiality of particulates like smoke, which is comprised of solids that are nonetheless dispersed so that they appear fluid or gaseous. Furthermore, the unchained camera enacts a dispersion of the gaze, whose transcendence had previously guaranteed epistemological stability.

Faust's steam bath. Still from *Faust*.

The film implies that this dispersion of the gaze ends with the dissolution of desire. The cloak ride ends in Italy, where with Mephisto's aid Faust seduces the Duchess of Parma at her own wedding, and the ensuing night of love leads Faust to forget the one-day deadline, trapping him in Mephisto's bargain. Faust's pursuit of pleasure, however, leads to dissolution rather than its satisfaction. After the episode in Italy, the film cuts to Faust sitting alone above a mountain range while he stares into the distance, surrounded by gently rising fog. Mephisto arrives to comment: "You have lived life to the fullest, Faust! From intoxication to intoxication . . . a frenzy without compare! But you are never satisfied!" The image of Faust here—motionless and listless, bathed in aerosols—combines distraction and material dispersion. Rather than lend force and concentration to Faust's striving, Mephisto has dissolved it.

This is the point at which a vision of *Heimat* reawakens Faust's attentiveness. Sitting in the mountains, Faust sees an image of home, which, as many critics have pointed out, appears like a cinematic image projected before him; furthermore, the scene links cinema with phantasmagoria, as the image materializes not on a solid screen but in a space previously occupied by mountain fog. In this moment, Faust seems to recover a sense of agency. Instead of following Mephisto, Faust dreams his own destination and pursues it. The

overwhelmingly visual character of his pursuit, however, as well as its initial appearance as phantasm, implies that he is still subject to the whims of
visual and corporeal attraction, and indeed this turns out to be the case. Faust
seduces Gretchen, an act that brings tragedy to her family and ultimately
leads both of them to be burned at the stake. While the film tries hard to
impress upon the viewer that the problem of Faust's wandering gaze is solved
by love—with Gretchen serving as a fixed object of the gaze, upon which a
stable and autonomous subjectivity could ground itself—the fact that both
are ultimately transmuted into smoke suggests ambivalence. On the one
hand, in a modernity characterized by visual attraction and attentional drift,
fixing the gaze could constitute a kind of death; on the other, we might also
see Faust and Gretchen as having become, in death, truly modern subjects,
drifting along with everyone else.

In a final turn, however, the film implies that entropy can be circumvented
through the technological reproduction enabled by film technology. Film
can show us smoke as it disperses, suggesting transience; simultaneously, of
course, a visual index of the ephemeral phenomenon has been preserved and
made reproducible. In other words, film serves as a hygienic screen, presenting us with an image of dispersion while also insulating us from it. In *Faust*,
this paradoxical, double being of cinema's mechanical eye allows the spectator to both experience processes of subjective and material *Zerstreuung*, at
the level of identification with the camera and with the protagonist; and to
observe them as if from the outside, like the angel and the devil experiment-
ing with Faust in the world below. By transposing entropic phenomena into
another medium, they are objectified, preserved, and made graspable. This
is precisely what happens to Gretchen and Faust at the end of the film—as
their material bodies dissolve into ash on the stake, they reappear as ghostly,
superimposed figures. In the moment of dissipation they are translated into a
new medium, preserved by a special effect that stages the ascension to heaven
as filmic reproduction.

The insistent presence of particulate matter in *Faust* is perhaps most significant for what it reveals about the dominant framework in which film images
were produced and understood. As such a flagrant exception to the rule,
Murnau's *Faust* makes the absence of particulate matter in film conspicuous.
As a standard practice, film production strove to avoid, manage, and excise
such materials, and thereby repress their troublesome implications for bodily
and subjective coherence. This production practice buttressed an aesthetic of
the image that privileged spatial transparency and clearly discernible boundaries between bodies and environments. As such, cinema in its dominant form
functioned within a broader hygienic apparatus that sought to preserve the
subject's corporeal and psychic integrity in the face of modern environmental
conditions. In *Faust*, this repressed dynamic is made visible and ostensibly
overcome through the magic of filmic reproduction.

More than any other filmmaker of the Weimar period, Murnau displays a fascination with breakdowns of hygienic order. His Nosferatu, for instance, punctures skin, invades minds, and threatens to collapse the walls separating the healthy, modern West from the contagious and primitive East. Faust's propulsive striving dissolves everything in its wake, as inevitably as the thermodynamic tendency toward increasing disorder. Both *Nosferatu* and *Faust* revel in images that obscure the fragile boundary between figure and ground, body and environment, achieved sometimes by special effects like superimposition, and at other times with profilmic elements like smoke or steam. Films like *Phantom* (1922) or *The Last Laugh* (1924), discussed in the next chapter, explore bodies and minds in extremis, using camera movement and the manipulation of lenses to mimic subjective states of vertigo, delirium, debility, and intoxication—states contrary to normative ideals of physical and cognitive health.

As this chapter has shown, Murnau's fascination with contagion and pollution is simultaneously an interest in the unhygienic possibilities of cinema itself. *Faust*'s invocation of pre-cinematic phantasmagoria makes sense here as a form of spectacle whose excitement lay in the apparent lack of separation between the space of illusion and the space of the audience. Films like *Nosferatu* and *Faust* encourage us to imagine cinema in this phantasmagoric mode, in which the movie screen functions as a doorway through which all manner of disruptive presences enter our world, rather than a window through whose hard glass the audience can safely gaze.

Crucially, the transgressions of Murnau's phantasmagoric cinema reveal how dominant film production practices and an aesthetic preference for "clean" and "clear" images reproduced a hygienic vision of the body, its environment, and the proper relationship between the two. In this vision of environmental order, waste materials like smoke were not fully eliminated—such a thing would be thermodynamically impossible—but were to be contained and channeled. To evoke Mary Douglas's famous definition of dirt, a hygienic environment was one in which no matter was out of place.[59] This did not just apply to inanimate matter, however, but to human bodies as well. The nineteenth-century thermodynamic revolution, Doane points out, "destabilized the boundary between the living and the nonliving, making the universe and the human body analogous to the extent that each serves as a system for the conservation, transformation, and deployment of energy."[60] The next chapter examines the place of the body within the hygienic imagination of environmental order, and, specifically, what happened when certain bodies were perceived to be sources of disorder.

Chapter 4

✦

Bodies Out of Place

Images of Disability and Aging

In the Vortex of Traffic, the 1924 traffic safety film discussed in chapter 2, features an episode titled "Uncle Paul Visits Berlin," in which a man from the country struggles to navigate the bustling Potsdamer Platz.[1] Exiting the train station, Uncle Paul is bewildered by the flow of streetcars, automobiles, and pedestrians. Because of his ignorance of streetcar etiquette, exiting passengers must push past him as he tries, unsuccessfully, to board. He is almost run over multiple times, trips over a dog's leash, and falls on the stairs of the subway station, all the while interrupting various forms of traffic. In the end, Uncle Paul begs a traffic cop to return him to the train station. Superficially, the film frames Uncle Paul as a foreigner to the city, playing on the common early cinematic motif of the country rube.[2] Much of the comedy, however, derives from Uncle Paul's age and bodily fragility. Kaleidoscopic point-of-view shots convey how the urban environment seems to exceed the man's ability to make sense of it perceptually. The actor Herbert Paulmüller, who was in his sixties at the time the film was produced, walks slightly hunched over, with an uncertain shuffle, in contrast to the more agile and comfortable pedestrians whose paths he constantly blocks. The experience of urban traffic seems not just perceptually overwhelming but physically exhausting. From the country or not, Potsdamer Platz is simply not meant for someone with a body like his. Not only is Uncle Paul unable to navigate the urban environment himself, but his presence disturbs the efficient flow of traffic, inconveniencing and endangering others. The traffic police remove him for his own good—and everyone else's, too.

Uncle Paul's removal from the urban street reveals how the environmental order imagined by modern hygiene was tied to a normative concept of a body that could move, labor, and reproduce under the conditions of urban industrial modernity. Indeed, laboring ability was often how hygiene defined health as such. In 1924, the social hygienist Ödön Tuszkai declared that "the state's most valuable possession is human life, or rather, health—that is, the ability to work [*die Gesundheit, d. i. die Arbeitsfähigkeit*] and the resulting achievements of that work."[3] By equating the value of life with the results of its labor, Tuszkai implies that the most valuable life would be the one that is most productive within the industrial economy. In other words, the most valuable body was the most able body. This ableist hierarchy reflected hygiene's service to the existing economic system and the goal of realizing or increasing the productive potential of the population as a whole, which necessarily devalued those deemed less productive according to industrial criteria. If hygiene worked to make the capitalist economy more efficient, part of this work involved codifying and ultimately reinforcing a material order—environments for dwelling, transit, labor, commerce, and so on—that privileged the able-bodied.

Drawing on Mary Douglas's understanding of dirt as "matter out of place," Rosemarie Garland-Thomson has argued that stigmatized forms of disability occupy the status of "an anomaly, a discordant element rejected from the schema that individuals and societies use in order to construct a stable, recognizable, and predictable world."[4] Disability theorists like Garland-Thomson, Lennard J. Davis, and others have pointed to the way stigmatized persons become intensely visible in spaces where they are perceived not to belong.[5] These persons cannot occupy what Garland-Thomson calls the position of the "normate," the identity conferred by socially constructed ideals of bodily and cognitive normalcy. Surrounding the normate is an "economy of visual difference," in which "those bodies deemed inferior become spectacles of otherness while the unmarked are sheltered in the neutral space of normalcy."[6] This chapter examines various figures who fall outside of the normate, which can apply to a wide variety of cases beyond what we would call disability per se—itself a fluid category that is highly dependent on context. Sickness, age, temporary states of impairment, and many other conditions can make a body appear anomalous. To borrow another term, I am concerned here with what Sally Chivers and Nicole Markotić call "problem bodies," which "both materialize and symbolize moments of interaction between the social and the physical."[7] As Chivers and Markotić suggest, disability as a paradigmatic example of bodily stigmatization serves as an important "category of analysis even in those blurred instances where disability may not overtly preside."[8] In the following I deal with screen representations of characters who are disabled, elderly, intoxicated, or sometimes even children, all of whom in particular contexts appear as problem bodies.

These non-normate figures tested hygiene's normative conception of environmental order. On the one hand, hygiene acknowledged the many ways that industrial modernity impacted the body, often producing sicknesses and disabilities that made navigating daily life even more difficult. On the other hand, by holding up productivity and efficiency as ideals, hygiene placed the able body at the center of its vision of the world. Specialized care institutions that developed in the nineteenth century—homes for the deaf, the blind, the physically disabled, the mentally ill, the elderly—were one way of solving this contradiction. These institutions represented a triumph of medical reason over the work- and poorhouses of the past, while at the same time cementing the exclusion of people already marginalized by industrial modernity's normative regime of ability. In the first half of this chapter, I examine two nonfiction films that advocated on behalf of such spaces, showing how Weimar cinema participated in the containment of problem bodies within the urban environment. At the same time, film offered new ways for the problem body to circulate in public, making it a site of contact as well as containment. I suggest that by representing spaces inhabited by non-normate residents, these largely didactic films also open themselves to alternative readings that challenge the urban environment's hostility to disabled and aging people, as well as the hygienic ideal of the whole and autonomous body.

Fiction films of the Weimar era also thematized the spatial exclusions that characterized urban modernity. In the second half of the chapter, I examine Karl Grune's *Die Straße* (*The Street,* 1923) and Murnau's *Der letzte Mann* (*The Last Laugh,* 1924), two classics of Weimar cinema well known for exploring the geography of class and gender in the metropolis. I argue that disability plays an important role in how these films represent the city's oppressive environmental dynamics. They show how disability could signify gender and class difference, but they also reveal its role as a uniquely modern axis of exclusion in a world obsessed with movement, efficiency, and work. Moreover, both films evince a concern with deviations from normative forms of perception, which they go so far as to simulate by filmic means. The coincidence of perceptual impairment with aesthetic experimentation suggests that part of cinema's attraction in this context lay not just in its novel forms of visual representation, but in the way transgressed norms of visual ability and sensorimotor coordination. Where Murnau's *Faust* emphasized the spectator's subjective dispersion, *The Street* and *The Last Laugh* enact spectatorial displacements, interrupting the viewer's normative relation to filmic space in ways the films liken to a form of impairment. These moments of spectacular disorientation gesture toward cinema as a place where viewers could safely experiment with the unhygienic pleasure of bodily vulnerability.

Rehabilitation and Retirement

Krüppelnot und Krüppelhilfe (*The Plight and Care of the Disabled*, which I will refer to as *Plight and Care*), first shown in 1920 at a conference of the Society for Disabled Welfare, advocated institutional rehabilitation for disabled people as a transitional experience on the way to a life of productivity.[9] It was produced by Curt Thomalla and Nicholas Kaufmann for the Ufa Medical Film Archive in collaboration with the orthopedist Dr. Konrad Biesalski. Biesalski served as director of the Oskar-Helene Home for the Treatment and Education of Invalid Children located in Berlin-Zehlendorf, which he styled as a model institution for modern orthopedics and care for the physically disabled.[10] Much of the film is devoted to daily life at the Oskar-Helene Home, which opened in 1914, but as Philipp Osten has shown, it incorporated footage from an earlier film Biesalski produced for the 1911 International Hygiene Exhibition in Dresden.[11]

The film was released just months before the Prussian Law on Disabled Welfare went into effect, which Biesalski helped draft. The law defined disability as an inability to work, compelled medical professionals and teachers to report cases of disability to Prussian authorities, stipulated public "Welfare Offices for the Disabled" in every city and county, and required the state to provide specialized institutional care for those in need.[12] The law contributed to the creation of the physically disabled as a distinct population that would be subject to oversight by state medical authorities. Moreover, the contours of this population would be defined in relation both to the industrial economy and to medical understandings of normality and abnormality. The legal formalization of disability during the early Weimar Republic came in the wake of concerns about how to reintegrate soldiers disabled by war, and accorded with a broader interest on the part of the German state and experts in the human sciences with the physical, sensory, and cognitive abilities of the population.[13] Deaths, both on the front and at home, as well as a striking decline in birthrates during World War I, had a significant demographic impact on the German population. This, in addition to the prevalence of physical and cognitive impairments among the soldiers who had returned, as Michael Hau notes, resulted in "calls for a 'human economy' (*Menschenökonomie*) that would make rational use of human resources in order to make up for war losses."[14]

The beginning of *Plight and Care* foregrounds the status of physically disabled people as problem bodies in the urban environment. In the absence of "timely and prudent care," the film's first intertitle explains, the disabled "find themselves in poverty and social misery (1) because of an inappropriate lifestyle, [and] lack of medical treatment and observation; (2) because of the inability to attend school; (3) because of the inability to be trained for employment." The initial sequence then shows us the path from lack of care to "poverty and social misery." A staged scene depicts a mother and two sons, one of whom leaves for school while the other sits on the floor—we see that the remaining child is unable to stand up on his own, and the mother lifts him into a carriage otherwise meant for a baby. The family is coded as working-class, appearing to occupy a top-floor apartment, and we can guess that the child has rickets, which was associated with the children of the tenements. An intertitle indicates that the boy is left alone for hours at a time, presumably because he is unable to go to school or perform household labor. The child is framed as not properly belonging in this space: he cannot navigate his physical environment, and consequently hinders the mother in her household labor.

Following this initial scene, medical images and documentary shots display the bodily effects of rickets on children when untreated. Finally, we see the consequences of this lack of care: "Without medical care and employment counseling, the adolescent disabled person completely ruins his health through overexertion and improper work . . . or he wastes away playing the barrel organ, hustling on the street, and begging." Apparently staged scenes with disabled actors, including a man with crutches and a barrel organ in a tenement courtyard, demonstrate each of these conditions. These are followed by a series of shots of beggars: a man with two canes at a kiosk in a busy city intersection, while people pass by all around, with heavy city traffic in the background; a man on outdoor steps who is given money; and a man with one leg on crutches outside of a storefront.[15] Here, again, disability obstructs efficiency. In this first sequence, then, the film tells us that disabled persons belong neither in the home nor in the street, where their lack of mobility and ability to work interfere with everyday spaces of social reproduction, transit, and commerce. Moreover, the people around them do not have sufficient expertise (or time) to provide proper care. In sum, physically disabled people hinder the efficient functioning of modernity's environmental order, to the disadvantage of themselves and society at large.

The solution, of course, is the institutional home, whose environment is tailored to the needs of the disabled children who live there. The film's depiction of life at the Oskar-Helene Home is situated within a framing device, another staged sequence in which a couple take a young girl, with a condition that visibly affects her mobility, to a public Welfare Office. Here they are referred to the Home, where a doctor diagnoses the child's condition, gives the family a treatment plan, and performs an operation. Then the perspective expands, as we leave the framing device behind and witness scenes of various children recovering from surgeries and undergoing other sorts of treatment, such as physical therapy, massage, and light therapy. Subsequent sequences offer cross-sections of daily life in the institution, focusing in particular on schooling, vocational training, and play.

This section of the film is particularly interested in prostheses. As an orthopedist, Biesalski himself designed prosthetics and was a key figure in the shift from prostheses that served aesthetic purposes to functional ones. Before World War I, most prosthetic devices were intended to mask the presence of disability, and thus were designed to mimic the outward appearance of the part they replaced. The wartime imperative of maximizing resources, however, made "restoring a soldier's ability to work, rather than his physical appearance . . . the primary goal of prosthetic design," writes Heather R. Perry.[16] Boaz Neumann notes that functional prosthetics were designed for mass production and in many cases such that "various accessories and devices could be attached, such as: rings, drills, hammers, screwdrivers and others."[17] These are the types we see in the scenes of vocational training, which show boys with specialized prostheses doing carpentry, locksmithing, and ironwork, while girls with similar devices weave and sew. The Oskar-Helene Home is thus a site where problem bodies are transformed into productive ones, ideally so that they are adapted to the material environment of urban modernity and the types of bodily labor it requires.

The final sequence of the film returns to the girl from the framing device, who is "cured and released." "Homes for the disabled make alms takers into taxpayers!" the film's final title declares. "Every year many millions in national wealth are saved as a result of the reduced welfare burden, and millions more [are] generated by the labor of disabled people who have become employable." *Plight and Care* thus compares two trajectories for the lives of physically disabled people—one with expert institutional care and one without—and implies that their return to mainstream spaces of everyday life is conditional upon their bodily fitness for work. In one respect, the film advocates a loosened definition of the normate, one which would include people with different kinds of bodies in the category of the productive citizen. It is easy to see, however, that predicating full citizenship on the ability to work reinforces an exclusionary distinction between deserving and undeserving subjects. It also adheres to the spatial logic of functionalization observed in the *Kulturfilme* in chapter 2, in which types of labor or activity defined the different environments of everyday life and who belonged in them.

The lecture that accompanied the premiere of *Plight and Care* explained the work the film was meant to perform, which was not primarily to reduce the stigma attached to disability per se, but to shape what Brendan Gleeson calls the social space of disability, the social forces that tend to push disability out of some spaces and into others.[18] According to the lecture, the film was meant "to enlighten the disabled themselves, their families, and the lay public in general, about how much can still be done to help the advancement and recovery of disabled people. It is especially necessary to eliminate the widespread distaste for and fear of homes for the disabled among the public and spread knowledge of these beneficial institutions."[19] In conjunction with the trajectory witnessed in the film, the lecture makes clear that *Plight and Care* was intended to further exclude disability from public areas and contain it in institutional spaces, at least until disabled bodies could be made to conform. The hygienic function of the institution was not just to provide therapy, but to remove problem bodies from spaces of work, domestic labor, and transit. The Oskar-Helene Home could better serve this function the more willing families were to give up their children for a period of treatment and training. Akin to *The City of Tomorrow*, discussed in chapter 2, *Plight and Care* contributes to the viewer's cognitive map of the modern city, demonstrating which sorts of bodies belong in which sorts of environments and when.

What *Plight and Care* does for disabled youth, Ella Bergmann-Michel's 1932 film *Wo wohnen alte Leute* (*Where Old People Live*) does for retirees.[20] The film portrays life at the Henry and Emma Budge Home, a retirement home designed primarily by the Swiss modernist architects Mart Stam and

Werner Moser. Like the kitchen designed by Margarete Schütte-Lihotzky discussed in chapter 2, the Budge Home was a New Frankfurt project. As Susan R. Henderson explains, the Home embodied one of many forms of "healing architecture" pursued by New Frankfurt architects, along with schools, medical clinics, and housing for working-class boys without other accommodation.[21] Like Wolff's film about the Frankfurt Kitchen, Bergmann-Michel's *Where Old People Live* exhibits the exemplary character of the Budge Home, proposing it as a model of modern hygienic architecture for the elderly. Places like the Budge Home reflected the ways in which older people found themselves excluded from a society organized around economic productivity and the laboring body. Changes in family structure and the labor market due to industrialization and a shift toward white-collar work left many older people without work or adequate care. After World War I, inflation compounded these trends by wiping out the savings of older middle-class Germans, raising the question of how this population would be cared for. In the 1920s, cities, private foundations, and pensioners' associations embraced the model of *Wohnheime* (residence homes) for retirees, which appealed to pensioners as a way to maintain middle-class dignity, and to cities as a way to relieve pressure on an overstretched housing stock.[22] Like *Plight and Care*, *Where Old People Live* contrasts the place it depicts with an unhealthy urban environment and aims to reduce the hesitancy of potential residents, implicitly distinguishing the Budge Home from the nineteenth-century poorhouse. The similar geographies mapped in the two films show that although many retirees would not be considered disabled pe se, older people and disabled persons across the life span could face similar exclusionary dynamics and logics of containment. While occupying different positions with regard to the normate, both could be perceived as problem bodies in the modern environments of everyday life.

Where Old People Live begins by showing the contemporary urban environment to which aging people are poorly suited. We see an aerial image of densely packed buildings, over which street traffic is lightly superimposed—a shot that is immediately replayed, but upside down. By mixing images at different scales and then flipping them, Bergmann-Michel effects a jarring perspectival shift that codes the urban environment as spatially confused, disorienting, and stressful. This is followed by traffic scenes, with an intertitle alerting us to the "NOISE!" of the street; vertical pans of tall buildings, whose stairs elderly inhabitants might have difficulty navigating; an older man reading the newspaper in his dark apartment; and a lone older woman walking through a long series of tenement courtyards. The Budge Home comes as salvation: we see it first as an animated schematic, its capital H shape strikingly rendered in perspective, titled with "RETIREMENT HOME" and labels marking its "green spaces" and "quiet." We then see the building's exterior from various angles, before going inside to explore its hallways, common areas, kitchen, heating room, and, finally, the residents' apartments. Unlike *Plight and Care*'s final scene of reintegration, Bergmann-Michel's film ends

Where the elderly shouldn't live. Still from *Where Old People Live* (dir. Ella Bergmann-Michel, 1932).

with a choreographed farewell of second-floor residents who wave to the camera from their balconies, indicating that this is not a space of rehabilitation, but one where the residents will happily live out their days.

More than *Plight and Care*, *Where Old People Live* focuses on the built environment, and understandably so given the profile of its designers and the emphasis on architecture and design in the New Frankfurt project overall. The film's prologue stressed the dizzying verticality of the urban environment; the Budge Home, and Bergmann-Michel's depiction of it, are conspicuously horizontal by comparison. Designed with the mobility of its residents in mind, the building's two residential wings are long, two-story constructions set in parallel and connected by a large, high-ceilinged common area for meals and gatherings. Much longer than it is high, the Budge Home is grounded in a way that the buildings shown in the prologue were not, rejecting the verticality required by the dense construction of urban neighborhoods. Moreover, while animated blueprints do show us the building in its totality, we never see documentary shots of the home from above, suggesting that the surrounding architecture is not high enough to provide an overhead perspective. By calling attention to the Home's horizontal stability, Bergmann-Michel sets it in opposition to the stressful dynamism of urban space, which its aging

The Budge Home. Still from *Where Old People Live*.

residents presumably wish to escape. This feeling of having fled from the city is reinforced by a sense of the Home's self-sufficiency—we are not shown any surrounding architecture, nor is the Home placed on a map that would situate it for the viewer in relation to the city at large. Only the arrival of a resident, who exits a car glimpsed through the glass doors of the Home's lobby and enters to a joyful greeting, offers a trace of what lies beyond.

Moving to the building's interior, the film highlights the use of glass to create an atmosphere of transparency, openness, and health. As good modernists, Stam and Moser valued glass for how it could open architecture to sunlight—a therapeutic gesture, especially in this context—and used it copiously in the Budge Home. As in discussions of hygienic architecture generally, sun was a major consideration for the architects in designing the building's layout and determining its geographic orientation.[23] The camera lingers on the healing sunlight that streams through floor-to-ceiling windows, and potted plants growing in one of the long residential-wing hallways suggest a natural vitality. While emphasizing its separation from the city, the film exhibits the Budge Home's selective openness to external nature. Multiple shots also display the use of glass dividers, which produce a visual openness across different spaces within the building itself. These uses of glass make it easier for personnel to observe the residents, but they are also meant to prevent isolation and encourage sociality. The balconies of the second-floor residents, for instance, are divided by glass, allowing neighbors to acknowledge one another.

Indeed, a logic of transparency governs the entire film, which renders an otherwise inaccessible institution open to the viewer's observing eye. We even get to access parts of the building that residents normally would not, such as the heating room and the kitchen, where we see "modern machines" wash shining pots and pans. Like *Plight and Care*, *Where Old People Live* offers the Budge Home to public view in order to demystify it and differentiate it from its institutional predecessors. Moreover, both films contribute to the viewer's picture of the overall urban landscape, communicating ideas about who does and does not belong in what kinds of spaces, and reinforcing the sense that mainstream spaces are not meant to accommodate non-normate subjects.

At the same time, in depicting non-normate spaces *Plight and Care* and *Where Old People Live* offer themselves to reading against the grain. First, by examining environments that are designed for particular kinds of bodies, they gesture toward the highly contingent nature of ability and able-bodiedness. In arguing against a medical model that locates disability solely in the body of the disabled person, scholars in disability studies have pointed to the ways the definition and experience of disability have varied historically, in relation to prevalent forms of labor, production and transportation infrastructure, the state of medical knowledge, the development of treatments and prosthetic technologies, norms of gender presentation and social interaction, and much more.[24] Seeing the accommodating spaces of the Oskar-Helene Home and the Budge Home makes clear how the physical environment can restore some kinds of ability. These architectures reveal how built space functions as an enabling or disabling force, leading us to consider how the so-called able body is itself environmentally conditioned.

In addition to their built environments, one cannot help but notice the highly social nature of these spaces. *Plight and Care* and *Where Old People Live* depict a sense of community in their respective settings, both among the inhabitants themselves as well as those tasked with their care. They do so in order to "eliminate the widespread distaste for and fear of" such places, as the lecture accompanying *Plight and Care* said, but in the process they end up highlighting the fundamentally hostile and isolating social dynamics of the world outside. Megan R. Luke notes that unlike Paul Wolff's New Frankfurt films (like *The Frankfurt Kitchen*, discussed in chapter 2), which focused on domestic spaces as sites of efficient production, *Where Old People Live* foregrounds the sociality of the Budge Home, focusing on shared spaces and almost always showing the residents in groups.[25] In a similar vein, *Plight and Care*'s most affecting passages are those that reveal moments of care, belonging, and play. Particularly striking is the scene of the Home's open-air school (*Waldschule*), in which we witness a long train of children, boys and girls of various ages—some walking, with and without crutches, others in wheel-chairs, still others on rolling beds—proceed out of the building and down a sloped yard to an outdoor classroom in a grouping of trees. These brief shots show us an institutional environment adjusted to the physical needs of the children, with its stairless architecture and care workers ensuring mobility, as well as solidarity between the children themselves, who help each other to move as a collective. Later shots of group outdoor play reinforce this sense of collective freedom experienced at the Home.

Both films thus underscore what Barbara Arneil has described as "interde-pendency," a word she uses to move beyond the equation of able-bodiedness with autonomy and disability with dependence. Interdependency instead draws attention to the "'constellation' of supports required by *all of us* (not just people with disabilities) to gain independence."[26] Despite posing a stark contrast between the places they depict and the world outside, *Plight and Care* and *Where Old People Live* invite an acknowledgment of the ways that ability and autonomy as such are bound up with various forms of envi-ronmental and social scaffolding. By revealing this scaffolding in a limited setting, they call the fiction of the normate body's independence and self-sufficiency into question.

Nonetheless, as educational films, *Plight and Care* and *Where Old People Live* chart a clear trajectory from problem bodies to care and containment, showing how the hygienic vision of urban environmental order was tied to a normative conception of bodily ability. In the following section I consider two Weimar melodramas that thematize disability and aging in the urban context. Rather than focus on containment, however, they stage scenes of bodily failure and incapacity as part of their depictions of class and mas-culinity in the modern city, and open space for a more explicit critique of normative able-bodiedness.

Disability, Aging, and Impairment in *The Street* and *The Last Laugh*

Karl Grune's 1923 urban melodrama *Die Straße* (*The Street*) contains a minor but memorable scene in which a young girl and her blind grandfa-ther encounter the dangers of modern traffic. Having left their apartment to search for the girl's father, the pair wander into a shopping boulevard filled with pedestrians, cars, and other vehicles. The girl is attracted by a shop window, but the window is placed too high for her to get a good look. A small dog—more her size—catches the girl's attention and she chases it into the busy intersection. There the streaming cars and carriages paralyze her with fear, until she is eventually rescued by a traffic cop, who takes her to the police station. The grandfather, unaware that the girl has been found, franti-cally shouts from the sidewalk and is knocked to the ground by a passing car. A passerby helps him up and accompanies him home.

This scenario is similar to the episode from *In the Vortex of Traffic* in which the aging Uncle Paul, bewildered by modern Potsdamer Platz, requires the assistance of a traffic cop just to get back to the train station. That film placed the onus of traffic safety largely on individuals, who were supposed to learn the rules of the road, assess risks, and exercise self-discipline—those who could not, like Uncle Paul or children looking for somewhere to play, should keep out. *The Street*, by contrast, offers a decidedly critical view of an urban environment that privileges able-bodied adults. Instead of laughing at Uncle Paul's nervous movements and exaggerated expressions of fear, the viewer feels the force with which the girl and her blind grandfather are excluded from public space. In large and small ways, the street demands acts of visual mastery and ambulatory mobility of which neither are capable: not only does the complexity and speed of traffic threaten to kill them, but the visuality of consumer culture rejects them as well. As problem bodies, their presence makes us aware of how the organization of vision and movement in the urban environment functions to marginalize non-normate subjects.

The scene is an example of the way that film melodramas of the Weimar period dramatized the exclusions and breakdowns of urban modernity. Films like *The Street* and F. W. Murnau's *The Last Laugh* are famous for their depictions of urban class division and masculinity under threat; they are also, I suggest, about modernity's normative regime of ability, which we see reflected in physical and social environments that are hostile to children and disabled or aging persons. More explicitly than the *Kulturfilme* discussed previously, they allow for an understanding of disability not as a bodily pathology in need of containment, but as an experience of exclusion produced within shifting social and material relations. This is not to say that fiction films did not also work to contain disability, dependency, and aging in other ways, such as through narratives of victimization, grotesque portrayals of physical difference, and the use of able-bodied actors to play disabled characters. At the same time, however, by situating disabled, aging, or otherwise dependent characters within the urban environment and the modern workplace, *The Street* and *The Last Laugh* point toward what Robert McRuer calls "the compulsory nature of able-bodiedness"—the way in which freedom under industrial capitalism is predicated on bodily and cognitive normality.[27] They also allow insight into disability's place within the period's class and gender imaginaries, in which disability could figure as a marker of otherness in relation to bourgeois masculinity.

Grune's *The Street* is a key text of Weimar cinema's engagement with urban modernity. The success of the film, which depicts two sets of characters struggling to navigate desire and deprivation in an anonymous city, prompted a series of subsequent "street films" dealing with similar themes, and has been cited as a forerunner of film noir.[28] The primary narrative concerns a nameless middle-class husband (Eugen Klöpfer), who rejects the mundanity of dinner with his wife for a night of excitement on the town, with disastrous consequences. He is seduced by a sex worker (Aud Egede Nissen), who plans to rob him together with her partner (Anton Edthofer) and their accomplices. The secondary plot follows the daughter of Nissen and Edthofer's characters and her blind grandfather (Max Schreck), whom the couple have left behind in their tenement apartment while they work at night. The young girl and her grandfather venture into the street but fail to find her parents. The narrative lines intertwine when the parents bring their marks, the wayward husband and "a gentleman from the country" (according to the film's censorship card), back to the apartment in order to rob them. The country gentleman resists and is killed. Police arrest Klöpfer's character for the murder, but the young girl implicates her own father, and the husband is allowed to return to his mundane domestic life. In *The Street*, tenement deprivation and working-class criminality clash with petit-bourgeois domesticity and middle-aged male sexual frustration. In the following I trace the motif of visual impairment in the film, which serves as a marker of both working-class hardship and male subjectivity on the verge of collapse. At the same time, the film's portrayal of impairment points to the urban environment itself as a disabling force that deprives its inhabitants of the visual capacity and mental sobriety they need to survive.

As embodied by the blind grandfather and his young granddaughter, disability and physical dependency underscore the dysfunction of their working-class milieu. As a site of crime and prostitution in which the boundaries between public and private, work and home, family member and stranger, have broken down, their apartment carries all the signs of urban hygienic disorder familiar from prewar discussions of the housing question, which saw the tenements as sites not just of poverty and hunger, but of chronic illness and disability as well. The grandfather's visual impairment and dependency signify the end point of an existence lived out in such an environment; the neglected granddaughter, meanwhile, provides narrative stakes as the character whose further development this environment threatens. Left behind by their able-bodied, working family members, these characters are marked unambiguously as victims of social circumstance. In this way, at least, *The Street* portrays disability in what Rosemarie Garland-Thomson calls the "sentimental mode," which "instructs the viewer to look down with benevolence."[29] The sentimental mode comports with the attitude of bourgeois social reform, which focused on those in need of rescue from working-class criminality, prostitution, neglect, and general moral laxity. Aligned by their exclusion from the productive sphere and by their consequent dependency, grandfather and granddaughter represent two ends of a trajectory of urban working-class degeneration.

Impairment is not contained solely within the working-class milieu, however. The protagonist's visual experience of the world, at least, seems not to conform to the parameters of normative vision. The opening scene, for instance, contrasts the husband's distorted image of the urban world outside with his wife's objective view of the same scene. While the man reclines on a sofa in their apartment, two silhouettes on the ceiling engage in a playful pantomime of flirtation that draws the protagonist to the apartment window. After a close-up of his entranced stare, we cut to a montage of a kind that would become typical in city-themed films of the 1920s, which presents the street as a space of male fantasy. Street traffic, a clown making grotesque faces, a patchwork of amusement park rides in motion, a smiling woman's face, dancing couples, fireworks—images flow by, entrancing the man. The phantasmatic character of his vision is further emphasized by his wife's very different view of the street. Seeing her perturbed husband at the window, the wife takes a look for herself. Another point-of-view shot, this time without cinematic tricks, presents a single, uninterrupted image of the street below. For the wife, the street is simply another space of everyday life: without internal frames or montage effects, the street appears plainly, as a continuation of everyday routines. Nonetheless, the husband remains entranced and leaves their apartment, where he immediately encounters a woman who fixes him in her gaze. Shocked at being an object of vision rather than its subject, the husband sees the woman's face transform briefly into a skull, in what can only be a hallucination.

The street montage and the husband's hallucinatory experience could be read as moments of Expressionist excess that illustrate his fantasies, rather than reflecting some sort of impairment. They do serve this function, but other aspects of the protagonist's behavior and later scenes point to a more literal motivation: drunkenness. He often seems to stumble, rather than walk confidently; he exhibits a lack of sexual inhibition, in his pursuit of the woman seeking to con him; he is prone to aggression, nearly attacking a man who shows interest in the same woman; and he experiences moments of hallucination. One moment in particular makes his intoxication visually explicit. Upon entering a nightclub, the husband views the dance floor from above and is overwhelmed with what he sees. A medium close-up shows the man with eyes wide, his head nodding drunkenly in a circular motion that mimics the turning of the dancers below. A point-of-view shot then literally makes the room spin: the image of the dance floor turns first counterclockwise, then clockwise, before returning to the medium close-up of the dazed protagonist, who raises a hand to briefly cover his eyes. We then see another shot of the spinning room, this time with the man's silhouette superimposed, which simultaneously emphasizes his vertigo while providing the viewer with a point of stability. The image spins before his eyes, slowly settling into horizontality like a boat rocked by a wave. While certainly not disabled in the way that the grandfather is, the protagonist's perception and self-control appear altered in such a way that makes him vulnerable in the urban environment.

Hygiene discourse linked alcohol with working-class disability, understanding intoxication as a temporary physical or cognitive impairment and alcoholism as a debilitating and potentially hereditary condition. As Hasso Spode writes, by the late nineteenth century, "the growing importance of laborers in the makeup of industrial society seemed less and less reconcilable with their lack of sobriety."[30] Physicians and reformers studied the physiological, hereditary, and social effects of alcohol abuse, as well as the economic and social causes of alcoholism, as part of the broader effort to understand and manage urban industrial pathology. Temperance and abstinence movements, meanwhile, worked to reduce or even eliminate the presence of alcohol in public life. As with other hygienic dangers, experts and reformers linked alcoholism to industrialization, urbanization, and the recklessness of capitalist profit-seeking.[31] Alcoholism was presumed to cause gradual physical degeneration and hereditary defects, but drunkenness also interfered with the imperatives of industrial labor. The industrial psychologist (and early film theorist) Hugo Münsterberg argued that the "decrease of certain memory powers, of the acuity in measuring distance, of the time estimation, and similar psychical disturbances after alcohol, must evidently be of high importance for industry and transportation."[32] *In the Vortex of Traffic* features an episode of drunk driving that kills a pedestrian and leads the driver to end her own life. From the perspective of hygienic experts, alcohol consumption, which Münsterberg called "one of the worst enemies of civilized life," was a force of environmental disorder and bodily degeneration.[33]

In *The Street*, the husband's drunkenness signals the transgression of class and gender differences that define his social position. More specifically, dysfunctional vision characterizes his descent into a working-class world of lawlessness and license, which ends in the tenement apartment occupied by the blind man and his granddaughter—a space of disability and dependency. This descent, moreover, is occasioned by public female sexuality, which first triggers hallucination and then leads him into the hands of con men. Like alcohol, prostitution was also considered a degenerative force, as a vector of sexually transmitted disease. That the protagonist's encounter with class and gender difference is accompanied by visual dysfunction shows how Weimar's conception of bourgeois masculinity is bound up with a normative conception of bodily ability. For the bourgeois male subject, the city, with its alcohol, women, and debilitated underclass, functions as a potentially disabling environment that threatens the vision and mobility that secure his social position.[34] Disability is associated with otherness, and impairment marks the failure to keep that otherness at bay. This dynamic is confirmed by a return to visual stability at the end of the film. Released from jail after being cleared of suspicion for murder, the man returns home to his patient wife, where they reconcile in front of the window that first prompted the husband's adventure. But instead of gazing out the window, his repentant eyes meet hers—the debilitating sights of the city no longer beckon.

The film does not wholly endorse this normative version of male subjectivity, however. Although the husband is the film's central figure, there are numerous moments in *The Street* that align the viewer with other characters and invite a critical perspective on his rigid concept of bourgeois masculinity. The wife's sober view out of the apartment window at the beginning of the film, for instance, deflates her husband's hallucinatory fantasy of the city's temptations, making the latter appear ridiculous. The husband falls victim to his own fantasies as much as to the predations of the street; rather than sympathize, we could just as easily laugh at the husband's fragility and gullibility. Our sense of the husband as victim is similarly offset by the scenes featuring the girl and her grandfather, who by comparison are truly subject to the disabling forces of modernity, despite their best collective effort. In this way *The Street* could be read as equating disability with victimization and dependency, but unlike representations in the sentimental mode, disability is not used here to buoy the moral standing of a savior figure. Instead, the girl and the blind grandfather serve as another point of identification within the narrative that undercuts the fantasy of bourgeois masculinity itself, which can only see bodily and cognitive incapacity as threats to subjectivity. Indeed, as I will outline later, *The Street* even suggests that incapacitation is one of cinema's attractions.

A similarly rigid link between masculinity and able-bodiedness informs F. W. Murnau's *Der letzte Mann* (*The Last Laugh*, 1924). The film stars Emil Jannings as a porter at the bustling, cosmopolitan Atlantic Hotel, who is demoted to the position of bathroom attendant because of his waning strength and speed. The man's identity, both at work and in his working-class milieu, is so tied to his status as head porter at the hotel that the demotion destroys him, both mentally and physically. Unable to bear the embarrassment of his reduced status, the man steals his former uniform to keep up appearances in front of the residents of the tenement in which he lives, but he is soon found out and humiliated. It appears that the ex-porter will live out the rest of his days in defeat in a hotel bathroom. In an epilogue, however, which a prefatory intertitle admits is an unrealistic act of mercy on the part of the screenwriter, we find out that the man has inherited great wealth from an American millionaire who died in the Atlantic Hotel's bathroom. The film ends with the man and his elderly friend, the hotel's night watchman, living it up in the dining room of their former workplace.

The Last Laugh paints a critical portrait of a world in which masculine status depends on an increasingly narrow definition of able-bodiedness. As critics like Sabine Hake and Judith Ellenbürger note, the film resonated with the Weimar era's discourse of rationalization, which valued the energy and malleability of youth. "In an age defined by rapid technological progress, the reorganization of all labor processes, as well as the vociferous demand for increased productivity, efficiency, and profit," Ellenbürger writes, "more and more often . . . younger people are employed and older people let go."[35] This had gendered implications to the extent that male identity was linked to work, an identity that was also threatened by the employment of women. And just as the recent war had put more women to work, according to Sabine Kienitz it had also demonstrated how masculinity "was dependent on the fitness of the body." Kienitz writes that the figure of the disabled soldier revealed that the able body was the "central element of a construction of male identity . . . that was expressed in contemporary images of mobility, the performance of labor, power, authority, and virility."[36] The porter's failing body thus evokes a whole network of modern threats to masculinity, from women's growing social power to workplace rationalization and the trauma of war.[37]

Unlike *The Street*, *The Last Laugh* does not mark the working-class milieu in which the porter lives as a space of dysfunction or physical degeneration. His neighborhood is home to a vibrant community of people of all ages, from playing children to chatting grandmothers. Its tight-knit interpersonal bonds differ starkly from the porter's workplace, which is inhabited by its uniformed staff and a constantly rotating group of well-dressed guests. The spaces mirror each other, however, in the strictness with which they enforce the able-bodied masculine norm. In the opening scene of the film, the porter has difficulty carrying an especially heavy suitcase, and rests momentarily on a bench in the lobby to catch his breath—which the (much younger) hotel manager notices. The following day, he is demoted to the position of bathroom attendant, presumably for two reasons: first, his weakness threatens the efficient circulation of guests; and second, perhaps more importantly, his body no longer fits the image of youthful, rationalized modernity the hotel wishes to project. Instead of representing the hotel as the lead porter, the first face the guests see, he is banished to the downstairs restroom. The porter's failure to live up to the able-bodied norm has consequences at home as well. In order to hide his demotion, he steals his old uniform and wears it to and from work, but when his neighbors discover the truth they mock and shun him mercilessly. It seems, then, that able-bodiedness allows a limited amount of contact across class difference—in that it allows the working-class porter to occupy bourgeois spaces, if only as a servant—but male incapacity cannot be tolerated anywhere.

In emphasizing the reactions of others to the porter's physical weakness and reduced status at work, *The Last Laugh* puts the social construction of disability on display. Aside from his struggle with a heavy suitcase in the opening scene, the porter's physical decline seems wholly a product of how he is perceived. He recovers fairly quickly from lifting the suitcase, but subsequent moments of social humiliation take a perceptible toll on the porter's body. For instance, after arriving at the hotel the next day and noticing that a younger porter has taken his place, he takes on a hunched posture that contrasts with his earlier upright gait. In the hotel manager's office, the porter reads a letter explaining that because of his frailty (*Altersschwäche*, literally "age weakness"), he will be demoted to the position of bathroom attendant—a moment whose shock is rendered by a blurred point-of-view shot of the letter. The porter attempts to demonstrate his strength by lifting a trunk in the manager's office, but fails and collapses to the ground. Once he stands up again, his body is transformed. His head hangs forward, his eyes stare blankly, and he walks with his knees bent in a shuffling gait. When standing still, he rocks slightly. His reduction in workplace status has a lasting corporeal effect. The aunt of his niece's husband, who comes to visit him at work, delivers a similar shock. When she finds him not at the hotel entrance but in the downstairs bathroom, her recognition lands like a physical blow. In a quick shot the camera speeds toward the woman's face behind the bathroom's glass door as she lets out a cruel, pointed laugh. A reverse close-up shows the porter recoil from the force of the laugh. In its aftermath, his head hangs even lower than before. He is physically weakened, and a well-dressed patron berates him for providing a less-than-vigorous shoeshine. Given the way these instances of humiliation affect the porter, *The Last Laugh* seems to locate the source of decline not in the porter's own body, as a medical view of disability would, but in masculinity's precarious dependence on a range of status markers and social deference.

In this way, the film unmasks the disavowed social construction of the able male body. Critics have noted in particular the porter's attachment to his uniform, as that which ensures his status. "The spectacular uniform with the gold tresses and shiny buttons gives him a military bearing," Hake writes. "It functions like an external armor that imposes a distinct form and structure on a malleable, amorphous body. Like a prosthesis—or an external crutch of sorts—the uniform holds him up and provides him with a sense of wholeness."[38] If the porter's debilitation results from his decline in social standing, rather than the other way around, we also become aware of the extent to which the normate subject position relies on external supports whose importance can be disavowed until they are removed.

Evoking disability without explicitly addressing it, Hake's language brings to mind the work of critics such as Lennard J. Davis and Margrit Shildrick, who have emphasized how illusions of wholeness and self-sufficiency cover over the body's fundamental vulnerability. Davis speculates that "the element of repulsion and fear associated with fragmentation and disability may in fact come from the very act of repressing the primal fragmentariness of the body."[39] *The Last Laugh* thematizes the anxiety provoked by the porter's body, which, once no longer contained by the prosthetic uniform, confronts those around him with the reality of the vulnerable body. According to Shildrick, disability produces a fear of contamination: "The disabled body, the body that resists the conscious control of the will, that is effectively out of control, may carry no infectious agents, and yet . . . it is treated as though it were contaminatory."[40] Because the uniform can no longer paper over it, the porter's fragility must be contained and removed from sight in other ways. At work, the position of bathroom attendant hides him from most of the guests.[41] Back at home, the other residents mock him from their windows, which forces him to seek shelter with his niece—though the scornful gazes of her husband and his aunt force him back out, to return the stolen uniform in secret.[42] The porter's family and superiors at work treat him as a contaminant and enact the social forces that conspire to push him out of the home and out of sight at work. Moreover, *The Last Laugh* implicates the viewer in this dynamic, as Jannings's performance registers the pain caused by the gazes that fall upon him; watching him generates pity, but also guilt in that the act of watching the film contributes to his shame.

As we saw in the *Kulturfilme* discussed in the first part of this chapter, these forces encourage a movement toward containing the aging or disabled body in separate institutional spaces. And in fact, *The Last Laugh*'s famously binary urban geography, consisting of the hotel and the tenement, is haunted by such a space. The letter demoting the porter explains that the previous bathroom attendant, the hotel's oldest employee, has gone to live in a care home (*Versorgungsheim*). Superimposed over the letter, we see the previous bathroom attendant turn in his coat, a scene presumably imagined by the porter as he reads, which anticipates his own relinquishing of the porter's uniform as well as his own approaching retirement. We can guess, then, that the porter does not just fear losing his status at work or at home—rather, as someone without a spouse or children, retirement could mean the end of his life in mainstream society. The hotel bathroom's isolation prefigures that of the care home, which is the implied end point of the porter's trajectory.

The care home is arguably where the film should actually end. Instead, *The Last Laugh* concludes with a satirical version of the "miracle cure" trope found in many early twentieth-century films about disability, which relieved viewers of the anxiety that a beloved protagonist might be stricken for life.[43] The miracle takes the form of an inheritance, bequeathed to the porter by a wealthy man who happened to die in the hotel's bathroom while he was working there. Consistent with the logic of Jannings's performance, ability follows from social status rather than the other way around—not only is the porter fantastically rich, but the outward signs of weakness and impaired mobility have vanished, and his original posture reappears. Money has replaced the uniform as the prosthetic support that contains the porter's vulnerable body and allows him to assume his former masculinity.[44] In so doing, it enables his return to the social space of the hotel from which he had been banished, this time as a patron of the restaurant. Even though he is a figure of mockery—the other hotel patrons laugh as they read the newspaper article recounting his inheritance—he is no longer treated as a contaminant to be shunned.

The Street and *The Last Laugh* dramatize the circulation and containment of disability in the city in ways that challenge a hygienic view of the body and its proper place in the urban environment. The modern city accommodated certain kinds of bodies more than others. The hygienic perspective expressed in films like *Plight and Care* and *Where Old People Live* proposed to solve this problem by moving those who did not fit into specialized environments,

Intoxication. Still from *The Last Laugh* (dir. F. W. Murnau, 1924).

temporarily or permanently, where they could be cared for without interrupting the material intercourse of everyday life. *The Street* and *The Last Laugh* explore the fallout of the modern regime of bodily normality, which produced forms of spatial and social exclusion and instilled a paralyzing pressure to perform. In *The Last Laugh* this pressure is particularly crucial to masculine subjectivity, given the porter's own overwhelming shame after his failure to live up to it. These urban melodramas suggest that hygienic modernity's impulse to contain aging and disability is bound up with a gendered fear of the vulnerable body—a fear these films play with at an aesthetic level as well.

Movie Intoxication

One of *The Last Laugh*'s most memorable sequences demonstrates the porter's psychic investment in the performance of able-bodiedness. At his niece's wedding—the family and guests do not yet know he has been demoted—the porter drinks heavily and falls asleep on a chair, where he dreams about lifting an extremely heavy trunk with a single hand. It flies off the ground and he carries it away, leaving the other porters in awe. In a show of strength he then carries the trunk through a space that contains elements of both the hotel and the tenement courtyard, where he fears losing status. The sequence depicts a stark contrast between the physical control the porter demonstrates in the dream and his intoxicated movements beforehand, when his body sways, his head nods, and eventually he is unable to stand, at which point he sits down and falls asleep. In this sequence, at least, Shildrick's remark that "the body that resists the conscious control of the will . . . is treated as though it were contaminatory" does not hold. The other drunken guests party along with him, and the groom's aunt, who will later discover the porter's demotion and initiate his social exclusion, kindly wakes him and helps him get dressed for work the next morning. The content of the dream indicates that part of the pleasure of intoxication, especially in socially acceptable contexts, is its offer of temporary release from the imperative of able-bodiedness.

Both *The Street* and *The Last Laugh* employ cinematic effects to mimic drunkenness for the viewer. As mentioned earlier, *The Street* rotates the image of a nightclub dance floor in a point-of-view shot to convey the protagonist's intoxication. *The Last Laugh* goes much further, using the mobile camera to produce dizziness and disorientation. Just before the porter's dream, in a shot made by turning Jannings and the camera together on a platform, we see the room spin behind him while the camera remains fixed on his face. A point-of-view shot then pans unsteadily around the room, mimicking the porter's bobbing head. This intoxicated vision continues into the dream itself, which uses blurry transitions, double images, and the shakiness of Karl Freund's unchained camera to create an overall sense of visual instability and disorientation. Rather than securing the viewer's mastery over filmic space, *The Last Laugh* uses intoxication and dream—another everyday experience of the loss of bodily control—to destabilize it.

The sequence echoes the earlier demotion scene, in which a point-of-view shot renders the porter's momentary visual impairment. When the porter reads the demotion letter in the manager's office, the camera moves in to inhabit his viewpoint and fully align us with his perspective. An insert shows the letter, over which the imagined scene of the previous bathroom attendant being shuffled off to the care home appears, and then a medium close-up shows the porter pause briefly as he struggles to understand the letter's implications. Then, in extreme close-up, the crucial sentence passes through the frame letter-by-letter: "The reason for these measures"—the camera scans quickly, finding the next line—"is your frailty." At the end of the word "frailty," the camera loses focus and returns to the beginning of the word, before refocusing and reading it again. Here, the camera represents the porter's senescence visually, both through the slowness of its reading and the blurring of the image.

These examples, in which the film enacts states of impairment by aesthetic means, suggest that a loss of perceptual ability was itself a cinematic attraction for audiences under a regime of compulsory able-bodiedness. Like the intoxicated porter, whose livelihood and social standing depend on his

Visual difficulty. Stills from *The Last Laugh*.

ability to perform, viewers sought escape in a context where a lack of bodily control could be experienced in a safe and socially acceptable way. In 1916 the writer Richard Guttmann discussed what he called "movie intoxication" (*Kinorausch*), explicitly analogizing film spectatorship to states of drunkenness and dreaming. Such states reduce the influence of "will and active consciousness," as well as "considerations of saving face and social necessity," which allow "instincts, drives, and desires [to] rush through his soul."[45] Emphasizing the passive aspect of spectatorship in a world that demands performance, Guttmann's intoxication metaphor resonates with films like *The Street* and *The Last Laugh*, which use moments of impairment to motivate spectacular cinematic effects.

I do not mean to suggest that these moments convey something resembling actual experiences of visual impairment, or even intoxication; nor do they offer non-normative vision as a valid, alternative perception of the world.[46] Rather, the link between disorienting visual effects and bodily failure in the narrative appeals to a fantasy of impairment that resists the compulsion to be able-bodied. Along these lines, the disability theorists Sharon L. Snyder and David T. Mitchell propose that representations of disability or disfigurement in "body genres" such as horror, comedy, and melodrama can "appeal to viewer concerns about the maintenance of bodily integrity" and "destabilize the viewer's own investments in ability."[47] Against the backdrop of urban modernity's ideal of hygienic able-bodiedness, *The Street* and *The Last Laugh* experiment with disorienting visual effects to allow viewers to experience bodily vulnerability in the limited space and time of the cinema. Rather than immediately contain the impaired body, these films stage bodily failure as both nightmare and fantasy. Key to this fantasy, however, is that it is temporary—hence the analogies between film spectatorship and transitory states like intoxication or dreaming. Ironically or not, both films also conclude with a return to physical normality.

As a site where viewers could flirt with bodily vulnerability, cinema could challenge the normative relation between body and environment encouraged by hygiene discourse, which emphasized visual mastery of one's surroundings. The mode of vision encouraged by the traffic-safety film *In the Vortex of Traffic* is a paradigmatic case in point—the episode featuring Uncle Paul, described at the beginning of this chapter, even includes a kaleidoscopic point-of-view shot of Potsdamer Platz not unlike the intoxicated cinematography of *The Street* or *The Last Laugh*. It is precisely this type of visual failure that *In the Vortex of Traffic* aimed to prevent. *The Street* and *The Last Laugh*, by contrast, revel in defamiliarizing vision through vertiginous movement, blurriness, speed, slowness, and other techniques that inhibit quick and seamless visual comprehension—techniques the films themselves mark as deviating from "healthy" or "sober" forms of seeing. At the aesthetic level, these films explored the way cinema could afford a release from a normative relationship to the perceptual world.[48] Cinema was an environment in which one could see blurriness in perfect focus, feel movement without moving, and stagger while seated upright. However temporary or contained, these moments of movie intoxication constituted a filmic counter-discourse to the hygienic emphasis on sensorimotor coordination and perceptual sobriety.

These last two chapters have looked at film's role in imagining that which hygiene considered out of place in its vision of modernity: problematic materials like smoke and dust, on the one hand, which obscured sight and challenged the sanitary boundaries between the self and its environment; and problematic bodies, on the other, whose deviation from able-bodied norms interrupted traffic and threatened what Shildrick calls the "normative construct of the self's clean and proper body."[49] We have seen how cinema was subject to and participated in projects of hygienic containment, but also how it could function as a bounded space of unhygienic dispersion, contagion, and intoxication. In the final chapter, I turn from aesthetic to political challenges to the hygienic project, whose concept of modernization through environmental reform and broad-based populational health came to seem increasingly implausible at the end of the Weimar Republic.

Chapter 5

✦

Landscapes of Exploitation

Environmental Disorder and Late Weimar Oppositional Filmmaking

With the economic crisis that began in 1929, the question of order—economic, political, social, material—took on existential proportions. With skyrocketing unemployment, industrial capitalism as it had existed since the late nineteenth century seemed more and more unsustainable. In the face of cascading disorder, the fascist Right promised to institute order on a racial foundation. National Socialism made racial biopolitics its ideological raison d'être, with scientific legitimation provided by experts in heredity and racial hygiene. In so doing, it claimed the terrain of hygiene for itself by imagining a national body both socially and spatially cleansed of otherness. This fascist imagination of hygiene forged a powerful association between hygiene and fascism that persists into the present.

As historians like Corinna Treitel and Edward Ross Dickinson have argued, however, biopolitics were (and are) not the exclusive domain of the Right.[1] On the contrary, at the end of the Weimar Republic, numerous leftist films participated in the politicization of health and drew attention to the material disorder that still plagued working-class districts and industrial workplaces. In this chapter I examine three such films, in order to show how biopolitics and the problem of environmental disorder informed late Weimar oppositional filmmaking. The first two, *Hunger in Waldenburg* (Phil Jutzi, 1929) and *Zeitprobleme: Wie der Arbeiter wohnt* (*How the Worker Lives,* Slatan Dudow, 1930), could be called critical hygiene films. They borrowed techniques of the documentary *Kulturfilm,* but instead of endorsing the narrative of hygienic progress and training their viewers, they pointed to the unhealthy conditions of their present and indicted the capitalist economic order. In so doing, they exposed the ideological character of mainstream hygiene discourse, which served to blunt the sharp edges of industrial capitalism without addressing the underlying causes of material disorder. Dudow's feature film *Kuhle Wampe* (1932), the best-known example of late Weimar leftist cinema, went a step further, moving to the green urban periphery in order to both critique and transform the therapeutic function typically ascribed to such environments. In different ways, all three films served as a corrective to the earlier *Kulturfilme* discussed in chapter 2.

I argue that these films constituted a reaction to both the dominant capitalist narrative of hygienic progress as well as the increasing racialization of health discourse at the end of the Weimar Republic. They demonstrate the place of health and environmental order in the broader fight over how to resolve the crises of capitalist modernity. If film could be used to envision a world of hygienic order, it was also a powerful tool for deconstructing and reframing such visions. At the same time, the films discussed below are conflicted documents. They struggled to critically reflect upon and articulate alternatives to a discourse that was thoroughly infused with eugenic ideas and dominated by experts, two forms of hierarchy that stood in tension with aspects of the emancipatory political project the films otherwise espoused. Forged in the culture of industrial capitalism, hygiene was premised on maximizing economic productivity—this was the key to its rhetorical appeal to those with economic and political power in German society. Its approach to health thus tended to obscure the links between material order and economic or political order; in other words, hygiene promised the former without having to touch the latter, even though political economy was the primary reason why the material landscapes of modernity looked the way they did. In this regard, hygiene was more easily an ally of the Right. The films discussed in this chapter connected economic and environmental order (or more frequently, disorder), but their affirmation of values like bodily autonomy, collective well-being, and environmental justice stood in tension with a hygienic imaginary they could not quite escape.

Critique of Hygienic Reason

The films discussed in this chapter were all produced within an alternative film culture that emerged on the German Left in the late 1920s. "In the early years of the Republic," Marc Silberman writes, "both the SPD and the KPD considered political art to be an extension of mass organising, and movies—a mass medium in the hands of big business—were not seen as art but as an opiate."[2] In the mid-1920s, however, better economic conditions, inspiration from Soviet cinema, and a growing awareness of the political importance of modern media like film and radio spurred attempts to challenge the dominant models of commercial film exhibition and production. The documentary and didactic aspects of the films I discuss in this chapter suggest, however, that late Weimar leftist filmmaking can be read not just against mainstream commercial cinema, but against mainstream *Kulturfilme* as well.

Like those films, *Hunger in Waldenburg*, *How the Worker Lives*, and *Kuhle Wampe* were concerned to different degrees with unhealthy environmental disorder. Unlike those films, however, they viewed the urban landscape primarily in class terms and blamed capitalist exploitation for the debilitating environmental blight to which the industrial working class was disproportionately exposed. In other words, they framed environmental disorder as a constitutive element of capitalist modernity, not as a problem that could be solved through the sophisticated management of bodies and materials in space. They thus also rejected, however implicitly, the premise that hygienic modernization could reconcile capitalist development with the needs of the human organism. In this section, I explore the different filmic and narrative means through which these films staged their critique. Though containing imagery of both blighted and harmonious urban landscapes, similar to those found in a film like *The City of Tomorrow*, they pointed to the limits of a technocratic project like hygiene when it was constrained by the fundamentally antagonistic social and economic relations of industrial capitalism.

Slatan Dudow's 1930 short film *How the Worker Lives* was intended to be the first installment of a newsreel series for Weltfilm, a documentary film production and distribution company founded by the proletarian aid organization Workers International Relief. The film aimed to publicize the poor living conditions in working-class neighborhoods, opening with the intertitle: "In the tenements of the city of millions, multiple families must share a lightless, unhealthy apartment. Damp basement apartments rob the worker of his health. The squalor of the apartments ruins the vitality of children. Amidst this reality this film was made." Before documenting unhygienic proletarian housing, the film offers an economic context, emphasizing the rampant unemployment and rent increases in the midst of the world economic crisis. A series of brief sequences follows: working-class and bourgeois neighborhoods in Berlin juxtaposed through editing; unhealthy tenement courtyards and a crowded, shallow pool for children, which intertitles refer to ironically as "the gardens for workers" and "our Baltic Sea," respectively; a comparison between the lives of a working-class family and their landlord; and, finally, an eviction enforced by the police.

How the Worker Lives offers an exemplary case of modernist montage used to dismantle a narrative of progress. *The City of Tomorrow* used similar images of tenements and garden city-style housing, but strung them into a linear progression, in which unhealthy urban disorder was superseded by hygienic order. *How the Worker Lives* instead emphasizes simultaneity, the co-existence of orderly and disorderly environments. In one sequence, the film cuts between shots of long rows of tenement housing, framed on the right, and an exclusive residential area (*Villenviertel*) of modern homes with grass and trees, framed on the left. Editing thus creates an imaginary space of confrontation, with hygienic urban design on the "left" and the working-class neighborhoods on the "right"—spaces that are actually segregated in the urban landscape but brought into conflict through filmic means. In the spirit of Eisensteinian montage, editing is used to create conflict rather than smooth it over, highlighting actually existing contradictions rather than ordering them into a historical progression. Both spaces are also shot at canted angles, so that the buildings in each seem to tip toward each other. Earlier in the film, Dudow used strange angles to visualize the claustrophobic and inhospitable tenements; here, even the posh parts of Berlin are off-kilter. Though they look quite different, their shared imbalance suggests that the impoverishment of one space throws the whole into disarray. Hygienic modernity exists, but only for some, while others are left behind; indeed, healthy living for the minority seems premised upon the exploitation of the majority. Yet, while examining the environmental conditions of Berlin working-class districts through a hygienic lens may reveal a particular dimension of capitalist exploitation, the film does not suggest more or better hygiene as the solution to these conditions.

This is reflected in the film's attitude toward expertise and state authority as well. Unlike the *Kulturfilme* of chapter 2, *How the Worker Lives* is unconcerned with bolstering confidence in hygienic expertise. Expert knowledge is useful to the extent that it can diagnose inequalities of health and their intersection with environmental conditions, but the film does not portray a success story of modernization. The police, likewise, do not function to mediate conflicting interests, as in the traffic safety film *In the Vortex of Traffic*, but to uphold class domination. At the end of the film, a family is evicted from their apartment, and when a neighbor attempts to resist, police arrive to remove him and enforce the landlord's property rights. Indeed, the film suggests that the landlords and the police that back them are themselves agents of material disorder, as we see the family's furniture and other belongings haphazardly piled onto the street. *How the Worker Lives* foregrounds existing social tensions while refusing to imply that medical expertise or agents of state violence could resolve them. The problem of eviction exposes how hygiene is ultimately subordinate to property and profit. While it promises a healthy modernity, it delivers only insofar as the economic dominance of capital remains unchallenged.

Like *How the Worker Lives*, Phil Jutzi and Leo Lania's 1929 film *Hunger in Waldenburg* (also sometimes called *Um's tägliche Brot*, or *Our Daily Bread*) foregrounds present contradictions, but frames them within a history and geography of exploitation. This film was the first feature-length production of the Volksfilmverband (VFV), an independent organization of film enthusiasts interested in fostering alternatives to the commercial cinema that dominated Weimar film culture. Founded in 1928 by a group that included Heinrich Mann, Béla Balázs, and Käthe Kollwitz, the VFV published the journal *Film und Volk* and eventually had chapters in numerous German cities that organized film screenings and other events. Although ostensibly a nonpartisan grassroots organization, the VFV's leading voices were well-known Social Democratic and Communist artists and intellectuals. By 1929, the group "understood itself . . . primarily as a proletarian revolutionary cultural organization, whose central task should be to create the 'social preconditions' for proletarian film in Germany."[3] Leo Lania, a playwright, journalist, Communist, and VFV board member, encouraged the group's turn toward film production, first with the experimental "Montagefilm" *Im Schatten der Maschine* (*In the Shadow of the Machine*, 1928), which he co-directed. *Hunger in Waldenburg*, for which Lania wrote the screenplay, was the next film produced under the auspices of the VFV.

Hunger in Waldenburg was directed by Phil Jutzi, who made many detective films after the war but turned to more politically engaged ventures in the mid-1920s. Jutzi helped prepare Soviet films (most famously *Battleship Potemkin*) for distribution in Germany at Prometheus-Film, a company cofounded by the young Communist and media specialist Willi Münzenberg. Jutzi also served as a cameraman on collaborations between Prometheus and Mezhrabpom-Film, a Soviet firm associated with the hunger relief group also cofounded by Münzenberg, the Workers International Relief. Jutzi became far better known for the proletarian melodrama *Mother Krause's Journey to Happiness*, which he directed later in 1929, and the 1931 film adaptation of *Berlin Alexanderplatz*. *Mother Krause's Journey to Happiness*, a Prometheus production, has received more critical consideration as an exemplar of leftist political melodrama in the late Weimar Republic, but *Hunger in Waldenburg*, a hybrid object that mixes Soviet-style editing with *Kulturfilm* didacticism, deserves attention as a response to the dominant mode of educational films in Germany. It also reflects Jutzi's documentary work, which included numerous shorts made around the same time for Weltfilm (another Münzenberg venture).[4] Jutzi was thus an important part of Münzenberg's effort to contest bourgeois-dominated media and strengthen the workers' movement by creating an alternative public sphere. On *Hunger in Waldenburg*, Münzenberg and Weltfilm are listed as producers "on behalf of" ("im Auftrag von") of the VFV.

Released in March 1929, the conditions depicted in *Hunger in Waldenburg* preceded the staggering rise in German unemployment which began later that summer, heralding the onset of the Great Depression. In other words, Waldenburg was starving before the stock markets crashed. The city and the surrounding region of Lower Silesia were no strangers to poverty and exploitation. In 1930, after *Hunger in Waldenburg* had failed to bring about substantive improvement in the conditions there, Emil Baumann-Dittersbach wrote in *Die Weltbühne* that "the Waldenburg district is an exorbitant historical case of mass exploitation over centuries."[5] Until the nineteenth century, weaving was the region's most important industry. Baumann-Dittersbach called the area Frederick the Great's "Prussian Peru," that is, a quasi-colony that was home to a heavily exploited population considered useful only for the value it produced.[6] This exploitation made Lower Silesia the site of periodic rebellions by weavers in the first half of the nineteenth century, one of which was famously dramatized in Gerhart Hauptmann's 1892 play *The*

Weavers. Industrialization reduced the weavers' numbers and shifted the region's industry significantly toward coal mining. The general immiseration faced by the people living in and around Waldenburg was interrupted only by a brief period of prosperity from the mid-nineteenth century until the economic crash of the 1870s. The end of World War I brought further economic pressure to the region when countries that had previously imported Silesian coal began developing their own domestic mining industries.[7]

The beginning of *Hunger in Waldenburg* invokes the region's longer history of exploitation. Immediately after the prefatory title, which stresses the film's presentness, the first image is actually that of a book—a "Chronik," or local historical chronicle—followed by two handwritten statements. The first is a ministerial report from 1819, which simply states that "the situation in Silesia cannot be described as one of crisis, as poverty has always prevailed there." The statement fades and is replaced by another, from the German president Paul von Hindenburg, who visited Waldenburg in 1928. The text shown in the film is an excerpt from a speech Hindenburg gave at the Waldenburg city hall at the end of the visit: "What I saw and heard in Waldenburg shook me. It cannot continue like this."[8] The texts place what follows into a historical continuum. While *Hunger in Waldenburg* insists on its simultaneity with the present, the viewer is also meant to have a sense of the duration of the region's poverty and its people's endurance. Given the authority of their writers, the texts also point to Waldenburg's quasi-colonial status, under which it was ruled and exploited by powers who long observed the desperate conditions there but, at best, did nothing to change them. The film portrays Waldenburg as a place of historical stagnation, untouched by the modern blessings of housing, nutritional, and industrial hygiene.

The failure of hygienic modernization to improve conditions in Waldenburg forms the implicit background of the documentary sequence that follows, which depicts a single day in the life of the Waldenburg coal miners and their families. It begins in a dark tenement apartment before dawn. With the help of a spotlight, the camera investigates the space, showing the apartment's disrepair and its feeling of constriction—a family of two adults and four children sleep in what seems to be only one or two rooms, some on improvised beds. The sun rises, and the family prepares for the day. Shots of men on their way to work are interspersed with the family's morning routine, while superimposed handwritten text occasionally provides statistical context: "48% of all homes consist of a single room"; "8.8% without breakfast." The images and statistics evoke social reform discourse around 1900 that decried the primitivity of urban working-class housing and nutritional conditions. As I will examine later, they reproduce a charitable gaze that works against the film's emancipatory ambition.

As the father walks to work, shots of morning street life show traffic and the run-down facades of the tenements. Belching smokestacks signal the start of the working day, introducing a factory montage of gears, belts, wheels, and

The blighted city. Still from *Hunger in Waldenburg* (dir. Phil Jutzi, 1929).

lines of workers. Then, down into the mine. The camera rides the elevator down the shaft, and we see the exhausting labor of coal mining, over shifts of nine hours, according to the on-screen text. Hacking, shoveling, spraying, drilling, pushing, dragging, "day in, day out." The images capture cramped conditions, darkness, and a constant onslaught of steam and smoke. The overall impression is that of bodies exhausted by labor and swallowed by the punishing conditions of the environment in which they work. In one image, a group of miners jog toward what we might recognize as the entrance mine shaft, were it not obscured by a river of smoke. They enter the torrent and disappear. We saw such images in Murnau's *Faust*, and indeed, both films resist a dominant studio aesthetic that upheld the fantasy of a clear boundary between the body and its environment. In *Faust*, however, the body's visual diffusion into particulates functioned as part of a metaphysical reflection on entropy; in *Hunger in Waldenburg* this serves to document a world of material labor and exploitation. As work ends, we witness the power of coal in a montage of spinning machine wheels, smokestacks, and chimneys pumping out smoke. Placed in the middle of this montage, an image of the miners, covered in coal dust, as they deposit their lamps and leave the factory, links the power that drives society to the labor of the miners of Waldenburg. Part of the miners' exploitation consists in the unhealthy environmental disorder in which they labor; industrial hygiene, if it is practiced here, is probably meant more to protect the company's infrastructure than its workers, who are easy to replace.

Before moving into a narrative section about a young weaver who migrates to the city for work, *Hunger in Waldenburg* expands its world briefly to include those literally on top, with a montage sequence that places the suffering of Waldenburg's working people in the context of religion, capital, and class. It begins with five successive shots, each of which pans upward to trace a vertical structure: the spire of the Schutzengelkirche, a Catholic cathedral; the tower of the Evangelical Church, built in the eighteenth century; a smokestack; a massive, snow-covered fir tree; and the facade of the Schloss Fürstenstein, one of the residences of the principality of Pless. The repeated upward pan mimics the tipping back of the head in order to look up, linking the film's analysis to a set of bodily and environmental relations through which power is instantiated. Then, between images of the region and its industry, intertitles read: "Masters / over town / over village / over plains and mountains / coal / and weaving loom: / The princes Pless." Superimposed text informs us that the Fürstenstein estate consists of 10,000 hectares, and that Pless holdings include an additional 60 manors comprising over 40,000 hectares. Idyllic, wintry images of the Fürstenstein estate and its castle follow, the whiteness of the snow underscoring their distance from the soot-drenched landscape below. Around 1800, the principality of Pless was acquired through marriage by the Hochbergs, a Prussian noble family who also commanded the vast wealth generated by coal mining on their land. (An intertitle specifying the size of the Hochberg fortune in *Hunger in Waldenburg* was excised by censors.)[9] The end of World War I split the Hochbergs' landholdings between Poland and Germany, but efforts to expropriate the German nobility failed and the Hochbergs continued to exercise considerable power in the Waldenburg region throughout the Weimar Republic. In *Hunger in Waldenburg*, the Fürstenstein castle and estate thus serve to illustrate not only the vast inequality in wealth between owners and workers, but a continuity of domination before and after the war. Quasi-feudal power relations survive, despite a purported revolution, propped up by a capitalist economy.

Like *How the Worker Lives*, here the film contrasts the unhygienic spaces of working-class life and industrial labor with the clean and safe environments inhabited by those in charge. In so doing both films re-signify the visual oppositions of hygiene familiar from the films discussed in chapter 2. The Berlin *Villenviertel* and the Pless estate may be well-lit and visually ordered, but they do not embody the "good" state in a didactic opposition between hygienic and unhygienic. Rather than examples of hygienic modernization to strive for, they symbolize obstacles to be overcome. Moreover, although aesthetically distinct from the tenements and the mine, they are not actually opposed to them: in fact, they are mutually constituting elements in a system founded on exploitation. The apparent cleanliness of one

The Fürstenstein estate. Still from *Hunger in Waldenburg*.

environment depends upon the damaging physical labor and environmental blight carried out elsewhere. The system of industrial capitalism, these films suggest, produces hygienic spaces for some and unhygienic spaces for (many) others.

Since the late nineteenth century, however, the creation of parks and mass transportation had significantly increased access to recreational green space for many people in German cities, including workers and their families. For city planners, parks and other types of green space were part of a broader vision of hygienic modernization. In his 1915 dissertation, the urban planner Martin Wagner called for "sanitary" rather than decorative green space, which could offer clean air and a place for exercise, sports, and other forms of healthy recreation.[10] For Wagner, such spaces would help "ensure the health of the body of the German people and . . . raise the German people's energy."[11] As Berlin's head planner from 1925 to 1933, Wagner worked with transit commissioner Ernst Reuter to enable greater access to the forests and lakes at the city's edges, expanding the *Ausflugskultur* (excursion culture) of the nineteenth century to the masses.[12]

The 1932 film *Kuhle Wampe, or Who Owns the World?* begins in working-class Berlin, but travels to the city's green periphery in order to ironize the latter's supposedly therapeutic function. Unlike *How the Worker Lives* or

Hunger in Waldenburg, Kuhle Wampe does not dwell on the city's material disorder, and instead begins with sequences of economic and legal ruthlessness. The film starts with a montage of newspaper headlines reporting the ever-increasing number of unemployed, ending with a page of help wanted advertisements from a local paper. We then see a group of young men with bicycles gather at a kiosk to check the latest job ads, before racing each other to the prospective employers, where they are nonetheless rebuffed over and over again. The group includes the Bönike family's son, who returns home for dinner. His mother and father, the latter also unemployed, express disappointment at their son's supposed laziness and impoliteness, while his sister Anni understands that there simply is not enough to work to go around. After dinner, with father gone to a bar and Anni out with her lover Fritz, the young man commits suicide by jumping out of the window of their high-floor tenement apartment. The family is subsequently ordered to leave their apartment for failure to pay rent. Anni calls Fritz, who suggests they move out to the tent colony Kuhle Wampe with him. These first scenes are dominated by gestures of rejection, ejection, expulsion: the unemployed bikers who are rebuffed by signs saying "workers will not be hired"; the son's jump out of the window; the judge ruling in favor of the Bönikes' landlord; the shrugging shoulders, regretful nods, and shutting doors that Anni encounters in a fruitless search for assistance from various welfare authorities and representatives of the state. In the deteriorating economic context of the late Weimar Republic, in which mass unemployment was accompanied by cuts to state assistance, the Bönikes have no place and are forced out of the city.

With their furniture strapped onto the top of Fritz's car, the family drives out to Kuhle Wampe. As we follow the car out of the city, a radio report on the soundtrack introduces us to the family's new home: "About one hour by bus from metropolitan Berlin, set among the grass and woods of the inviting shores of Müggel Lake, not far from the Müggel Hills, is the tent colony Kuhle Wampe, Germany's oldest weekend colony. It was established in 1913 with 10 or 20 tents. After the war it expanded to such a degree that it now consists of 93 tents in which 300 persons are housed." As the family sets up their tent, we see images of leisure in nature: people walk bicycles and carry canoes through tree-lined paths; others sun themselves and doze in beach chairs; men play chess and cards; and a woman knits while listening to pre-war marches on the radio. Indeed, in normal times, these would have been signs of hygienic modernization: common people regenerating their bodies and spirits in a therapeutic environment, before heading back to work during the week. In the midst of an economic crisis, however, these images appear thoroughly ironic. Kuhle Wampe's status as a "weekend colony," as described in the radio report, depended on a system in which people worked in the city during the week. Its therapeutic function now meaningless under changed economic circumstances, Kuhle Wampe has become a place of permanent excursion. A shot of a mock gravestone reading "Here rests our last hope for

Life at the tent colony. Still from *Kuhle Wampe* (dir. Slatan Dudow, 1932).

work: Kuhle Wampe" indicates that the inhabitants themselves are aware of their predicament. Hygienic lifestyle prescriptions only make sense within a functioning economy; country air and recreational sport cannot pay the rent.

Nor will they feed children. After joining Fritz at Kuhle Wampe, Anni becomes pregnant. Soon after, they pass by a group of schoolchildren, who elicit an associative montage from Anni's point of view that links images of child care, economic struggle, abortion, and death. Shots of advertisements for children's soap, baby food, and toys in display windows evoke the capitalist valorization of childbearing, as well as the demographic targeting of mothers by profit-seeking industry. The glossy ads are undercut, however, by multiple images of the passing children superimposed on one another in close-up, suggesting an endless procession of hungry mouths. The motif of repetition joins the rows of identical commodities to the children themselves, associating industrial production with human reproduction. Given the use of doubled images, one could add filmic reproduction as well, which copies the children over and over and unleashes a stream of images. Other shots call up the specter of unemployment and the death of Anni's brother: a work performance record; a funeral home; looming tenement windows; people surrounding her brother's body covered by a sheet in a courtyard; a cab taking the body away. In this montage, *Kuhle Wampe* targets the contradiction of

a system that would encourage population growth for the sake of economic
productivity, but which does not provide people with a way to sustain their
livelihood. Claiming to foster life, this system causes premature death. The
montage portrays overpopulation as a form of material disorder analogous
to capitalism's profusion of commodities, which are likewise placeless in the
general immiseration of the early 1930s. (At the end of the film, train passengers discuss the burning of millions of pounds of coffee in Brazil, which was
done to maintain the commodity's price. As with Anni's brother, economic
rationality dictated its destruction.) Hygiene can only create material order,
can only put things and people into place, if political and economic conditions permit. Later I will discuss *Kuhle Wampe*'s population politics further,
but here it suffices to note the film's portrait of a society that purports to
value health while creating misery and death.

Kuhle Wampe's juxtaposition of a failed economic system and lack of state
support with the tainted idyll on the city's edge resonates with the arguments
of some experts who recognized the economic and political underpinnings of
health. As the social hygienist Julius Moses wrote in 1931, "unemployment
means missed income, poor nutrition, unhealthy dwelling and inadequate
clothing. It results in psychological depression."[13] As long as the underlying
conditions remained, Moses lamented, nothing would fundamentally change.
"The physician can certainly treat the symptoms of unhealthy conditions in
individual cases," Moses wrote, "but not their political causes."[14] In the last
instance, he suggests, health is a matter of politics, not medicine or hygiene.
Indeed, by highlighting the constitutive environmental disorder of capitalist
modernity, all three films discussed here frame health as a matter of political
contestation. In that case, if these films are meant to have political effects, it
bears examining where they draw lines of conflict, what kinds of agency or
political subjectivity they foreground, and how they position their implied
spectator.

Charity or Solidarity?

"It must be one of the most urgent tasks for the Communist Party in the area
of agitation and propaganda," wrote Willi Münzenberg in his 1925 book
Conquer Film! "to wrest away from the enemy such a significant medium of
propaganda, which has until today been the sole property of the ruling class,
and use it against him."[15] In 1923, five years before his role in making *Hunger
in Waldenburg*, Leo Lania wrote admiringly about Münzenberg's work with
the Workers International Relief, the Communist-aligned mutual aid group
he had cofounded. For Lania, the group's "class character" distinguished it
from the aid offered by Allied governments, religious groups, and other charitable organizations after the war.[16] Lania praised Münzenberg's ability to
communicate the difference between the WIR and "the collection plates of

bourgeois charity . . . so that [the masses] recognize it is not alms they receive, but fraternal aid, to which they as comrades-in-arms have a claim, and of which they must prove themselves worthy through their deeds, their further action in support of the common cause."[17] Lania's comments suggest that the provision of health and the material order that supports it are also inflected by class relations. Like mainstream cinema, charitable enterprise functioned to pacify rather than empower, and thereby preserve industrial capitalism. Charity thus had a certain affinity to hygienic discourses that treated populations as objects of administrative expertise, rather than as active historical subjects.

In raising issues of health and hygiene, leftist filmmakers were confronted not just with the problem of adapting mainstream cinematic forms (like the *Kulturfilm* or the feature film), but of entering a discursive terrain dominated by experts who were typically aligned with the state. From pre-World War I social reform to postwar *Kulturfilme*, environmental disorder had been figured as an apolitical, technocratic problem whose solution would benefit the *Volkskörper*, and in turn the nation's economic productivity and military readiness. Such a discourse was necessarily in tension with a project that would foreground class antagonism and working-class agency, rather than positing a unified national body that is a passive object of administration. As films concerned with health and urban industrial disorder, *Hunger in Waldenburg*, *How the Worker Lives*, and *Kuhle Wampe* thus risked reinscribing a charitable or administrative gaze. Challenging the hierarchy implicit in modern hygienic discourses necessitated reframing the issue of health in relation to a film's mode of address: would the viewer be positioned as a student of the film's expertise, as in the *Kulturfilme* of chapter 2? As an onlooker, who gazes with pity and advocates expert intervention? Or as a potential comrade-in-arms?

Hunger in Waldenburg's opening documentary scene of the sleeping family treats them and their home as objects of observation and evaluation. In this scene the camera implicitly adopts the position of housing inspector, the hygiene expert who examines not just the state of the building but also the family's sleeping arrangements and whether they have done their part to maintain clean living spaces.[18] The camera's view is lit by a spotlight apparently attached to it, which glides over floors, walls, and faces. Lighting the apartment so that it could be shot without the spotlight would have broken *Hunger in Waldenburg*'s particular code of realism—no one is awakened by the bright light shining in their face, suggesting some level of staging—but this nighttime scene has a feeling of intrusion, as if we have broken into the apartment. In taking up the view of the hygiene expert, we approach the family from outside and above, not as people with whom we feel solidarity. The scene strongly echoes images produced in the 1910s and early 1920s by municipal authorities that sought to document living conditions in the tenements.[19] Inspired by bourgeois reform approaches to the housing question, such images were meant to elicit pity and technocratic rather than political solutions, treating their working-class subjects as victims who had little if any agency to resist their own exploitation.

In 1925, Lania published a report on Waldenburg in *Die Weltbühne* that was strongly influenced by the prewar reform imaginary, and painted a similarly passive image of the city's working-class population. In Lania's account, the people themselves embody the disease and degeneration that comes with the worst of pre-hygienic industrial modernity: "The men: used up, broken-down figures, at 40 years old they appear to be 60. Children with the faces of old men, with rickets, retarded in growth and mental development. All are lethargic and listless, animated by a single thought: bread."[20] This passage uncomfortably echoes visions of working-class racial degeneration common among prewar reformers. Though he blames their pitiable state on conditions beyond their control, Lania does paint the working-class inhabitants of Waldenburg as physically and mentally primitive, reduced to a passive existence. While the text does not focus especially on the physiognomy of its subjects, it does often suggest that they live a kind of animalistic existence— sleeping in dense, dark quarters, working underground, acting out base drives like hunger and rage—which appears pitiful and alien to the reader.

Hunger in Waldenburg's ambiguous relationship to hygienic expertise can be seen in its use of statistics, which differs from how statistics appear in other *Kulturfilme*—to a certain extent. Those films were largely narrated from the position of the hygiene expert, explaining to the viewer how health and life could be maintained in urban contexts. They served the double function of communicating hygienic knowledge and legitimating the authority of scientific hygiene for mass audiences. In *Hunger in Waldenburg*, hygienic expertise plays a subordinate role in the narration, exemplified in the use of statistics. Indeed, rather than bolstering confidence in the ability of public health authorities and the welfare state to blunt the health effects of industrialization, the statistics offered in the film demonstrate their utter failure. At the same time, the insistent enumeration of statistics in the film—"3.2% of all schoolchildren without shoes. 21.4% without coats. Out of 350 school-girls, 33 are tuberculitic. Of 510 boys, 297 are sick. Of 5,296 schoolchildren, 256 have rickets, 203 tuberculosis."—allows the voice of medical expertise to dominate our interpretation of the film's images. By keeping the focus on bodily sickness, the film implies that a proper solution to the conditions in Waldenburg would be medical rather than political. Moreover, this expert view has the effect of othering the people of Waldenburg. The film quotes Waldenburg's municipal doctor, who, referring to the nutritional norms for children developed by the Austrian pediatrician Clemens von Pirquet, declared that "were I to apply Pirquet's standards here, the results would show almost 90% malnutrition, but going hungry has become such an art in this population for centuries that other measurements are to be applied." Here the film means to communicate the severity of the region's historical privation, but it ends up revealing how medical expertise normalizes economic and environmental injustice through a kind of racialization. The doctor posits a bodily difference among "this population" as a result of adaptation to centuries of exploitation. Although calling hunger an "art" implies cultural rather than bodily adaptation, the claim that Pirquet's statistical norms cannot be applied suggests that the people of Waldenburg have somehow become physiologically different.[21] By othering the Waldenburgers in this way, the film allows medical expertise to reduce the scope of its social critique.

The medical gaze also tends to reduce the viewer's sense of the Waldenburgers' own agency and survival strategies. There is a dearth of resistance in *Hunger in Waldenburg*, especially when one considers the region's history of revolt. In 1927 Friedrich Zelnik directed *The Weavers*, a major film adaptation of Gerhart Hauptmann's play, which translated a nineteenth-century Silesian rebellion into contemporary visual terms. In some moments, Zelnik's film consciously emulates Soviet portrayals of proletarian uprising—as did Fritz Lang's *Metropolis*, also from 1927, whose spatialization of class and images of strenuous physical labor are (perhaps inadvertently) echoed in *Hunger in Waldenburg*.[22] Revolution, obviously, is costly to stage, and would not have reflected the situation in Waldenburg in January 1929. Nonetheless, the film leaves the overwhelming impression of an utterly pacified working class. The only significant moment of resistance comes at the end of the film's second half, which follows the son of a family of weavers who moves to the city in search of mining work. Hungry and desperate, the man is taken in by a young widow, who agrees to let him stay with her and her children for a few days. When it appears that the landlord will evict the widow and her family, the young man fights him. At first, others stand watching from the doorways of their apartments, poised to join in solidarity—instead, however, they back away, closing their doors. The landlord knocks the man down a flight of stairs, as impressions of his journey flash up, and the film ends with this image of defeat.

For the journalist and writer Willi Bredel, later a founding member of the German Academy of Arts in East Germany, *Hunger in Waldenburg* conveyed a sense of impossibility. In a review for the *Hamburger Volkszeitung* (a paper he edited at the time), Bredel denied that the film offered an authentic view of proletarian life and complained of its lack of revolutionary purpose: "The film shows misery, misery, misery—but with no way out—completely fatalistic, completely resigned."[23] The film's reliance on medical statistics and an objectifying gaze blunts the more radical possibilities implied by its juxtaposition of the disordered proletarian milieu with the Fürstenstein castle. Though sensitive to the economic causes of material disorder, *Hunger in Waldenburg* turns its subjects into objects of pity rather than potential comrades—an attitude compounded by Waldenburg's location on Germany's eastern periphery. The presumably metropolitan viewer looks at the country's less civilized margins, and the history of exploitation there invoked at the beginning of the film comes to seem natural and eternal.

How the Worker Lives resembles *Hunger in Waldenburg* in many ways. Both depict unhygienic proletarian housing; both thematize unemployment, rent, and eviction; and both make use of modernist montage to foreground social antagonism. *How the Worker Lives*, however, avoids the other film's charitable gaze and sense of defeatism. As noted above, Dudow's film also deemphasizes hygienic expertise. The statistics it provides do not concern illness but unemployment and rent, and thereby more clearly ground its images of proletarian life in their economic context. More importantly, perhaps, the film does not elicit the viewer's sense of pity. We certainly see images of extreme deprivation, but in their midst we also witness scenes of care, play, and resistance. Children playing in dark courtyards and swimming in overcrowded pools smile, jump, run, and shove; people being evicted fight back; subjects in close-up look directly into the camera. Dudow's film captures the poor hygienic conditions of Berlin's working-class housing while also allowing the vitality of its inhabitants to shine through. Furthermore, in contrast to the finality of the young weaver's death in *Hunger in Waldenburg*, the film ends in a state of tension. The last intertitle we read as furniture is being thrown onto the street tells us: "That is no solution!" Having articulated a conflict whose solution has not yet arrived, *How the Worker Lives* invites its viewer to join the fight.

This ethos of solidarity comes to the forefront in Dudow's *Kuhle Wampe*, which is deeply concerned with how to forge solidarity under the material conditions of urban modernity. Given the film's gradual flight to the urban periphery, it seems that in the city itself there is little space for such bonds. Indeed, it is this fact that leads to the death of Anni's brother. In the opening sequence, his bicycle is one among many that crowd the frame as they race from site to site in search of work. The city's existing material and economic order produces scarcity, driving a desperate competition between workers, whose survival in turn depends on being faster or stronger or otherwise better than the next man. Solidarity seems impossible here, and the Bönikes are forced out of the city.

There are hints of a different kind of life in the Kuhle Wampe tent colony, where the material pressure of the urban center is relieved to a certain extent. Here, at least, the family has space in which to live; indeed, here they and others excluded from the city have room to make their own order. As Kristin Poling notes, Berlin's margins have historically served as places of improvised refuge for those unable to find shelter in more developed areas. During a particularly acute housing shortage after national unification in 1871, when Berlin became Germany's capital, people shut out of the housing market erected shantytowns "just beyond the recently removed city gates to the east and south. . . . On vacant land (most of it owned by the city), evicted families constructed huts from scrap wood, straw, and old furniture."[24] Though much further from Berlin's center than these *Gründerzeit* shantytowns—the city had since expanded its edges and its transportation network—the Kuhle

Wampe tent colony is one instance in a longer history of improvised settlement by those excluded by uneven processes of urbanization. The colony thus embodies an alternative, more democratic form of place-making than the one operating within the city, which is determined by capitalist speculation and various practices of hygienic ordering, however inadequate (planning, water provision, waste removal, and so on).

At Kuhle Wampe the inhabitants can make a place for themselves, but ironically, the place they make mimics the one they left. The tent colony's inhabitants cling to outmoded behavioral scripts and class aspirations, a situation the film, in a further level of irony, compares to the cyclical seasons of nature. The family's arrival at Kuhle Wampe is followed by a sequence depicting a date between Anni and Fritz. He picks her up at the family's tent and they go walking in the forest, where it is implied they have sex. A shot of the couple walking into the woods is followed by a montage of the natural landscape around the Müggel Lake, bookended by another shot, with an identical setup to the first, of the couple reemerging. The montage consists of trees, bushes, and other plants all blowing in the wind, with a bit of sky and clouds, and throughout we hear Helene Weigel's rendition of the song "On Nature in Springtime" ("Das Frühjahr kommt"). The text of the song roughly parallels the scene over which the song plays, describing two lovers in nature. Like the visual track, which turns to nature instead of following Anni and Fritz, the song's description of (human) seduction is supplanted by images of the natural world, which offer their own kind of sex scene: "Boundless is the growth of trees and grasses in spring. / Incessantly fruitful is the forest / are the meadows and the fields. / And the earth gives birth to the new / heedless of caution." The sequence mocks the codes of commercial cinema, which use elision to imply sex within the narrative but avoid depicting it visually. The lack of close-ups between Fritz and Anni, the bombast of the song, and its depiction of nature as a threatening, "heedless" force drain the sequence of any erotic charge. Rather than love between two individuals, their relationship appears as the mechanical unfolding of a romantic script that has become second nature. In this, Fritz and Anni reflect the function of Kuhle Wampe itself. Relatively removed from the desperate conditions in the city, the place allows its inhabitants to live out an empty simulation of their previous life, according to social norms whose economic premises are quickly disappearing. At Kuhle Wampe, people can act naturally, so to speak, as if nothing has changed. Rather than health or regeneration, the tent colony's bucolic setting represents the indifference and irrationality of nature.

A form of solidarity that is truly antagonistic to the status quo does emerge on the urban periphery, but only once Anni breaks things off with Fritz (whom she was about to marry after becoming pregnant, in a concession to petit bourgeois custom) and reaffirms her connection to the workers' movement. As Theodore Rippey points out, the film displaces a clear resolution to the Anni-Fritz plot, which a more conventional film would center, by a turn to the political collective—specifically, to the display of a "revolutionary, collective corporality that Kuhle Wampe counterposes to the conservative, atomized corporality depicted in the opening act and the engagement party."[25] Anni's friend Gerda invites her to stay with her and participate in the sports festival that coming weekend. The following scene shows the athletes preparing for the upcoming event, making banners and printing flyers for different Berlin neighborhoods. Fritz comes looking for Anni, and we learn that her place in this politicized milieu is not new, but a return. "She's with us and works here," Anni's comrade Kurt tells Fritz. "She was here before, too, before you came along and took her." They convince Fritz, who has recently been laid off, to join them at the festival.

The festival sequence begins in the city streets, cutting between motorcycles racing and workers marching and singing the Solidarity Song. Then we move to the urban periphery. We see Anni with a group of singing marchers, and a brief shot appears to show annoyed residents of Kuhle Wampe, whose routine the young workers have disturbed. This is followed by a montage of motorcycle racing, rowing, and swimming competitions, accompanied by its own song, which praises the sacrifice and spirit necessary for the workers to escape the city and stage such an event: "Coming out of the crowded tenements / the darkened streets of embattled cities / you come together / to struggle together / . . . / and learn to win." The crosscutting in the editing suggests simultaneous athletic events, unites the various athletes, and orients them to a common goal (or *Ziel*, as the banner marking the finish line of the rowing competition reads).[26] Within the film, the athletics sequence echoes the opening race for work, in which young men on bicycles rushed from workplace to workplace, only to be turned away. There, the relation between the job seekers was competitive, each struggling to beat out the others in a world of scarce resources. Within the city, pockets of solidarity—however fragile, even at the level of the family, as we see in the case of the Bönikes—exist within a fundamentally competitive world. In an inversion that evokes the older, carnivalesque sense of festival, the Workers' Sport event subordinates competition to a framework of solidarity, conveyed by the opening march and concluding rally that bookend the athletics.

The festival's use of the city's green periphery exceeds the hygienic function ascribed to it in discourse on urban leisure spaces. For planners, green space was meant to be therapeutic, a place where people could regenerate their spirit and strength before returning to work. The festival may indeed serve this function, but more importantly, it uses the green periphery to strengthen its participants' identification with the workers' movement and their sense of collective agency. By and large, hygiene aims to reproduce what is, and does so by assigning everything a place and keeping it there. At the festival, the collective appropriates the openness of the city's margins in order to make its own place. In this, the young workers resemble the inhabitants of Kuhle Wampe. The latter, however, sought only to re-create the place that economic

Visualizing the collective. Still from *Kuhle Wampe*.

conditions had ejected them from, whereas the workers are in the process of creating a place that is wholly new, and had been impossible to form fully within the city itself.

The natural openness of the festival's setting also serves an aesthetic function, as a background against which the collective can be visualized. In the competition sequence, the motorcyclists, rowers, and swimmers exert themselves on tree-lined roads and calm water—flat, visually undifferentiated surfaces on (or in) which the competitors can be seen clearly. Shots of the rowers' finish line and the festival flag, filmed from below against the sky, reinforce the motif of visual inscription on a blank surface. Here we find echoes of a hygienic visual code that foregrounds the healthy body's distinction from its material environment, contrasting the overcrowding and indistinction of urban space with the neutral background of nature. *The City of Tomorrow* used this code in order to advocate for a hygienic loosening of urban space, which would produce healthier workers but implicitly preserve existing property and class relations. *Kuhle Wampe* adopts the visual freedom allowed by the urban periphery, its hygienic blankness, in order to envision a political collectivity that might overturn those relations. In other words, the "crowded tenements" may be a milieu in which incipient solidarities are formed, but the film suggests that their conditions also constrict political imagination. The urban-nature interface thus also appears in *Kuhle Wampe*, at least in the case of the Workers' Sport festival, as a place where both the material and imaginative constraints of urban disorder can temporarily be overcome, allowing experiments to happen and futures to be prefigured.[27]

In other words, nature functions here as a stage, or a screen, and in the gathering that marks the end of the festival we see both. At the back of a large crowd, who are arranged stadium-style, the competitors file in to applause and stand in front of a massive, light-colored banner that reads: "Solidarity." As a background, the cloth screen allows them to stand out and distinguishes them from the rest of the crowd. The athletes are marked as a collective within the collective who, in this moment, are worthy of recognition for their common effort. Attention quickly turns, however, to a small stage, where the agitprop group Red Megaphone (*Das rote Sprachrohr*) is performing. With large, conical megaphones, they announce: "We are the Red Megaphone / Megaphone of the masses we are. / We speak what oppresses you. / We are the Red Megaphone." Here, too, a blank field enables the perception of visual distinctions, between both groups and individuals. Filmed from above, the stage marks a spatial and visual separation between performers and audience, but it also highlights the movements of individual performers as they cross from one end to the other, stage antagonisms, dissolve groupings, and re-form them. The scene they perform depicts a family facing eviction, and the neighbors as they gather to successfully resist the landlord and police. On the empty white stage, we and the festival-goers witness a process of collective formation that mirrors the arc of the film as a whole up to this point, from eviction to collective agency. Water, ground, sky, banner, stage—these flat, blank surfaces against which configurations of people can be more clearly recognized echo the function of the movie screen itself. As we saw in chapter 2, the apparatus of cinema can be put to use to envision hygienic order, in which environmental disorder is cleared away and the distinction between bodies and their surroundings is maintained. *Kuhle Wampe* implies that this same operation of visual distinction can be pushed beyond its hygienic use to envision new political collectives. In the film, the environment of the urban periphery becomes the site or ground of a political dispositif through which a class comes to see itself, an experience the film aims to replicate in the cinema.

Environmental or Collective Fitness?

Hunger in Waldenburg, How the Worker Lives, and *Kuhle Wampe* reckoned with capitalist modernity's failure to provide humane living conditions for working-class people. Dudow's films in particular suggested that hygienic expertise alone would not improve this state of affairs, given that the better off already live in bright, clean, and spacious environments, while millions still live in tenements. According to *Kuhle Wampe*, modernity's material disorder could only be solved by the organized, collective action of those who have been its victims—by "those who don't like" the world as it is ("die, denen sie nicht gefällt"), as one of the festival participants says in the film's final line. In the context of the late Weimar Republic, these films' leftist critique of urban disorder and their implied solutions should also be understood in relation to visions of racial order and disorder on the Right, which increasingly dominated hygienic debate and structured German society after 1933. I argue that the films' emphasis on material environments was a rejoinder to racial hygiene's logic of polluted and polluting bodies. Nonetheless, *Kuhle Wampe*'s concern with reproduction and physical strength resonated with a eugenic ideology that was shared to different degrees across the political spectrum.

In the book thus far, I have largely dealt with environmental hygienic discourses that aimed to produce ordered spaces fit for human habitation, transit, work, and recreation. Body-centered hygiene, meanwhile, was also concerned with making a population fit for life under industrial capitalism.[28] The care of the body through the practice of personal cleanliness, a healthy diet, and physical fitness was the focus of much of the popular health education during the Weimar period, because individuals had more control over their own bodies than the environments in which they lived and worked. Body-centered practices also included sexual hygiene, explained in sexual enlightenment films like *Die Geschlechtskrankheiten und ihre Folgen* (*Venereal Diseases and Their Consequences*, 1920), *Falsche Scham* (*False Shame*, 1926), *Geissel der Menschheit* (*Scourge of Humanity*, 1926), *Der Fluch der Vererbung* (*The Curse of Heredity*, 1927), and *Feind im Blut* (*Enemy in the Blood*, 1931).[29] Such films were particularly keen to educate viewers about the dangers of diseases that could be transmitted from mother to child, such as gonorrhea, which could cause blindness in newborns, and syphilis, which caused various facial and dental abnormalities, among other symptoms. These films and sexual hygiene more broadly treated those with sexually transmitted diseases as potential agents of disorder, whose circulation in society needed to be limited, whether voluntarily or by the state.[30]

Anxiety about congenital defects was an expression of the eugenic impulse behind discourses of bodily hygiene, especially during the Weimar period. Health professionals of all sorts lamented the state of the *Volkskörper* after the war, which they understood as responsible for malnourishment, chronic illness and disability, high rates of tuberculosis and venereal disease, and a low birthrate. "The collapse of the political order was matched by a breakdown of the people's physical constitution," writes Paul Weindling, and medical officials aimed "to breed a healthy and fit future generation to compensate for the war losses."[31] Forms of racial hygiene that distinguished strongly between purported human races were relatively marginal for most of the 1920s, but bodily hygiene was thoroughly eugenic in its concern for both the quantity and the quality—that is, the level of fitness—of human life. Many aspects of the Weimar social welfare state were aimed at improving the health of the existing population and encouraging those deemed fit to reproduce, while discouraging those deemed unfit. The economic crisis which began in the late 1920s provided an opening for more radical eugenic ideas to move to the forefront of public health debate. "The economic crisis brought about a change of heart on welfare," Weindling writes. "The mid-twenties dream of equal rights and improved living standards ended. Positive measures with equal entitlement for all in need were too costly."[32] In an environment of scarce resources, eugenicists argued, state benefits should support those who contribute (or could potentially contribute) most to the nation's economic productivity. Rather than mitigate the material disorder of urbanization and industrialization generally, eugenics would provide the criteria that determined which populations were fit, and which were not, in order to ensure an efficient distribution of resources.

Against this backdrop of increasingly radical eugenic ideas, the emphasis that films like *Hunger in Waldenburg* and *How the Worker Lives* placed on the material environment becomes more striking. At first glance, their concern with working-class housing seems to simply reiterate the argument made in prewar debates of the "housing question": that poor health and social disorder could be traced to unhygienic living conditions. This may be true, but such an argument gained urgency once again during the period of mass unemployment and welfare retrenchment at the end of the Weimar Republic. Selective eugenics found an ally in economic austerity, which placed a burden on individuals to demonstrate that they were fit, and therefore deserving of society's support. By insisting on the environment as a factor in material and social disorder, Jutzi and Dudow's films push back against the state's abandonment of the most vulnerable.

In the previous chapter, we saw a weaker form of eugenics at work in the logic of institutionalization applied to elderly and physically disabled people, whom the *Kulturfilme* discussed there portrayed as out of place in the urban environment. To solve this disorder, these films advocated for specialized institutions whose spaces and operation would be tailored to the abilities of their inhabitants. The more radical, negative eugenic stance, which came to dominate health policy under National Socialism, would designate the very existence of certain categories of disabled people as something out of place, a form of intolerable disorder within the *Volkskörper* to be eradicated through sterilization or murder. Dudow's films, particularly *How the Worker Lives*, invert the eugenic formula by decentering individual bodies and portraying the material environment as unfit. In *How the Worker Lives*, we see children doing what they are supposed to be doing—that is, playing—while the streets and tenement courtyards in which they do it are wholly inadequate. In *Kuhle Wampe*, the Bönikes may leave for the tent colony because they have no place in the city, but the film takes pains to demonstrate the economic and legal structures that have squeezed the family out.

Things become more complicated when we consider *Kuhle Wampe*'s reproductive politics. The film was made during a time of intense reproductive rights activism, when, as Atina Grossman recounts, "a brief and unparalleled alliance among liberal and radical lawyers, doctors, intellectuals, artists, Social Democrats, Communists, and diverse constituencies of women" targeted the prohibition on abortion under paragraph 218.[33] The law had been liberalized in the mid-1920s to allow for medically necessary abortions. Amid widespread unemployment and welfare cuts, however, a renewed push against the law was spurred on by a 1930 papal decree against abortion and the 1931 arrests of Else Kienle and Friedrich Wolf, both physicians and outspoken abortion advocates. At one level, *Kuhle Wampe* again emphasizes economic rather than bodily disorder, in this case as Anni's motivation for terminating her pregnancy. She imagines that if she were to have a child, its life would resemble that of her brother, whom the collapsed economy left with little hope. In Wolf's 1929 play *Cyankali* and its 1930 film adaptation, the protagonist Hete comes to a similar conclusion and procures cyanide to induce miscarriage, but dies due to an incorrect dosage.[34] These depictions of reproductive rights as an economic issue can be contrasted with the sexual enlightenment films mentioned above, which play on the fear of bearing children with disabilities.

In her survey of Weimar abortion stories on stage and screen, Cornelie Usborne finds *Kuhle Wampe*'s focus on Anni's decision-making to be exceptional. Rather than foregrounding medical arguments, as most filmic depictions did, Usborne argues for the film's feminism, which suggests that Anni's abortion leads to her "liberation . . . from a degrading 'enforced' engagement and from the petty bourgeois conventions of her parents' generation. Anni is thus free to realize her own potential in the world of work, politics and leisure."[35] This reading resonates with the place of rights-based discourse in the activism of 1930–31, which was captured by the prominent slogan "your body belongs to you."[36] On the other hand, the montage triggered when Anni sees a group of schoolchildren, which uses superimposed images to suggest a frightening overabundance of children, indicates that there is more at play in *Kuhle Wampe*'s depiction of abortion. The montage is one of material proliferation and excessive (re)production. Too many products, too many images, too many babies—children are shown as part of capitalist modernity's unsustainable environmental disorder.

At first glance, the reproduction montage might indicate an affinity between *Kuhle Wampe* and hygienic or eugenic anxieties about urban overcrowding and overpopulation. Given the aim of maximizing labor power, especially after the losses of World War I, hygiene experts worried about the health effects of overcrowding. Urban planners advocated schemes like that envisioned in *The City of Tomorrow*, which proposed to disperse urban "herding together" (*Zusammenpferchung*) through the creation of satellite cities, thereby allowing the metropolitan population to grow safely.

Eugenicists placed greater emphasis on the purported quality of the population and feared the overproduction of children by people they considered
minderwertig, "of lesser value." The framing of reproduction as a matter of
collective concern was common among advocates of abortion as well, who
often employed a eugenic logic. Atina Grossmann points out that the emphasis around 1931 on individual rights and a woman's control of her own
body was exceptional among sex reformers across the political spectrum.
"In a needs-based discourse of collective welfare, whether of class, *Volk*, or
nation," she writes, "sex reformers managed to argue that legalization combined with widespread contraception would ultimately reduce not only the
number of unwanted and unfit babies but also the number of abortions."[37]
Given *Kuhle Wampe*'s interest in the production of collectives, then, it would
not be surprising to find echoes of hygienic or eugenic ideas in the film's treatment of abortion, beyond its invocation of women's individual rights.

Eugenics, moreover, influenced thinking about population on the Left as
well as the Right in the early twentieth century. Karl Kautsky, for instance, a
friend of Friedrich Engels and an important figure in the early history of the
German Social Democratic Party, married criticism of life under capitalism
with advocacy for racial hygiene. According to Kautsky, racial degeneration
was rampant because of the way capitalism produced debilitating living and
working conditions for the working class, while at the same time prolong-
ing life through the advance of science and thereby preventing the "struggle
for existence" that would weed out the unfit. Eugenic selection, he argued,
could only fight a losing battle under capitalism, because it would not change
the conditions that would continue to produce sick and disabled children.
Kautsky thus proposed that only under socialism could racial hygiene truly
transform the human species for the better: "thus will socialism bring to
humanity not only material wealth and leisure, but health and vitality as
well, and exterminate sickness as a mass phenomenon."[38]

Is *Kuhle Wampe*'s representation of abortion characterized by eugenic
anxiety? The lyrics of "On Nature in Spring," which invoke the "incessant
fruitfulness" of nature, do seem to imply that human reproduction should
be brought under some form of rational control. The reproduction montage,
moreover, particularly in the shots of superimposed faces of children looking
directly into the camera, mobilizes a kind of unsettling affect found in xeno-
phobic and eugenic visual discourses of invasion and unchecked proliferation.
At the same time, however, there is little to indicate a fear of racial degeneration. Anni's brother—the person whose life she fears her own child would
recapitulate—is not portrayed as sickly or lazy, despite what their father suggests. On the contrary, as Anni is well aware, her brother spends the entire
day biking around the city in search of work. Like the film's early sequences,
rather, the reproduction montage returns to the motif of placelessness. Anni
worries that, like her brother, and to a certain extent like her whole family,
her child would have no economically viable life in the place they used to live.

Population anxiety. Still from *Kuhle Wampe*.

Instead of racialized fears of degeneration and overpopulation, then, *Kuhle Wampe* points to a Marxist analysis of surplus population (*Übervölkerung*). "Modern industry's whole form of motion," Marx writes, "depends on the constant transformation of a part of the working population into unemployed or semi-employed 'hands.'"[39] The surplus population includes workers made redundant by advances in technology and efficiency; those forced to work below living wages; and those unable to work due to age or impairment (often the result of industrial labor itself).[40] For Marx, this industrial reserve army is a constitutive part of capitalist political economy, and serves as an available labor force for new enterprise while at the same time depressing wages and helping to maximize the exploitation of the employed. Inevitably, a part of this population will be utterly impoverished. The production of poverty "is included in that of the relative surplus population, its necessity is implied by their necessity; along with the surplus population, pauperism forms a condition of capitalist production, and of the capitalist development of wealth."[41] Against the eugenic imaginary of overpopulation and racial degeneration, *Kuhle Wampe* poses the fear of becoming surplus. Having seen it happen to her brother, Anni is terrified at the thought that her child would be structurally disposable. In the film's geography, then, the urban periphery is where surplus populations gather. As discussed earlier,

Kuhle Wampe's portrayal of the tent colony satirizes the hygienic conception of natural or semi-natural environments as therapeutic, and instead functions as a receptacle for those pushed out of the urban core. It is also where workers—those who could at any moment themselves become surplus—are able to strengthen their bonds of solidarity.

Though in these ways *Kuhle Wampe* turns away from hygienic and eugenic discourses, it is significant that the film nonetheless articulates the strength of the workers' solidarity through a spectacle of physical fitness. Mass sport, of the kind seen in the sport festival sequence, was a key element of Weimar-era biopolitics and was promoted by health experts, civic groups, and political factions alike. "Along with social welfare, better nutrition, and improved housing," Michael Hau writes, "medical professionals, psychologists, and physical educators believed sport mobilized psychological performance potentials that raised people's enthusiasm for physical and mental work, in addition to it overtly strengthening the physical constitution and health of people."[42] The expert discourse on the value of athletics also emphasized solidarity—of a kind. Stressing the adverse health effects of World War I, athletics advocates saw physical fitness as a hygienic good for the nation, and understood a healthy *Volkskörper* as an important resource in the economic and political competition between nations.

Beginning in the 1890s, the workers' sport movement called into question the nationalism that permeated both bourgeois sports organizations as well as expert discourse on athletics, for which the nation was the spoken or unspoken analytical horizon. While sharing the hygienic concern for urban environmental and working conditions, workers' sport organizations saw the "strengthening of the body . . . not only as a valuable correction to the general strains and the debilitating influences of heavy physical work," W. L. Guttsman writes. "Its body-building function was also regarded as a valuable preparation for the class struggle."[43] Workers' sport thus tended to deemphasize competition between athletes, and instead used sport as a medium of class solidarity. Members of the Berlin Fichte Workers' Sport Association, a group founded in 1890 and subsequently disbanded by the Nazis, appear as competitors and extras in *Kuhle Wampe*'s athletics festival. In the spirit of the workers' sport tradition, the festival serves to articulate a class body that is implicitly distinct from the national body imagined by dominant hygienic discourses. This political collective, as Christoph Schaub argues, is "egalitarian, interactive, decentered, non-uniform, gender-integrated, devoid of leader figures . . . in which the participants constantly change their roles"—as distinct both from the nineteenth-century imaginary of the mob and the fascist mass subordinated to a single leader.[44]

For all this, the collective is nonetheless composed of eminently able and healthy bodies—fit bodies. Theodore Rippey sets the film's portrayal of mass sport in contrast to industrial capitalism, which subordinates the body to profit, as well as to the racialized body of fascist aesthetics, but the able body still serves as the ideal one for anti-capitalist struggle. Indeed, the meta-phorical reduction of collective or systemic antagonism to a physical struggle by or between bodies seems to be a common denominator between capitalist, fascist, and anti-capitalist imaginaries. Under capitalism, the fit body emblematizes the nation's competitive readiness within the global economic and geopolitical order; under fascism, the *Volkskörper*'s battle for racial dominance; and in *Kuhle Wampe*, the working class's fight against the existing economic order. In each case, the physically and mentally fit body stands in for the collective's agency and capacity for struggle against its respective antagonists.

These films show how difficult it was to think beyond capitalist modernity's concepts of health and order, which were deeply entangled with hierarchies of knowledge and eugenic fitness. By relying on expert knowledge to diagnose the health effects of exploitation, *Hunger in Waldenburg* reproduced the patronizing image of a pacified, pitiable working class; by representing the potential for working-class solidarity and strength in terms of physical fitness, meanwhile, *Kuhle Wampe* bore traces of a eugenic imaginary that figured collective agency by way of idealized fit and able bodies. Nonetheless, these films on the whole articulated a structural, anti-capitalist critique that understood unhealthy environments as a necessary symptom of the political-economic order, which could not be remedied simply by putting things into their right place. Although they did not problematize the concept of health per se, the films suggested that a healthy modernity would be impossible under capitalism. The mirage on the horizon of the hygienic project, in other words, could only be realized with the abolition of class society.

From Hygiene to Blood and Soil

For its part, Nazism proposed to solve the contradiction between urbanization and health in a wholly different way. To conclude this chapter, I turn to an early Nazi film that outlined a fascist alternative to visions of healthy modernity, whether achieved by hygienic reform or socialist revolution. Although Nazism would vigorously take up the language of hygiene in its imagination of racial struggle, its program of territorial expansion marked the end of modernization as envisioned by late nineteenth-century experimental hygiene and its successors.

The 1933 film *Blut und Boden* (*Blood and Soil*), directed by Rolf von Sonjevski-Jamrowski, Hans von Passavant, and Walter Ruttmann, recasts the disorder of the end of the Weimar Republic in fascist ideological terms. Produced as part of a public relations effort in support of the Nazis' "Reich Hereditary Farm Law" (Reichserbhofgesetz), the film concerns many of the same problems raised in *Kuhle Wampe* and other leftist films of the period—the displacement of working families, the irrationalities of a global market

economy, urban unemployment and homelessness, human reproduction—
but frames them in a narrative of racial decline and potential regeneration.
Like *Hunger in Waldenburg* or *How the Worker Lives*, *Blood and Soil* is
also clearly in the *Kulturfilm* tradition. It combines staged, documentary, and
montage sequences; it visualizes statistics and large-scale phenomena with
animation; and it aims to inform the public about a matter of political or
social importance, and ultimately to instill a sense of social responsibility
in the audience. Ruttmann, best known for his Weimar-era avant-garde animated shorts and the montage film *Berlin: Symphony of a Great City* (1927),
produced a number of *Kulturfilme* in the 1930s and early '40s related to
public health, beginning with *Enemy in the Blood* in 1931.[45] When compared
to earlier examples, both of the mainstream and oppositional varieties, *Blood
and Soil* demonstrates some of the ways that Nazism adapted hygiene discourse for its own ends, integrating some aspects while downplaying others.

After setting the scene with a montage of farm work during harvest season, *Blood and Soil*'s narrative begins at the dinner table of a German peasant
family, whose conversation establishes their millennium-long connection to
the land—in contrast to "the Jews," who have lived in Germany for a mere
200 years. The opposition between Jewish nomadism and Aryan connection
to the soil sets up the subsequent tragedy of the economic crisis, which has
forced German peasants into debt and foreclosure. The family reads about a
foreclosure in the newspaper and expects a similar fate unless they can pay
off their debts. At this point, a montage sequence gestures toward the larger
economic context, with images of ships, cargo, and a market with stereotypi-
cally Jewish traders, after which Svend Noldan's animation visualizes how
German agriculture has been wiped out by global trade. Like the Bönikes in
Kuhle Wampe, the peasant family receives no mercy from those who could
forestall their dispossession—in this case a banker who refuses to provide
credit, with which the family could purchase new machinery and increase
the farm's profitability. The farm is auctioned off and the family must move
to the city. Another montage sequence (which contains images repurposed
from Ruttmann's *Berlin Symphony*) renders the nightmarish economic and
material disorder of the modern industrial city, showing newspapers, traffic,
factory production, and crowds of unemployed men. Animation then explains
the consequences of this disorder for the racial *Volkskörper*, claiming that
"among city folk, there are too few births," so that without migration from
the countryside, the population of Berlin would shrink to a mere 90,000 by
2050: "Verstädterung führt zum Volkstod"—urbanization leads to the death
of the *Volk*. The answer, according to the film, is the agricultural development
of Germany's less-populated eastern regions, which it calls the nation's "natural settlement area" (*naturgegebene Siedlungsraum*). The film concludes by
imagining the "regeneration of the German peasantry" in this eastern territory, in the form of energetic farmers, smiling children, and columns of Nazi
youth singing and marching in formation on idyllic wooded paths.

In many ways, *Blood and Soil* echoes the modernist urban planning film *The City of Tomorrow*. *Blood and Soil* similarly laments the environmental disorder brought on by capitalist modernity, visualizes statistical and geographical processes by way of graphs and animation, and concludes with a sunny vision of harmony between a new generation and the places it inhabits. Both films even employed the same animator, Sven Noldan. *Blood and Soil*'s expansionist racial imaginary distinguishes it in a few key respects, however. Most obviously, where *The City of Tomorrow* imagined the possibility of hygienic urbanization, *Blood and Soil* is fundamentally at odds with urbanization as such, and posits a spiritual connection between the land and the Aryan peasantry that is destroyed by the growth of cities. This view of cities reflected that of the Reich minister of food and agriculture, Walther Darré, who, as Thomas Lekan writes, considered cities "infertility machines": "they siphoned peasants away from rural areas, transforming them into alienated proletarians without organic bonds to the soil and nation and subjecting them to poverty and diseases that lowered the birth rate."[46] Darré's ideas shaped the Reich Hereditary Farm Law, decreed less than two months before the premiere of *Blood and Soil*, which was intended to protect farms from foreclosure and thereby "sustain the peasantry as the lifeblood [*Blutquelle*] of the German *Volk*."[47]

The project of hygienic modernization at the center of this book was fundamentally urban in orientation. Although the goal of populational health resonated with the aim of national reconstruction after World War I, hygiene's roots in the late nineteenth century as a response to urbanization kept it anchored within a municipal framework and committed to reconciling the growth of cities with the material and social needs of the human organism. *Blood and Soil* departs from hygiene's municipal environmentalism and shifts into a national frame, in which populations are to be distributed territorially in order to survive. The seeds of Nazi expansionism, which must ultimately exceed the bounds of the nation so that the racial *Volk* may grow, are already visible in this shift. Lekan notes that blood and soil ideology differed from the discourse of *Heimat* preservation which it often appropriated, in that it reversed the latter's emphasis on landscape as that which shaped the inhabitants of a region. Instead, it was "racial character" which "determined the state of the landscape."[48] This understanding of race as primary accorded with an expansionist logic whereby foreign territories could be transformed into German *Lebensraum*, instead of German settlers being changed by foreign landscape. *Blood and Soil*, consequently, is less concerned with preserving landscape or regional character than with agricultural development. The film similarly rejects the hygienic version of environmental determinism, which viewed landscape as a therapeutic space for regeneration, separate from the sphere of labor. Here, labor and racial regeneration coincide in the act of developing the landscape, making it productive, and thereby integrating it as *Lebensraum*.

Blood and Soil thus marks a turn away from what I have termed the "hygienic apparatus." This apparatus was assembled in the second half of the nineteenth century in order to manage the material effects of urbanization and industrialization, which threatened to create environments hostile to human life and labor. The future it envisioned, in part with the aid of cinema, was one of further urbanization guided by the twin ideals of health and efficiency, in which the material forces of capitalist modernity had been reconciled with the needs of the human organism. In the form of *Kulturfilme*, cinema helped articulate this vision to mass audiences and taught them to apprehend their environments hygienically, in everyday acts of observation that distinguished between safe and dangerous, clean and dirty, healthy and unhealthy, ordered and disordered. *Blood and Soil* indexes the way that Nazism racialized such distinctions and turned them from a project of rational urbanization to one of genocidal expansion. Experimental hygiene had come to shape urban everyday life in significant ways, and the hygienic apparatus continued to operate, but after the economic crisis and the arrival of fascism it no longer offered a credible vision of progress. Leftist films at the end of the Weimar Republic proposed one way of reconstructing that vision; *Blood and Soil* proposed another.

Afterword

✦

Hygiene and Media, Then and Now

As I finished the first draft of this book, the COVID-19 pandemic gave questions of hygiene new urgency. The virus was a jarring reminder of the material interactions that compose social life and the spaces in which they take place. The transmissibility of disease forces us to become hyper-aware of our situatedness within shared environments, where we touch the same surfaces and breathe the same air as others. Suddenly, our bodies come to feel frighteningly porous and vulnerable, and our surroundings, once taken for granted, thicken into something fraught. Many became conscious in ways they had never been before of the material traffic of daily life, of what came and went in the spaces they inhabited, and they sought ways to monitor and control this traffic.

Though cinema in its traditional form is not nearly as culturally important as it once was, the example of Weimar cinema can attune us to the different dynamics, potentials, and meanings of technological media in times of hygienic anxiety. This is true for situations of more immediate danger, when the fear of contagion predominates, as well as for the slow boil of ecological collapse. Though a hundred years distant from Weimar cinema, we still inhabit a modernity characterized by environmental degradation, states invested in the health of populations (to varying degrees), and medical and environmental expertise. These and other broad commonalities make past cases a resource for thinking about how media technologies will figure in ongoing and future efforts to manage environmental dangers—including pandemics, which seem likely to become more common events.

Movie theaters still exist for the time being, and recent events have echoed the period a century ago when the material traffic that took place in cinemas triggered hygienic worry. In 2020, for instance, at a time when some pandemic restrictions were still in place in the United States, many theaters tried to adapt the theater environment to the new conditions. The "CinemaSafe" guidelines developed by the National Association of Theatre Owners prescribed maintaining social distance in the auditorium, increasing ventilation and air filtration, wearing masks, moving to contactless payment systems, and more.[1] Like their counterparts in the early twentieth century, these practices tried to insert elements of dispersion into the cinema experience—now aided by digital media, for things like payment and seat assignments—in order to defuse the inherently risky gathering it traditionally requires. While reinforcing the dominance of home viewing, hygienic danger also spurred experimentation with new practices of collective spectatorship, such as online "streaming parties," virtual film festivals, and less risky spaces for gathering physical audiences.[2] By the same token, some critics suggested that once the danger of infection has passed, community cinemas could be spaces for "therapeutic interactions," where local arts groups "could help rebuild the confidence of people feeling safe to gather in larger numbers again."[3] Such proposals recall the discussions about therapeutic theater design in the mid-1920s, though at that time it was the theater's built environment that would provide a healing contrast to the fatiguing spaces of the world outside; now it is hoped that the very act of gathering can provide comfort in an atomized society that is even further isolated by quarantine.

Film and media scholars have long analyzed the historical trend away from collective forms of reception and toward individualizing media technologies such as television and the internet. The pandemic brought this development into sharper relief and revealed the hygienic functions the latter could serve, by allowing communication across distance. Much more than cinema ever could have done, the new media were used directly to negotiate the crisis and enable work and social reproduction by mediating the traffic of social life. The digital realm of networked televisions, home computers, webcams, and personal devices has been central to how individuals, businesses, and governments managed the pandemic. Remote work, virtual classrooms, online shopping, social media, telemedicine—for many, laptop and cellphone screens became antiseptic barriers through which they interacted with the world. Personal devices also provided new opportunities for hygienic surveillance, such as apps that could monitor symptoms or whether one had been in proximity to a contagious person. The ubiquity of these technologies incentivized public and private actors to further develop their potential to observe and regulate the kinds of human traffic that impact health. (In hindsight, we might also ask how earlier, more dispersed technologies like radio, the telephone, and television have been used historically as hygienic media.) The pandemic has also provided a preview of how media might be put to use in environments around the globe as they become less and less hospitable to human habitation. In this regard, as one of the first places where large numbers of people experienced a climate-controlled environment, movie theaters may once again become relevant. Though not well-suited to pandemics, cinema does provide a model for an increasingly air-conditioned world.

Though differently than cinema, new media technologies also facilitate gathering in ways that produce hygienic anxiety. Current discourses on the dangers of digital media echo the mixture of moral and hygienic anxiety that characterized the reception of film in the early twentieth century. Besides concerns about their effect on attention and psychological development—a fear that has accompanied virtually every new communication technology since print—social media and the internet have also proven their ability to assist physical gatherings, ranging from acts of righteous protest to vigilante violence. As was the case a century ago, the prospect of disease transmission once again offered a rhetorical tool for legitimizing elite fear of the rabble. At the same time, the health mis- and disinformation that are propagated on social media weaken efforts to combat disease and death. Effectively a broadcast medium, cinema in the early twentieth century could serve as a site for mass education where health experts could exercise unchallenged authority. Institutions of governance used film, along with other forms of communication and exhibition, to produce images of bodies and populations, legitimate their own power, inculcate the value of physical and mental health, transmit racist and ableist ideologies, demonstrate habits of bodily care, and much more. Today's networked forms of communication, by contrast, maintain some of cinema's educational potential but also present a significant challenge to the contemporary hygienic apparatus. One no longer needs access to film production equipment, studio space, and distribution companies to make videos that can be uploaded and shared. Though the actual social and political roots of mistrust in expertise go much deeper, social media will be a key hygienic battleground because of their place in the economy of communication.

Beyond these communicative dynamics, media can also challenge the hygienic at the aesthetic level, in the ways they engage the body and the senses. While important aspects of film exhibition and production were subjected to principles of health and safety, Weimar-era filmmakers continued to display a fascination with the non-normative traffic that cinema could facilitate between spectator and screen, which expressed itself in images of plague, smoke, and intoxication. The current popularity of zombie- and vampire-themed media would suggest that the thrills of contagion and bodily vulnerability still hold an allure. At the same time, the ideal of "health" has even greater disciplinary power than ever. A dominant neoliberal framing that equates physical health (according to normative criteria of ability) with freedom and makes both a matter of personal responsibility enacts a rigid set of prescriptions for individual lifestyle and behavior, which are increasingly difficult to fulfill. Mediated forms of communication and aesthetic creation offer a mode of presumably safe contact that can nonetheless facilitate otherwise stigmatized experiences and fantasies. The decline of the cinematic dispositif prompts reflection on the aesthetic forms that resistance to the hygienic might now take, given the very different possibilities of experience and interaction that newer media technologies offer. Indeed, in various ways these new technologies have redefined what it means to be able-bodied, for instance, in that navigating work and daily life require operating a mobile phone. These shifting norms of ability may generate their own transgressive impulses in turn, which will look very different from the movie intoxication of the Weimar period.

At the end of the Weimar Republic, film was one medium in which oppositional artists could articulate a political critique of health inequality and environmental disorder. They demonstrated that hygienic modernity had not yet arrived for many working-class Germans, who continued to be exposed to unsafe work and living spaces. Their project serves as a reminder of the uneven distributions of vulnerability that dominant narratives of health and environmental issues often obscure by individualizing responsibility or focusing on technological panaceas, such as vaccines, the digital revolution, or green energy. For instance, the incredible protective power of digital media in a time of contagion, which enabled remote work, schooling, and shopping, also depended on new experiences of risk for others. The clicks and taps happening on screens at home exposed restaurant workers, grocery store workers, personal shoppers, warehouse workers, delivery drivers, and many others to risk in the world outside. The distributions of wealth and resources, divisions of labor, and the possibilities afforded by digital mediation combined to make some people less and others more vulnerable to disease. These examples raise the question of how media technologies are implicated in distributing environmental exposure; as well as how they might be mobilized to represent and challenge such structures of vulnerability.

Weimar cinema's intersections with the modern apparatus of hygiene exemplify the crucial but necessarily ambivalent position that technological media occupied within responses to urbanization and industrialization in early twentieth-century Germany. Cinema's immense usefulness as a technology of hygienic education and separation was predicated precisely on the potentially dangerous contacts between people, images, and ideas that it facilitated. While they could be used in certain ways to stabilize the environments of everyday life, these forms of contact also opened up a dizzying range of material, social, aesthetic, and imaginative possibilities that confounded projects of governance and pointed beyond the order that the hygienic apparatus served to uphold. Although "hygiene" no longer means what it once did, this dynamic resonates amid the ongoing ecological and media-technological changes of today. While contemporary media technologies may provide some protection in an increasingly uninhabitable world, whatever transformative possibilities they may have lie elsewhere.

NOTES

Introduction

1. v. d. Hude and Hennicke, "Das Central-Hôtel in Berlin," *Zeitschrift für Bauwesen* 31 (1881): 180.

2. v. d. Hude and Hennicke, "Das Central-Hôtel," 184.

3. Wilhelm Ostwald, *Energetische Grundlagen der Kulturwissenschaft* (Leipzig: Dr. Werner Klinkhardt, 1909), 90–91.

4. Eva Horn, "Air Conditioning: Die Zähmung des Klimas als Projekt der Moderne," *Sinn und Form* 67, no. 4 (2015): 460.

5. Frank Uekötter, *Umweltgeschichte im 19. und 20. Jahrhundert* (Munich: Oldenbourg, 2007), 15.

6. Theodor Weyl, *Die Einwirkung hygienischer Werke auf die Gesundheit der Städte mit besonderer Rücksicht auf Berlin* (Jena: Gustav Fischer, 1893), 2.

7. Lewis Mumford, *Technics and Civilization* (New York: Harcourt, Brace, 1934), 169.

8. Mumford, *Technics and Civilization*, 248.

9. Mumford, *Technics and Civilization*, 258.

10. Mumford, *Technics and Civilization*, 251. Lisa Cartwright points to the importance of "cinema as an institution and an apparatus for monitoring, regulating, and ultimately building 'life' in the modernist culture of Western medical science." Cartwright, *Screening the Body: Tracing Medicine's Visual Culture* (Minneapolis: University of Minnesota Press, 1995), xi.

11. Joachim Radkau, *The Age of Ecology: A Global History*, trans. Patrick Camiller (Cambridge: Polity, 2014), 32.

12. See Greg Eghigian, *Making Security Social: Disability, Insurance, and the Birth of the Social Entitlement State in Germany* (Ann Arbor: University of Michigan Press, 2000), 59–61.

13. Eduard Reich, *System der Hygieine*, vol. 1 (Leipzig: Friedrich Fleischer, 1870), xvi; English quoted from George Rosen, "What Is Social Medicine? A Genetic Analysis of the Concept," *Bulletin of the History of Medicine* 21 (1947): 702–3.

14. Philipp Sarasin, *Reizbare Maschinen: Eine Geschichte des Körpers, 1765–1914* (Frankfurt am Main: Suhrkamp, 2001), 22.

15. Sarasin, *Reizbare Maschinen*, 23–25.

16. *International Hygiene Exhibition. Guide* (Dresden, 1911).

17. William Rollins, "A Nation in White: Germany's Hygienic Consensus and the Ambiguities of Modernist Architecture," *German Politics and Society* 19, no. 4 (2001): 11–16.

18. Alfons Labisch, *Homo Hygienicus: Gesundheit und Medizin in der Neuzeit* (Frankfurt: Campus Verlag, 1992), 166–67.

19. Didem Ekici, "The Physiology of the House: Modern Architecture and the Science of Hygiene," in *Healing Spaces, Modern Architecture, and the Body*, ed. Sarah Schrank and Didem Ekici (London: Routledge, 2017), 51.

20. See Dieter Schott, "The *Handbuch der Hygiene*: A Manual of Proto-Environmental Science in Germany of 1900?" in *Environment, Health and History*, ed. Virginia Berridge and Martin Gorsky (Basingstoke, UK: Palgrave Macmillan, 2012), 69–92.

21. Jean-Louis Baudry, "The Apparatus," trans. Jean Andrews and Bertrand Augst, *Camera Obscura* 1, no. 1 (1976): 104–26.

22. See François Albera and Maria Tortajada, "Introduction to an Epistemology of Viewing and Listening Dispositives," in *Cinema beyond Film: Media Epistemology in the Modern Era*, ed. François Albera and Maria Tortajada (Amsterdam: Amsterdam University Press, 2010), 9–22.

23. Noam M. Elcott, *Artificial Darkness: An Obscure History of Modern Art and Media* (Chicago: University of Chicago Press, 2016), 11.

24. Michel Foucault, "The Confession of the Flesh," in *Power/Knowledge: Selected Interviews and Other Writings 1972–1977*, ed. Colin Gordon, trans. Colin Gordon et al. (New York: Pantheon Books, 1980), 194.

25. Foucault, "Confession of the Flesh," 195. Randall Halle has recently proposed a renewal of apparatus theory in film studies, which takes account of the Foucauldian concept of the dispositif and links cinema to questions of social reproduction. See Halle, *The Europeanization of Cinema: Interzones and Imaginative Communities* (Urbana: University of Illinois Press, 2014), chap. 1.

26. Here I paraphrase Elcott, who says that "a dispositif is little more and nothing less than judicious coordination." *Artificial Darkness*, 17.

27. Chris Otter points to the way urban hygienic reform was intertwined with liberal subjectivity in Victorian England: "The respectable mastered their passions in public spaces conducive to the exercise of clear, controlled perception: wide streets, squares and parks." These were spaces with "material conditions in which sight can prevail, civil conduct be exposed to view, and those eminently Victorian qualities of reserve and distance maintained." Otter, "Making Liberalism Durable: Vision and Civility in the Late Victorian City," *Social History* 27, no. 1 (2002): 3.

28. See Georg Toepfer, "Umwelt," in *Historisches Wörterbuch der Biologie: Geschichte und Theorie der biologischen Grundbegriffe* (Stuttgart: J. B. Metzler, 2011), 3:584–86.

29. Inga Pollmann, *Cinematic Vitalism: Film Theory and the Question of Life* (Amsterdam: Amsterdam University Press, 2018), 101.

30. As I have framed it here, *hygiene* resonates with both older and more recent meanings of the term *Kulturtechnik*. Beginning in the late nineteenth century, the word *Kulturtechnik* referred to agricultural engineering techniques that aimed to make land more productive. A century later, however, it could signify certain fundamental cultural operations, such as reading and writing, whose mastery reflects the acquisition of culture or *Bildung*. See Bernhard Siegert, "Cultural Techniques: Or the End of the Intellectual Postwar Era in German Media Theory," *Theory, Culture & Society* 30, no. 6 (2013): 56–57.

31. Detlev J. K. Peukert, *Max Webers Diagnose der Moderne* (Göttingen: Vandenhoeck & Ruprecht, 1989), 74–75.

32. Andreas Killen, *Homo Cinematicus: Science, Motion Pictures, and the Making of Modern Germany* (Philadelphia: University of Pennsylvania Press, 2017), 139.

33. Rollins, "A Nation in White," 10.

34. Michael Cowan, *Walter Ruttmann and the Cinema of Multiplicity: Avant-Garde—Advertising—Modernity* (Amsterdam: Amsterdam University Press, 2014).

35. Matthew Gandy, "Rethinking Urban Metabolism: Water, Space and the Modern City," *City* 8, no. 3 (2004): 364.

36. Cowan's work on Ruttmann reflects this shift; see also Vinzenz Hediger and Patrick Vonderau, eds., *Films That Work: Industrial Film and the Productivity of Media* (Amsterdam: Amsterdam University Press, 2009).

37. Michel Foucault, *The History of Sexuality*, vol. 1, *An Introduction*, trans. Robert Hurley (New York: Pantheon Books, 1978), 139. For discussions of the concept's usefulness for understanding German modernity, see Edward Ross Dickinson, "Biopolitics, Fascism, Democracy: Some Reflections on Our Discourse about 'Modernity,'" *Central European History* 37, no. 1 (2004): 1–48; and Corinna Treitel, *Eating Nature in Modern Germany: Food, Agriculture and Environment, c. 1870 to 2000* (Cambridge: Cambridge University Press, 2017).

38. Anton Kaes shows how thoroughly the trauma of World War I shaped Weimar cinema in *Shell Shock Cinema: Weimar Culture and the Wounds of War* (Princeton, NJ: Princeton University Press, 2009).

39. See, for instance, Anja Laukötter, *Sex-richtig! Körperpolitik und Gefühlserziehung im Kino des 20. Jahrhunderts* (Göttingen: Wallstein, 2021).

40. Important contributions include: Jost Hermand, *Grüne Utopien in Deutschland: Zur Geschichte des ökologischen Bewusstseins* (Frankfurt am Main: Fischer Taschenbuch Verlag, 1991); Catherine E. Rigby, *Topographies of the Sacred: The Poetics of Place in European Romanticism* (Charlottesville: University of Virginia Press, 2004); Thomas M. Lekan, *Imagining the Nation in Nature: Landscape Preservation and German Identity, 1885–1945* (Cambridge, MA: Harvard University Press, 2004); and Axel Goodbody, *Nature, Technology and Cultural Change in Twentieth-Century German Literature: The Challenge of Ecocriticism* (Basingstoke, UK: Palgrave Macmillan, 2007).

41. Anson Rabinbach, *The Human Motor: Energy, Fatigue, and the Origins of Modernity* (New York: Basic Books, 1990), 63.

42. With regard to Weimar cinema, the most extensive work as yet is Seth Peabody, "Environmental Fantasies: Mountains, Cities, and Heimat in Weimar Cinema" (PhD diss., Harvard University, 2015), https://dash.harvard.edu/handle/1/17467382.

43. Brian R. Jacobson, "Introduction: Studio Perspectives," in *In the Studio: Visual Creation and Its Material Environments* (Berkeley: University of California Press, 2020), 7.

44. Jennifer Fay, *Inhospitable World: Cinema in the Time of the Anthropocene* (Oxford: Oxford University Press, 2018), 4.

45. Tom Crook, *Governing Systems: Modernity and the Making of Public Health in England, 1830–1910* (Berkeley: University of California Press, 2016), 9.

46. Crook, *Governing Systems*, 9.

47. Benjamin Ward Richardson, *Hygeia: A City of Health* (London: Macmillan, 1876).

Chapter 1

1. Adolf Sellmann, "Das Geheimnis des Kinos," *Bild und Film* 1, no. 3 (1912): 65.

2. Annemone Ligensa, "Triangulating a Turn: Film 1900 as Technology, Perception and Culture," in *Film 1900: Technology, Perception, Culture*, ed. Klaus Kreimeier and Annemone Ligensa (New Barnet, UK: John Libbey, 2009), 5.

3. Victor Noack, *Der Kino: Etwas über sein Wesen und seine Bedeutung* (Gautzsch b. Leipzig: Felix Dietrich, 1913), 3.

4. On the category of *Schund*, see Kara L. Ritzheimer, *"Trash," Censorship, and National Identity in Early Twentieth-Century Germany* (New York: Cambridge University Press, 2016).

5. Sabine Hake, *The Cinema's Third Machine: Writing on Film in Germany, 1907–1933* (Lincoln: University of Nebraska Press, 1993), 50.

6. Killen, *Homo Cinematicus*, 82.

7. Anne I. Hardy, *Ärtze, Ingenieure und städtische Gesundheit: Medizinische Theorien in der Hygienebewegung des 19. Jahrhunderts* (Frankfurt: Campus Verlag, 2005), 245.

8. See Labisch, *Homo Hygienicus*, 143.

9. Ferdinand Hueppe, "Wohnung und Gesundheit," in *Weyl's Handbuch der Hygiene*, 2nd ed. C. Fraenken, vol. 4, *Bau- und Wohnungshygiene* (Leipzig: J. A. Barth, 1914), 23

10. Victor Noack, *Wohnungsnot und Mieterelend: Ein Erbstück des alten Staates* (Berlin: Ernst Wasmuth, 1918), 8–9.

11. Noack, *Der Kino*, 8.

12. "Bericht über das Ergebnis der Kinobesuche in Cöln durch Beauftragte von der Volksgemeinschaft zur Wahrung von Anstand und guter Sitte," in *Verhandlungen der verfassungsgebenden Deutschen Nationalversammlung*, vol. 341 (Berlin: Julius Sittenfeld, 1920), 2511.

13. See Hardy, *Ärtze, Ingenieure und städtische Gesundheit*, 131–41.

14. Friedrich H. Lorenz, "Soziale Tuberkulosebekämpfung," *Öffentliche Gesundheitspflege* 52, no. 2 (1920): 52.

15. Victor Noack, " 'Schlafburschen' und 'Möblierte,' " *Sexual-Probleme*, no. 6 (1912): 392.

16. On the turn to environmental explanations in nineteenth-century criminology, see Andrew Lees, *Cities, Sin, and Social Reform in Imperial Germany* (Ann Arbor: University of Michigan Press, 2002), 163–70.

17. "Bericht über das Ergebnis der Kinobesuche in Cöln," 2511.

18. Erich Wernicke, "Die Wohnung in ihrem Einfluss auf Krankheit und Sterblichkeit," in *Krankheit und soziale Lage*, ed. M. Mosse and Gustav Tugendreich (Munich: J. F. Lehmanns Verlag, 1913), 110.

19. Jill Suzanne Smith, *Berlin Coquette: Prostitution and the New German Woman, 1890–1933* (Ithaca, NY: Cornell University Press, 2013), 6–9.

20. Wilhelm von Drigalski, "Deutsche Jugendnot," *Öffentliche Gesundheitspflege* 6, no. 11 (1921): 377.

21. According to Kaspar Maase, "das Kinoproblem erschien weitgehend als Jugend(schutz)problem." Maase, "Massenkunst und Volkserziehung: Die Regulierung von Film und Kino im deutschen Kaiserreich," *Archiv für Sozialgeschichte* 41 (2001): 41.

22. Robert Gaupp, "The Dangers of Cinema," in *The Promise of Cinema: German Film Theory, 1907–1933*, ed. Anton Kaes, Nicholas Baer, and Michael Cowan, trans. Eric Ames (Berkeley: University of California Press, 2016), 225.

23. In the U.S. context, Kirsten Ostherr finds a similar discourse around film spectatorship as contagion in the 1920s and '30s. See Ostherr, *Cinematic Prophylaxis: Globalization and Contagion in the Discourse of World Health* (Durham, NC: Duke University Press, 2005), 31–39.

24. Waldemar Schweisheimer, *Die Bedeutung des Films für die soziale Hygiene und Medizin* (Munich: Georg Müller Verlag, 1920), 69.

25. Schweisheimer, *Die Bedeutung des Films*, 72.

26. Schweisheimer, *Die Bedeutung des Films*, 74.

27. Schweisheimer, *Die Bedeutung des Films*, 76–77. As Killen points out, "deep anxiety about the circulation of false or dangerous forms of knowledge in public life" made enlightenment films ambivalent objects among medical experts. Killen, *Homo Cinematicus*, 46.

28. *Different from the Others* (1919), a film that argued against the criminalization of homosexuality, played an outsized role in the censorship debates. See James D. Steakley, "Cinema and Censorship in the Weimar Republic: The Case of *Anders als die Andern*," *Film History* 11, no. 2 (1999): 181–203.

29. Hans Schliepmann, *Lichtspieltheater: Eine Sammlung ausgeführter Kinohäuser in Gross-Berlin* (Berlin: Ernst Wasmuth, 1914), 6.

30. Schliepmann, *Lichtspieltheater*, 7.

31. James Leo Cahill, "How It Feels to Be Run Over: Early Film Accidents," *Discourse* 30, no. 3 (2008): 294.

32. Gustav Effenberger, *Die Welt in Flammen: Eine Geschichte der großen und interessanten Brände aller Jahrhunderte* (Hannover: Rechts-, Staats- und Sozialwissenschaftlicher Verlag, 1913), 731. The excerpt is taken from Goethe's collection *Zahme Xenien*.

33. Michel Foucault, *Security, Territory, Population: Lectures at the Collège de France, 1977–78*, trans. Graham Burchell (New York: Palgrave Macmillan, 2007), 64.

34. Foucault, *Security, Territory, Population*, 63–64.

35. See Nitzan Lebovic and Andreas Killen, "Introduction," in *Catastrophes: A History and Theory of an Operative Concept*, ed. Nitzan Lebovic and Andreas Killen (Berlin: De Gruyter, 2014), 1–14.

36. K. B. Lehmann, *Arbeits- und Gewerbehygiene*, vol. 4.2 of *Handbuch der Hygiene*, ed. Max Rubner, M. v. Gruber, and M. Ficker (Leipzig: S. Hirzel, 1919), 90.

37. "Bericht über die Verwaltung der Feuerwehr," Verwaltungsbericht des Magistrats zu Berlin für das Etatsjahr 1908 (Berlin: Magistrat zu Berlin, 1910), 8.

38. Joseph Garncarz, "Perceptual Environments for Films: The Development of Cinema in Germany, 1895–1914," in *Film 1900: Technology, Perception, Culture*, ed. Klaus Kreimeier and Annemone Ligensa (New Barnet, UK: John Libbey, 2009), 147.

39. See Konrad Polthier, "Brandsicherheitswachen der Feuerwehr in Versammlungsstätten mit Bühnen und Szenenflächen," *Schadenprisma* 6, no. 4 (1977): 56–59.

40. "Bericht über die Verwaltung der Feuerwehr," Verwaltungsbericht des Magistrats zu Berlin für das Etatsjahr 1909 (Berlin: Magistrat zu Berlin, 1911), 8–9.

41. "Bericht über die Verwaltung der Feuerwehr," Verwaltungsbericht des Magistrats zu Berlin für das Etatsjahr 1912 (Berlin: Magistrat zu Berlin, 1914), 5.

42. "Bericht über die Verwaltung der Feuerwehr 1912," 6.

43. "Bericht über die Verwaltung der Feuerwehr 1912," 7.

44. Eckhard Müller, "Entwicklung des baulichen Brandschutzes bei Versammlungsstätten," *Schadenprisma* 6, no. 4 (1977): 53–54.

45. See "Polizei-Verordnung betreffend die bauliche Anlage und die innere Einrichtung von Theatern, Circusgebäuden und öffentlichen Versammlungsräumen," *Centralblatt der Bauverwaltung*, November 30, 1889; and "Polizeiverordnung über die bauliche Anlage, die innere Einrichtung und den Betrieb von Theatern, öffentlichen Versammlungsräumen und Zirkusanlagen," *Zentralblatt der Bauverwaltung*, April 21, 1909.

46. Reproduced in *Leitfaden für Kinooperateure und Kinobesitzer*, 4th ed. (Leipzig: Otto Klemm, 1919), 270–73, here 272.

47. *Leitfaden für Kinooperateure und Kinobesitzer*, 272–73.

48. See, for example, the 1912 Berlin ordinance, *Leitfaden für Kinooperateure und Kinobesitzer*, 259–64.

49. On zoning, see Dieter Schott, "Industrialisierung und städtische Umwelt in Deutschland," in *Umwelt und Geschichte in Deutschland und Großbritanien*, ed. Franz Bosbach, Jens Ivo Engels, and Fiona Watson (Munich: K. G. Saur, 2006), 101–3.

50. Reproduced in *Leitfaden für Kinooperateure und Kinobesitzer*, here 261–62.

51. Der Preussische Minister für Volkswohlfahrt, *Vorschriften über die Anlage und Einrichtung von Lichtspieltheatern sowie für die Sicherheit bei Lichtspielvorführungen* (Berlin: Carl Heymanns Verlag, 1926), 15–16. Electricity had a reputation as a cleaner and safer light source than gas. See Wolfgang Schivelbusch, *Disenchanted Night: The Industrialization of Light in the Nineteenth Century*, trans. Angela Davies (Berkeley: University of California Press, 1995), 50–52.

52. *Leitfaden für Kinooperateure und Kinobesitzer*, 263.

53. *Leitfaden für Kinooperateure und Kinobesitzer*, 273.

54. *Leitfaden für Kinooperateure und Kinobesitzer*, 265.

55. "It has been well known for a long while," declared the industrial psychologist Hugo Münsterberg in 1913, "how intimate the relations are between fatigue and industrial accidents." Hugo Münsterberg, *Psychology and Industrial Efficiency* (Boston: Houghton Mifflin, 1913), 213. On the science of fatigue, see Rabinbach, *The Human Motor*.

56. Der Preussische Minister für Volkswohlfahrt, *Vorschriften über die Anlage und Einrichtung*, 14.

57. Der Preussische Minister für Volkswohlfahrt, "Erlaß, betreffend die Überwachung der Lichtspieltheater," *Zentralblatt der Bauverwaltung* 43, no. 33/34 (April 25, 1923): 204.

58. Der Preussische Minister für Volkswohlfahrt, *Vorschriften über die Anlage und Einrichtung*, 12.

59. On inspection as a feature of modern municipal government, see Chris Otter, *The Victorian Eye: A Political History of Light and Vision in Britain, 1800–1910* (Chicago: University of Chicago Press, 2008), chap. 3.

60. Gunning developed the notion of the cinema of attractions in the 1980s in dialogue with other reassessments of early cinema by scholars such as Charles Musser and André Gaudreault. Gunning's important essays include "The Cinema of Attractions: Early Film, Its Spectator and the Avant-Garde," in *Early Cinema: Space—Frame—Narrative*, ed. Thomas Elsaesser (London: British Film Institute, 1990), 56–62; "An Aesthetic of Astonishment: Early Film and the (In)Credulous Spectator," in *Viewing Positions: Ways of Seeing Film*, ed. Linda Williams (New Brunswick, NJ: Rutgers University Press, 1994), 114–33; and "'Primitive' Cinema—A Frame-up? Or The Trick's on Us," *Cinema Journal* 28, no. 2 (1989): 3–12.

61. I draw on Frank Kessler's definition of *dispositif* outlined in Frank Kessler, "The Cinema of Attractions as Dispositif," in *The Cinema of Attractions Reloaded*, ed. Wanda Strauven (Amsterdam: Amsterdam University Press, 2006), 61–62. Timothy Barnard discusses the transition from showman to operator in "The 'Machine Operator': Deus Ex Machina of the Storefront Cinema," *Framework* 43, no. 1 (2002): 40–75.

62. Schliepmann, *Lichtspieltheater*, 7.

63. Schliepmann, *Lichtspieltheater*, 7.

64. Walter Thielemann, "Notausgänge in Kinotheatern," *Kinematograph*, May 28, 1919.

65. Robert Heynen, *Degeneration and Revolution: Radical Cultural Politics and the Body in Weimar Germany* (Leiden: Brill, 2015), 389.

66. See, for instance, Eckard Michels, "Die 'Spanische Grippe' 1918/19: Verlauf, Folgen und Deutungen in Deutschland im Kontext des Ersten Weltkriegs," *Vierteljahrshefte für Zeitgeschichte* 58, no. 1 (2010): 20; and Wolfgang U. Eckart, "Kino, Hunger, 'Rassenschmach': Exemplarische Dokumentar- und Propagandafilme aus dem Nachkriegsdeutschland, 1919–1924," in *Das Vorprogramm: Lehrfilm / Gebrauchsfilm / Propagandafilm / unveröffentlichter Film in Kinos und Archiven am Oberrhein 1900–1970*, ed. Philipp Osten et al. (Heidelberg: A25 Rhinfilm, 2015), 316–20.

67. Mendelsohn's poetic opening speech is reproduced in Lotar Holland, "Universum," *Filmtechnik* 4, no. 24 (November 24, 1928): 468.

68. Andor Kraszna-Krausz, "Das moderne Lichtspielhaus," *Filmtechnik* 2, no. 26 (December 25, 1926): 509.

69. Adolf Behne, *Neues Wohnen – Neues Bauen* (Leipzig: Hesse & Becker, 1927), 11.

70. Kraszna-Krausz, "Das moderne Lichtspielhaus," 509.

71. Rollins, "A Nation in White," 4.

72. On Pettenkofer's experiments and the broader physiological reimagining of architecture in the nineteenth century, see Ekici, "The Physiology of the House."

73. Leo Witlin, "Das Aufbauprinzip von großen Lichtspielhäusern," *Filmtechnik* 2, no. 26 (December 25, 1926): 510.

74. Witlin, Das Aufbauprinzip," 510.

75. Hanns Jakob, "Form und Hygiene des Filmtheaterbaues," *Filmtechnik* 2, no. 26 (December 25, 1926): 512.

76. Jakob, "Form und Hygiene des Filmtheaterbaues," 512.

77. K. Retlow, "Die Projektionswand," *Filmtechnik* 2, no. 26 (December 25, 1926): 522.

78. H. Reichenbach's chapter on illumination in *Weyl's Handbook of Hygiene*, for instance, discusses eyestrain and eye damage in relation to light intensity and color, as well as sudden changes in intensity. Reichenbach, "Beleuchtung," in *Weyl's Handbuch der Hygiene*, 2nd ed., ed. C. Fraenken, vol. 4, *Bau- und Wohnungshygiene* (Leipzig: J. A. Barth, 1914), 89–166.

79. Jakob, "Form und Hygiene des Filmtheaterbaues," 512.

80. August Gärtner, *Leitfaden der Hygiene für Studierende, Ärtze, Architekten, Ingenieure und Verwaltungsbeamte*, 8th ed. (Berlin: S. Karger, 1920), 457.

81. Jakob, "Form und Hygiene des Filmtheaterbaues," 512.

82. Gärtner, *Leitfaden der Hygiene*, 301.

83. Theodor Weyl, "Die Ursachen der Luftverschlechterung in bewohnten Räumen," in *Weyl's Handbuch der Hygiene*, 2nd ed., ed. C. Fraenken, vol. 4, *Bau- und Wohnungshygiene* (Leipzig: J. A. Barth, 1914), 261.

84. Stindt's early book-length contribution to film theory was *Das Lichtspiel als Kunstform: Die Philosophie des Films, Regie, Dramaturgie und Schauspieltechnik* (Oldenburg i. O.: Gerhard Stalling, 1924).

85. Georg Otto Stindt, "Die Luft im Kino," *Filmtechnik* 2, no. 26 (December 25, 1926): 513.

86. Retlow, "Die Projektionswand," 521.

87. Salvatore Basile, *Cool: How Air Conditioning Changed Everything* (New York: Fordham University Press, 2014), 113–19.

88. Stindt, "Die Luft im Kino," 513.

89. Georg Otto Stindt, "Kalte und warme Farben," *Filmtechnik* 3, no. 16 (August 6, 1927): 304.

90. Stindt, "Kalte und warme Farben."

91. Sarah Street and Joshua Yumibe, *Chromatic Modernity: Color, Cinema, and Media of the 1920s* (New York: Columbia University Press, 2019), 129.

92. On the value of whiteness in architectural modernism, see Rollins, "A Nation in White."

93. See Peter Boeger, *Architektur der Lichtspieltheater in Berlin: Bauten und Projekte 1919–1930* (Berlin: Arenhövel, 1993), 27–28.

94. Fritz Wilms, *Lichtspieltheaterbauten* (Berlin: Friedrich Ernst Hübsch Verlag, 1928), vii–viii.

95. Wilms, *Lichtspieltheaterbauten*, viii.

96. Wilms, *Lichtspieltheaterbauten*, viii.

97. Wilms, *Lichtspieltheaterbauten*, ix.

98. Leo Witlin, "Mercedes-Palast in Neukölln," *Filmtechnik* 3, no. 6 (March 19, 1927): 107.

99. Witlin, "Mercedes-Palast in Neukölln," 105.

100. On "fresh air as advertisement" see Christoph Bignens, *Kinos: Architektur als Marketing* (Zürich: Hans Rohr, 1988), 81–84.

101. Elcott, *Artificial Darkness*, 17.

102. In addition to Elcott's work, noteworthy contributions include François Albera and Maria Tortajada, eds., *Cinema beyond Film: Media Epistemology in the Modern Era* (Amsterdam: Amsterdam University Press, 2010); Martin Lefebvre and André Gaudreault, eds., "Cinema & Technology," special issue, *Recherches Sémiotiques / Semiotic Inquiry* 31, no. 1–2–3 (2011); Albera and Tortajada, eds., *Cine-Dispositives: Essays in Epistemology Across Media* (Amsterdam: Amsterdam University Press, 2015); and Jocelyn Szczepaniak-Gillece, *The Optical Vacuum: Spectatorship and Modernized American Theater Architecture* (Oxford: Oxford University Press, 2018).

103. In his 1926 *Sittengeschichte des Kinos* (*Moral History of the Cinema*), Konrad Haemmerling noted the moviegoing public's attraction to darkness: "Come in ladies and gentlemen, our cinema is the darkest in the whole city!" *Sittengeschichte des Kinos* (Dresden: P. Aretz, 1926), 209. Haemmerling published the book under the pseudonyn Curt Moreck.

Chapter 2

1. Rudolf Abel, "Die nächsten Aufgaben der öffentlichen Gesundheitspflege," *Öffentliche Gesundheitspflege* 51, no. 1 (1919): 10.

2. Abel, "Die nächsten Aufgaben," 7.

3. This was the estimate of the important German nutrition scientist Max Rubner in 1918. See Corinna Treitel, "Max Rubner and the Biopolitics of Rational Nutrition," *Central European History* 41, no. 1 (2008): 22.

4. Paul Weindling, *Health, Race, and German Politics between National Unification and Nazism, 1870–1945* (Cambridge: Cambridge University Press, 1989), 414.

5. Curt Thomalla, "Hygiene und soziale Medizin im Volksbelehrungsfilm (I)," *Zeitschrift für Medizinalbeamte* 35, no. 21 (1922): 593.

6. Emphasizing the legitimacy of hygiene, as opposed to lay practices and quackery, was part of a longer-term effort by hygienists to establish their expertise. See Alfons Labisch, "Doctors, Workers, and the Scientific Cosmology of the Industrial World: The Social Construction of 'Health' and the 'Homo Hygienicus,'" *Journal of Contemporary History* 20 (1985): 603–4; and Killen, *Homo Cinematicus*, chap. 5.

7. Curt Thomalla, "Hygiene und soziale Medizin im Volksbelehrungsfilm (III)," *Zeitschrift für Medizinalbeamte* 35, no. 23 (1922): 635.

8. On Thomalla's biography and filmmaking practice from after World War I into the Nazi period, see Killen, *Homo Cinematicus*, 8–14, 46–48, 62–64, and 145–49.

9. For descriptions of these films, see Curt Thomalla, "Hygiene und soziale Medizin im Volksbelehrungsfilm (II)," *Zeitschrift für Medizinalbeamte* 35, no. 22 (1922): 606–10. I discuss *How Do I Stay Healthy?* later in this chapter, and *The Plight and Care of the Disabled* in chapter 4.

10. Thomalla, "Hygiene und soziale Medizin im Volksbelehrungsfilm (I)," 591.

11. See Klaus Kreimeier, "Ein deutsches Paradigma: Die Kulturabteilung der Ufa," in *Geschichte des dokumentarischen Films in Deutschland*, ed. Peter Zimmermann, vol. 2, *Weimarer Republik (1918–1933)*, ed. Klaus Kreimeier, Antje Ehmann, and Jeanpaul Goergen (Stuttgart: Reclam, 2005), 69.

12. See Kreimeier, "Ein deutsches Paradigma," 104–5.

13. Thomalla, "Hygiene und soziale Medizin im Volksbelehrungsfilm (I)," 592.

14. Klaus Kreimeier, "Komplex-starr: Semiologie des Kulturfilms," in *Geschichte des dokumentarischen Films in Deutschland*, ed. Peter Zimmermann, vol. 2: *Weimarer Republik (1918–1933)*, ed. Klaus Kreimeier, Antje Ehmann, and Jeanpaul Goergen (Stuttgart: Reclam, 2005), 93–94.

15. Thomalla, "Hygiene und soziale Medizin im Volksbelehrungsfilm (II)," 607.

16. Thomalla, "Hygiene und soziale Medizin im Volksbelehrungsfilm (II)," 606.

17. See Labisch, "Doctors, Workers, and the Scientific Cosmology of the Industrial World," 609–12.

18. Ulf Schmidt, "'Der Blick auf den Körper': Sozialhygienische Filme, Sexualaufklärung und Propaganda in der Weimarer Republik," in *Geschlecht in Fesseln: Sexualität zwischen Aufklärung und Ausbeutung im Weimarer Kino 1918–1933*, ed. Malte Hagener (Munich: edition text & kritik, 2000), 24.

19. See Anja Laukötter, "Wissen als Animation: Zur Transformation der Anschaulichkeit im Gesundheitsaufklärungsfilm," *montage AV: Zeitschrift für Theorie und Geschichte audiovisueller Kommunikation* 22, no. 2 (2013): 79–96.

20. Unfortunately, the second part of this film doesn't seem to have been preserved.

21. Curt Thomalla, "The Development of the Medical Film and of Those Dealing with Hygiene and General Culture in Germany," *International Review of Educational Cinematography* 1, no. 4 (1929): 448.

22. Thomalla, "Development of the Medical Film," 447.

23. Adolf Rath, "Wohnungsaufsicht," in *Weyl's Handbuch der Hygiene*, 2nd ed., ed. C. Fraenken, vol. 4: *Bau-und Wohnungshygiene* (Leipzig: J. A. Barth, 1914), 57.

24. Ekici, "The Physiology of the House," 50.

25. Rath, "Wohnungsaufsicht," 70–71.

26. See Christine Frederick, *Household Engineering: Scientific Management in the Home* (Chicago: American School of Home Economics, 1923); and Bruno Taut, *Die neue Wohnung: Die Frau als Schöpferin*, 3rd ed. (Leipzig: Klinkhardt & Biermann, 1925).

27. Margarete Schütte-Lihotzky, "Rationalisierung im Haushalt," *Das neue Frankfurt* 1, no. 5 (1927): 120.

28. See Thomas Elsaesser, "Die Kamera in der Küche: Werben für das neue Wohnen," in *Umwidmungen: Architektonische und kinematographische Räume*, ed. Gertrud Koch (Berlin: Vorwerk 8, 2005), 36–56.

29. Very similar diagrams appear in Frederick, *Household Engineering*.

30. Behne, *Neues Wohnen – Neues Bauen*, 7.

31. "Mit der traditionellen Küche ist auch die traditionelle Hausfrau, deren Erkennungszeichen die Kittelschürze war, aus dem 'Neuen Frankfurt' verschwunden." Christiane Keim, "'Neue Welten der Sichtbarkeit schaffen': Der Lehrfilm 'Die Frankfurter Küche' als Teil der medialen Repräsentation des 'Neuen Frankfurt' in den 1920er-Jahren," in *Architektur im Film: Korrespondenzen zwischen Film, Architekturgeschichte und Architekturtheorie*, ed. Christiane Keim and Barbara Schrödl (Bielefeld: transcript, 2015), 86.

32. On the bodily and racial aesthetics of health in late nineteenth- and early twentieth-century Germany, see Michael Hau, *The Cult of Health and Beauty in Germany: A Social History, 1890–1930* (Chicago: University of Chicago Press, 2003).

33. Adrian Forty, *Objects of Desire* (New York: Pantheon Books, 1986), 156.

34. Rollins, "A Nation in White," 20.

35. Curt Thomalla, "Film Propaganda in Favour of Protection against Accidents," *International Review of Educational Cinematography* 2, no. 7–8 (1930): 954.

36. Thomalla, "Film Propaganda," 954.

37. Thomalla, "Film Propaganda," 951–53.

38. Karl Tramm, "Die Verhütung der Unfälle durch Propaganda," *Industrielle Psychotechnik* 1, no. 5–6 (1924): 149.

39. Kade, "Zur Frage der Verkehrsbeschulung der Jugend," *Die Polizei* 24 (1927): 594.

40. Andreas Killen, "Accidents Happen: The Industrial Accident in Interwar Germany," in *Catastrophes: A History and Theory of an Operative Concept*, ed. Nitzan Lebovic and Andreas Killen (Berlin: De Gruyter, 2014), 84.

41. Dietmar Fack, *Automobil, Verkehr, und Erziehung: Motorisierung und Sozialisation zwischen Beschleunigung und Anpassung 1885–1945* (Leverkusen: Leske + Budrich, 2000), 272.

42. Sara Hall, "Open Your Eyes! Public Ordering and the Policing Gaze," *Modernism/modernity* 15, no. 2 (2008): 292.

43. Thomas Elsaesser, "Die Stadt von morgen: Filme zum Bauen und Wohnen," in *Geschichte des dokumentarischen Films in Deutschland*, ed. Peter Zimmermann, vol. 2: *Weimarer Republik (1918–1933)*, edited by Klaus Kreimeier, Antje Ehmann, and Jeanpaul Goergen (Stuttgart: Reclam, 2005), 388.

44. On the film's production, see Maximilian von Goldbeck and Erich Kotzer, "Die Stadt von Morgen: Ein Film vom Städtebau," *Städtebau* 25, no. 12 (1930): 237–39.

45. Thomas Etzemüller, "Social engineering als Verhaltenslehre des kühlen Kopfes. Eine einleitende Skizze," in *Die Ordnung der Moderne: Social Engineering im 20. Jahrhundert*, ed. Thomas Etzemüller (Bielefeld: transcript, 2009), 30.

46. See Jens Lachmund, *Greening Berlin: The Co-Production of Science, Politics, and Urban Nature* (Cambridge, MA: MIT Press, 2013), 20–26.

47. Ariane Leendertz, "Ordnung, Ausgleich, Harmonie: Koordinaten raumplanerischen Denkens in Deutschland, 1920 bis 1970," in *Die Ordnung der Moderne: Social Engineering im 20. Jahrhundert*, ed. Thomas Etzemüller (Bielefeld: transcript, 2009), 130–31.

48. Leendertz, "Ordnung, Ausgleich," 131.

49. K. Krüger, "Zeitlupe und Zeitraffer," in *Das Kulturfilmbuch*, ed. Edgar Beyfuss and Alexander Kossowsky (Berlin: Carl P. Chryselius'scher Verlag, 1924), 193.

50. On time-lapse techniques in this film, see Janelle Blankenship, "'Film-Symphonie vom Leben und Sterben der Blumen': Plant Rhythm and Time-Lapse Vision in *Das Blumenwunder*," *Intermédialités*, no. 16 (2010): 83–103.

51. In *Dialectics of Nature*, Friedrich Engels wrote that "the whole Darwinian theory of the struggle for life is simply the transference from society to organic

nature of Hobbes' theory of *bellum omnium contra omnes*, and of the bourgeois economic theory of competition, as well as the Malthusian theory of population." Engels, *Dialectics of Nature*, ed. and trans. Clemens Dutt (New York: International Publishers, 1960), 208. See also Georg Toepfer, "Konkurrenz," in *Historisches Wörterbuch der Biologie: Geschichte und Theorie der biologischen Grundbegriffe* (Stuttgart: J. B. Metzler, 2011), 2:277–89.

52. Michael Hau, *Performance Anxiety: Sport and Work in Germany from the Empire to Nazism* (Toronto: University of Toronto Press, 2017), 51.

53. Gabriele Moser and Jochen Fleischhacker, "People's Health and Nation's Body: The Modernisation of Statistics, Demography and Social Hygiene in the Weimar Republic," in *The Politics of the Healthy Life: An International Perspective*, ed. Esteban Rodríguez-Ocaña (Sheffield, UK: European Association for the History of Medicine and Health Publications, 2002), 155–56.

54. Cowan, *Walter Ruttmann*, 100.

55. Jeanpaul Goergen, "Werben für eine neue Stadt: Stadtplanung und Dokumentarfilm im Wiederaufbau der Bundesrepublik," in *Architektur im Film: Korrespondenzen zwischen Film, Architekturgeschichte und Architekturtheorie*, ed. Christiane Keim and Barbara Schrödl (Bielefeld: transcript, 2015), 116.

56. Otter, *The Victorian Eye*, 74.

57. Otter, *The Victorian Eye*, 75.

58. Crook, *Governing Systems*, 284.

59. Extreme close-ups of bacterial growth in *Hygiene of Domestic Life* have a similar effect, showing something that might elude everyday perception.

60. On the color (or lack thereof) of hygiene, see Rollins, "A Nation in White." Susan R. Henderson discusses hygienic architecture and planning in *Building Culture: Ernst May and the New Frankfurt Initiative, 1926–1931* (New York: Peter Lang, 2013).

Chapter 3

1. Anselm Wagner, "Historie versus Hygiene: Staub in der Architektur(theorie)," in *Staub: Eine interdisziplinäre Perspektive*, ed. Daniel Gethmann and Anselm Wagner (Vienna: Lit, 2013), 91.

2. Frank Uekötter, *The Age of Smoke: Environmental Policy in Germany and the United States, 1880–1970* (Pittsburgh, PA: University of Pittsburgh Press, 2009), 1.

3. Rollins, "A Nation in White," 14.

4. On the history of thermodynamics, see especially Crosbie Smith, *The Science of Energy: A Cultural History of Energy Physics in Victorian Britain* (Chicago: University of Chicago Press, 1998).

5. See Anne Hoormann, *Lichtspiele: Zur Medienreflexion der Avantgarde in der Weimarer Republik* (Munich: Fink, 2003), 187, 190.

6. See Frances Guerin, *A Culture of Light: Cinema and Technology in 1920s Germany* (Minneapolis: University of Minnesota Press, 2005), 113–25.

7. Lotte H. Eisner, *Murnau* (Berkeley: University of California Press, 1973), 165.

8. Andor Kraszna-Krausz, "Faust," *Filmtechnik*, no. 22 (1926): 444.

9. Pinthus's review is reproduced in Hans-Michael Bock and Michael Töteberg, eds., *Das Ufa-Buch: Kunst und Krisen, Stars und Regisseure, Wirtschaft und Politik: Die internationale Geschichte von Deutschlands grösstem Film-Konzern*

(Frankfurt am Main: Zweitausendeins, 1992), 117. *Faust* was not generally well received.

10. Mark Cioc, "The Impact of the Coal Age on the German Environment: A Review of the Historical Literature," *Environment and History* 4, no. 1 (1998): 107.

11. John Robert McNeill, *Something New under the Sun: An Environmental History of the Twentieth-Century World* (New York: W.W. Norton, 2000), 85.

12. McNeill, *Something New under the Sun*, 113–16.

13. See, for instance, Julius von Schroeder and Carl Reuss, *Die Beschädigung der Vegetation durch Rauch und die Oberharzer Hütterauchschäden* (Berlin: Paul Parey, 1883). Schroeder and Reuss helped draw attention to the problem of *Waldsterben* (forest decline) in the late nineteenth century.

14. For a comparative overview of smoke control efforts in Germany and the United States, see Uekötter, *The Age of Smoke.*

15. Louis Ascher and Ernst Kobbert, "Verhütung von Rauch und Ruß in den Städten," in *Weyl's Handbuch der Hygiene*, 2nd. ed., C. Fraenken, vol. 2, *Städtereinigung* (Leipzig: J. A. Barth, 1914), 45.

16. Heim and Nier, "Die Bekämpfung des Staubes im Hause und auf der Straße," *Deutsche Vierteljahrsschrift für öffentliche Gesundheitspflege* 39, no. 1 (1907): 112.

17. Lehmann, *Arbeits- und Gewerbehygiene*, 112.

18. Volkmar Kohlschütter, *Nebel, Rauch und Staub* (Bern: Akadem. Buchhandl. v. Drechsel, 1918), 3.

19. Alex Kossowsky, "Das Filmgelände der Decla-Bioscop," in *Babelsberg: Ein Filmstudio 1912–1992*, ed. Wolfgang Jacobsen (Berlin: Argon, 1992), 40–41.

20. Guido Seeber, "Rauch und Nebel," *Filmtechnik* 4, no. 14 (1928): 263.

21. Brian R. Jacobson, "Fire and Failure: Studio Technology, Environmental Control, and the Politics of Progress," *Cinema Journal* 57, no. 2 (2018): 23.

22. Urban Gad, *Der Film: Seine Mittel – Seine Ziele* (Schuster & Loeffler, 1921), 48.

23. Felix Pfitzner, "Das moderne Filmatelier," *Der Film* 10, no. 39 (September 27, 1925): 52.

24. Brian R. Jacobson, *Studios before the System: Architecture, Technology, and the Emergence of Cinematic Space* (New York: Columbia University Press, 2015), 17.

25. Jacobson, *Studios before the System*, 18.

26. Gad, *Der Film*, 83.

27. See Elcott, *Artificial Darkness.*

28. Echoes of the phantasmagoric showman and early cinema trickster can be found in many films of the 1910s and 1920s. In the German context, well-known examples are the character of Scapinelli (John Gottowt) in *The Student of Prague* (1913), and Caligari (Werner Krauss) in *The Cabinet of Dr. Caligari* (1919). *Faust's* Mephisto is no exception, as the many appearances, disappearances, and transformations he instigates are usually accompanied by clouds of smoke.

29. Fulgence Marion, *The Wonders of Optics*, trans. Charles W. Quin (New York: Charles Scribner's Sons, 1869), 184.

30. Marion, *The Wonders of Optics*, 189–90. "Vitriol" likely refers to sulfuric acid; "aquafortis" is nitric acid.

31. Seeber, "Rauch und Nebel," 262.

32. Gundula Kreuzer, "Wagner-Dampf: Steam in *Der Ring des Nibelungen* and Operatic Production," *The Opera Quarterly* 27, no. 2 (2011): 180.

33. Kreuzer, "Wagner-Dampf," 185.

34. Kreuzer, "Wagner-Dampf," 185.

35. Eisner, *Murnau*, 69.

36. Eisner, *Murnau*, 166. Given the availability of unusable film stock in studios, burning celluloid for smoke effects was relatively common. Guido Seeber suggests rolling up 30–50 meters of film on the end of a cord, lighting it, and dousing it in a water container. "After a short time, if you remove the roll of film from the water," he writes, "it will begin to release an extremely powerful smoke into the open air. A yellow smoke—one not very comfortable for the lungs!—pours out. One can achieve very good effects with this technique for a short time, but when using it, one must keep in mind that it does, to a certain extent, present a danger to health." Seeber, "Rauch und Nebel," 262–63.

37. Eisner, *Murnau*, 165.

38. Rabinbach, *The Human Motor*, 62.

39. Hermann von Helmholtz, "On the Interaction of Natural Forces," *London, Edinburgh and Dublin Philosophical Magazine and Journal of Science* 11 (4th series), no. 75: Supplement (1856): 503.

40. Murnau alludes to these in *Nosferatu* as well. See Kaes, *Shell Shock Cinema*, chap. 3.

41. It is possible that the revered German dramatist Gerhart Hauptmann, who wrote verse intertitles for *Faust* that were not used in the final version of the film, saw this link as well. His title for this scene, in the voice of Mephisto, read: "Gift'gen Wrasen, faule Gase / Stoß' ich aus durch Maul und Nase" (Poisonous gases, foul flows / do I emit from mouth and nose). By the late nineteenth century, "Wrasen" was a common term for excess steam in factory production. Gerhart Hauptmann, "Worte zu Faust," in *Hätte ich das Kino! Deutsche Schriftsteller und der Stummfilm*, ed. Ludwig Greve, Margot Pehle, and Heidi Westhoff (Munich: Kösel, 1976), 266. The head of Ufa at the time deemed Hauptmann's verse too elevated for the typical moviegoer, who he claimed had the intellectual abilities of an eight-year-old. See the letter from Hans Neumann reproduced in *Hätte ich das Kino!* 265.

42. It is beyond the scope of my argument to address the links between Murnau's film and the earlier Faust texts that inspired it. Nonetheless, this chapter stands in a long tradition of writings on the Faust story that reflect on the relationship between humanity, technology, and nature. Goethe's *Faust*, in particular, has been a touchstone for ecocritical debate for decades, from Promethean readings that endorsed Faust's battle with nature as heroic, to Jost Hermand's praise for Goethe's "grüne Weltfrömmigkeit" in the early 1990s. More recent ecocritical assessments continue this debate. Kate Rigby, for instance, sees in Faust an "adversarial construction of the relationship between humanity and the natural world"—an anthropocentric, hierarchical, and patriarchal relation of mastery. For Heather Sullivan, meanwhile, who reads the play alongside other texts by Goethe in which weather figures centrally, Faust does not ascend to heaven but merely the upper atmosphere, where he will circulate among the elements. "The tragedy," she writes, "appears less a final affirmation of Faust's skills as 'modern developer' than a portrayal of elemental forces in whose flows we exist." Like

Sullivan, I emphasize the ways in which Faust is airborne, but in relation to a new historical moment in which the "elemental forces" are no longer easily identifiable as either natural or artificial. See Jost Hermand, *Im Wettlauf mit der Zeit: Anstösse zu einer ökologiebewussten Ästhetik* (Berlin: Edition Sigma, 1991); Rigby, *Topographies of the Sacred*, 211; and Heather Sullivan, "Ecocriticism, the Elements, and the Ascent/Descent into Weather in Goethe's *Faust*," *Goethe Yearbook* 17 (2010): 55. For an overview, see Axel Goodbody, *Nature, Technology and Cultural Change*, chap. 2.

43. Lekan, *Imagining the Nation in Nature*, 22.

44. Seth Peabody notes that engineers proposed to solve the pollution problem through techniques of "separation and dilution," such as tall smokestacks, on the assumption that "if the polluting element is far enough away . . . there is no cause for concern." He finds such a logic at work in *Metropolis*; in *Faust*, however, the constant return of smoke runs counter to the optimism of the engineers. Seth Peabody, "Infrastructure, Water, Ecology: Fritz Lang's *Metropolis* as Ecological Archive," *Colloquia Germanica: Internationale Zeitschrift für Germanistik* 53, no. 2–3 (2021): 261.

45. Michel Serres, "Turner Translates Carnot," in *Hermes: Literature, Science, Philosophy*, ed. Josué V. Harari and David F. Bell (Baltimore, MD: Johns Hopkins University Press, 1982), 58.

46. Mary Ann Doane, *The Emergence of Cinematic Time: Modernity, Contingency, the Archive* (Cambridge, MA: Harvard University Press, 2002), 138.

47. Doane, *The Emergence of Cinematic Time*, 115.

48. Jonathan Crary, *Suspensions of Perception: Attention, Spectacle, and Modern Culture* (Cambridge, MA: MIT Press, 1999), 13–14.

49. Kracauer's most-cited writings on distraction include the essays "Cult of Distraction: On Berlin's Picture Palaces" and "The Little Shopgirls Go to the Movies" in Siegfried Kracauer, *The Mass Ornament: Weimar Essays*, ed. and trans. Thomas Y. Levin (Cambridge, MA: Harvard University Press, 1995), 323–28 and 291–304; as well as Kracauer, *The Salaried Masses: Duty and Distraction in Weimar Germany*, trans. Quintin Hoare (London: Verso Books, 1998), especially the chapter "Shelter for the Homeless." Walter Benjamin's accounts of spectatorship and urban subjectivity in the "Kunstwerk" essay and his discussions of Baudelaire have been touchstones in contemporary discourse on modernity. See Walter Benjamin, "The Work of Art in the Age of Its Technological Reproducibility: Second Version," in *Walter Benjamin: Selected Writings*, ed. Howard Eiland and Michael William Jennings, trans. Edmund Jephcott and Harry Zohn, vol. 3, *1935–1938* (Cambridge, MA: Belknap, 2002), 101–33; and Benjamin, "On Some Motifs in Baudelaire," in *Walter Benjamin: Selected Writings*, ed. Howard Eiland and Michael William Jennings, trans. Harry Zohn, vol. 4, *1938–1940* (Cambridge, MA: Belknap, 2003), 313–55.

50. Walter Benjamin, "Das Kunstwerk im Zeitalter seiner technischen Reproduzierbarkeit (zweite Fassung)," in *Gesammelte Schriften*, ed. Rolf Tiedemann and Hermann Schweppenhäuser (Frankfurt am Main: Suhrkamp, 1991), 7.1:380.

51. The phrase "Zerstreuung der Energie" appears first in Felix Auerbach's translation of Maxwell's 1871 *Theory of Heat*. James Clerk Maxwell, *Theorie der Wärme*, trans. Felix Auerbach (Breslau: Maruschke & Berendt, 1877), viii. From Maxwell's original: "Of this energy, however, only a part is available

for the purpose of producing mechanical work, and though the energy itself is indestructible, the available part is liable to diminution by the action of certain natural processes, such as conduction and radiation of heat, friction, and viscosity. These processes, by which energy is rendered unavailable as a source of work, are classed together under the name of the Dissipation of Energy." Maxwell, *Theory of Heat* (London: Longmans, 1871), v.

52. See Jonathan Crary, *Techniques of the Observer: On Vision and Modernity in the Nineteenth Century* (Cambridge, MA: MIT Press, 1990).

53. Crary hints at this parallel briefly: "Philosopher Alfred Fouillée succinctly expressed the problem: 'Concentration of the will and of attention on anything will lead to exhaustion of attention and to a paralysis of the will.' In this sense attention had certain thermodynamic qualities by which a given force could assume more than one form." Crary, *Suspensions of Perception*, 47.

54. Scott Curtis and Andreas Killen offer detailed accounts of anxieties among medical professionals about the effects of cinema on spectators. See Curtis, *The Shape of Spectatorship: Art, Science, and Early Cinema in Germany* (New York: Columbia University Press, 2016); and Killen, *Homo Cinematicus*.

55. Elcott, *Artificial Darkness*, 88, 144.

56. Siegfried Kracauer recounts this part of the production in "Calico-World: The UFA City in Neubabelsberg," in *The Mass Ornament: Weimar Essays*, ed. and trans. Thomas Y. Levin (Cambridge, MA: Harvard University Press, 1995), 284–85.

57. Eisner, *Murnau*, 62–63.

58. Friedrich Wilhelm Murnau, ". . . der frei im Raum zu bewegende Aufnahmeapparat," in *Friedrich Wilhelm Murnau*, ed. Fred Gehler and Ullrich Kasten (Berlin: Henschel, 1990), 141.

59. See Mary Douglas, *Purity and Danger: An Analysis of Concepts of Pollution and Taboo* (New York: Praeger, 1966), 36.

60. Doane, *The Emergence of Cinematic Time*, 116.

Chapter 4

1. As Sabine Hake writes, "with its complicated spatial layout, rich history, and multiple uses, Potsdamer Platz brought out the dilemmas of urban planning in Weimar Berlin more clearly than any other place." As an example of "classic urbanity in its pure form," Potsdamer Platz fascinated Weimar-era critics and artists. Uncle Paul's inability to navigate it can be understood to represent the exclusionary effects of urban modernity as such. Hake, *Topographies of Class: Modern Architecture and Mass Society in Weimar Berlin* (Ann Arbor: University of Michigan Press, 2008), 52.

2. On "rube films," see Thomas Elsaesser, "Discipline through Diegesis: The Rube Film between 'Attractions' and 'Narrative Integration,' " in *The Cinema of Attractions Reloaded*, ed. Wanda Strauven (Amsterdam: Amsterdam University Press, 2006), 206–23.

3. Ödön Tuszkai, "Menschenökonomie: Die öffentliche Hygiene auf volkswirtschaftlicher Grundlage," *Archiv für soziale Hygiene und Demographie* 15 (1924): 4.

4. Rosemarie Garland-Thomson, *Extraordinary Bodies: Figuring Physical Disability in American Culture and Literature* (New York: Columbia University Press, 1997), 33.

5. Lennard J. Davis writes that "disability, in this and other encounters, is a disruption in the visual, auditory, or perceptual field as it relates to the power of the gaze. As such, the disruption, the rebellion of the visual, must be regulated, rationalized, contained." Davis, *Enforcing Normalcy: Disability, Deafness, and the Body* (London: Verso, 1995), 129.

6. Garland-Thomson, *Extraordinary Bodies*, 8.

7. Sally Chivers and Nicole Markotić, "Introduction," in *The Problem Body: Projecting Disability on Film*, ed. Sally Chivers and Nicole Markotić (Columbus: Ohio State University Press, 2010), 11.

8. Chivers and Markotić, "Introduction," 12.

9. Here, and in subsequent translations of quotations and names of institutions, I have used "disabled" for the German word *Krüppel*. Like its English cognate, the term was used derogatorily in everyday language and continued to carry this stigmatizing connotation in medical and legal discourse, despite the efforts of some to resignify it. On the history of the term, see Klaus-Dieter Thomann, "Der 'Krüppel': Entstehen und Verschwinden eines Kampfbegriffs," *Medizinhistorisches Journal* 27, no. 3–4 (1992): 221–71.

10. On Biesalski and the Oskar-Helene Home, see Philipp Osten, *Die Modellanstalt: Über den Aufbau einer "modernen Krüppelfürsorge," 1905–1933* (Frankfurt am Main: Mabuse-Verlag, 2012).

11. Osten reconstructs the timeline of the film's creation in "Ärzte als Filmregisseure: Ein Ufa-Kulturfilm aus dem Berliner Oskar-Helene-Heim für die Heilung und Erziehung gebrechlicher Kinder, aufgenommen in den Jahren 1910 bis 1920," *Filmblatt*, no. 37 (2008): 36–55.

12. Osten, *Die Modellanstalt*, 391–92.

13. Heather R. Perry speaks of the "invention of disability" in this moment, in which German orthopedists "argued that the nation's disabled ex-servicemen could be just as self-sufficient as able-bodied Germans, and urged their compatriots to dispense with their 'old-fashioned' attitudes regarding 'cripples.'" Perry, *Recycling the Disabled: Army, Medicine, and Modernity in WWI Germany* (Manchester, UK: Manchester University Press, 2014), 119.

14. Hau, *The Cult of Health and Beauty*, 125.

15. The image of the disabled man as a barrel organ player or beggar had been a stereotype since the nineteenth century and circulated frequently during the Weimar Republic. See Carol Poore, *Disability in Twentieth-Century German Culture* (Ann Arbor: University of Michigan Press, 2007), 7.

16. Perry, *Recycling the Disabled*, 55.

17. Boaz Neumann, "Being Prosthetic in the First World War and Weimar Germany," *Body & Society* 16, no. 3 (2010): 98.

18. Brendan Gleeson describes the social space of the industrial city in chapter 6 of his *Geographies of Disability* (London: Routledge, 1999).

19. "Lehrfilme zum Krüppelkongreß," *Film-Kurier* 2, no. 196 (September 3, 1920): n.p.

20. In the film itself, the title is posed as a question, with the title card reading "Wo wohnen alte Leute?" ("Where do old people live?"). Reference works commonly omit the question mark, however. For the sake of clarity, in this chapter I use the English title listed on the 2010 Edition Filmmuseum DVD collection of Ella Bergmann-Michel's late Weimar documentaries.

21. See Henderson, *Building Culture*, especially chapter 6, "Architectural Healing."

22. See Hans-Joachim von Kondratowitz, "Das Alter – eine Last: Die Geschichte einer Ausgrenzung, dargestellt an der institutionellen Versorgung des Alters 1880–1933," *Archiv für Sozialgeschichte* 30 (1990): 119.

23. Mart Stam and Werner Moser, "Das Altersheim der Henry und Emma Budge-Stiftung in Frankfurt a.M.," *Das neue Frankfurt* 4, no. 7 (1930): 157–76.

24. The literature is too extensive to be cited here. For an overview, see Tom Shakespeare, *Disability: The Basics* (New York: Routledge, 2018), chap. 1. Shakespeare adopts a "multi-factorial" approach that tries to account for environmental, social, and biological aspects of disability.

25. Megan R. Luke, "Our Life Together: Collective Homemaking in the Films of Ella Bergmann-Michel," *Oxford Art Journal* 40, no. 1 (2017): 43. Luke notes a similar focus in Bergmann-Michel's film *Erwerbslose kochen für Erwerbslose* (1932), about a soup kitchen initiative in the wake of the economic crisis.

26. Barbara Arneil, "Disability, Self Image, and Modern Political Theory," *Political Theory* 37, no. 2 (2009): 234.

27. On McRuer's concept of compulsory able-bodiedness, see *Crip Theory: Cultural Signs of Queerness and Disability* (New York: New York University Press, 2006), introduction.

28. See, for instance, Anton Kaes, "29 November 1923: Karl Grune's *Die Straße* Inaugurates 'Street Film,' Foreshadows Film Noir," in *A New History of German Cinema*, ed. Jennifer M. Kapczynski and Michael D. Richardson (Rochester, NY: Camden House, 2012), 128.

29. Rosemarie Garland-Thomson, "Seeing the Disabled: Visual Rhetorics of Disability in Popular Photography," in *The New Disability History*, ed. Paul K. Longmore and Lauri Umansky (New York: New York University Press, 2001), 346.

30. Hasso Spode, *Die Macht der Trunkenheit: Kultur- und Sozialgeschichte des Alkohols in Deutschland* (Opladen: Leske und Budrich, 1993), 203.

31. The sanitation advisor for the city of Wiesbaden wrote in 1913 that "alcoholism, as a widespread phenomenon and index of social conditions, is obviously closely related to the capitalist boom in the drink trade, the boom in potato and hops-growing, the increase in industrial workers, their financial compensation, and the growth of large cities, which these workers seek out and inhabit in droves; the easy and widespread availability of alcohols, and the economic freedom of a class of bar- and innkeepers led to an extraordinary increase in the consumption of spirits." B. Laquer, "Der Einfluss der sozialen Lage auf den Alkoholismus," in *Krankheit und soziale Lage*, ed. M. Mosse and Gustav Tugendreich (Munich: J. F. Lehmanns Verlag, 1913), 473.

32. Münsterberg, *Psychology and Industrial Efficiency*, 226.

33. Münsterberg, *Psychology and Industrial Efficiency*, 230.

34. Margrit Shildrick argues that "the normative construct of the self's clean and proper body is under constant threat, on the one hand from the potential of internal leakage and loss of form, and on the other, from the circulation of all those dangerous bodies—of women, of racial others, of the sick, of the monstrous— who both occupy the place of the other and serve to define by difference the

self's own parameters." Shildrick, *Embodying the Monster: Encounters with the Vulnerable Self* (London: Sage, 2002), 71.

35. Judith Ellenbürger, *Fun Works: Arbeit in der Filmkomödie von den Lumières bis Chaplin* (Paderborn: Fink, 2015), 99.

36. Sabine Kienitz, *Beschädigte Helden: Kriegsinvalidität und Körperbilder 1914–1923* (Paderborn: Ferdinand Schöningh, 2008), 21. On the articulation of masculinity with ability and Weimar discourses of rehabilitation, see also Caroline Weist, "Castration and Critique: Resisting Rehabilitation in Ernst Toller's *Hinkemann*," *Monatshefte* 112, no. 3 (2020): 367–91.

37. Anjeana Hans links gender anxiety at the workplace directly to war trauma: "A woman's employment . . . suggested an inability on the part of the man to work and pointed back to his mutilated body; at the same time, it implied not only new responsibilities but also a potentially profound loneliness for these women whose former partners had thus 'returned mutilated.' " Anjeana Hans, *Gender and the Uncanny in the Films of the Weimar Republic* (Detroit, MI: Wayne State University Press, 2014), 23.

38. Sabine Hake, "Who Gets the Last Laugh? Old Age and Generational Change in F. W. Murnau's *The Last Laugh* (1924)," in *Weimar Cinema: An Essential Guide to Classic Films of the Era*, ed. Noah Isenberg (New York: Columbia University Press, 2009), 127. Hake is not alone in using disability metaphors when discussing *The Last Laugh*—Ellenbürger compares the porter's demotion to an "amputation." *Fun Works*, 94.

39. Davis, *Enforcing Normalcy*, 141.

40. Shildrick, *Embodying the Monster*, 73.

41. The night watchman, who is also aging and whose body moves similarly to the porter's, has a job that likewise keeps him out of sight.

42. Notably, the aunt, who seems to be about the same age as the porter, is not treated in the same way. In the world of *The Last Laugh*, it seems that the vulnerable male body, no longer able to live up to the masculine ideal, is particularly intolerable.

43. On the miracle cure trend, see Martin F. Norden, *The Cinema of Isolation: A History of Physical Disability in the Movies* (New Brunswick, NJ: Rutgers University Press, 1994), 58–68. German examples include *Der Gang in die Nacht* (Murnau, 1921) and *Orlacs Hände* (Robert Wiene, 1924). In both cases, Conrad Veidt plays the miraculously cured character.

44. The old night watchman whom the porter has befriended does not move differently than he does earlier in the film, and still bears signs of slowness and weakness—presumably because he lacks the porter's newly acquired wealth. He is only allowed in the restaurant by dint of their friendship.

45. Richard Guttmann, *Die Kinomenschheit: Versuch einer prinzipiellen Analyse* (Vienna: Anzengruber, 1916), 6, 7.

46. Carrie Sandahl proposes drawing on the phenomenology of disabled experience as a generative impulse for rethinking theatrical form. Sandahl's proposal develops out of a self-aware disability politics that is absent from *The Last Laugh* or *The Street*. Sandahl, "Considering Disability: Disability Phenomenology's Role in Revolutionizing Theatrical Space," *Journal of Dramatic Theory and Criticism* 2, no. 2 (2002): 17–32.

47. Sharon L. Snyder and David T. Mitchell, *Cultural Locations of Disability* (Chicago: University of Chicago Press, 2006), 165.

48. As Inga Pollmann argues, cinema's non-normative perception, which "bends the spatiotemporality of the world as we know it," fascinated early film theorists, as well as the biologist Jakob von Uexküll, whose theory of *Umwelt* pointed to the way an organism's sense faculties structure its environment. Pollmann, *Cinematic Vitalism*, 132. In addition to animals (most famously the tick), Uexküll used examples of sensory disability to illustrate differences between *Umwelten*, suggesting that discourses on perceptual difference in this period were bound up with modernity's normalization of the body and its abilities.

49. Shildrick, *Embodying the Monster*, 71.

Chapter 5

1. See Treitel, *Eating Nature in Modern Germany*; and Dickinson, "Biopolitics, Fascism, Democracy."

2. Marc Silberman, "Political Cinema as Oppositional Practice: Weimar and Beyond," in *The German Cinema Book*, ed. Tim Bergfelder, Erica Carter, and Deniz Göktürk (London: British Film Institute, 2002), 166.

3. Richard Weber, ed., "Der Volksfilmverband: Von einer bürgerlichen Bündnisorganisation zur proletarischen Kulturorganisation," in *Film und Volk: Organ des Volksfilmverbandes* (Cologne: Gaehme, Henke, 1975), 18. On the history of the VFV, see also Bruce Murray, *Film and the German Left in the Weimar Republic: From Caligari to Kuhle Wampe* (Austin: University of Texas Press, 1990).

4. Such as *1. Mai – Weltfeiertag der Arbeiterklasse* and *Blutmai 1929*, both from 1929; and *100,000 unter roten Fahnen: Solidaritätstag der I.A.H., Bezirk Berlin-Brandenburg 1930* and *Die Todeszeche* from 1930.

5. Emil Baumann-Dittersbach, "Waldenburg (I)," *Die Weltbühne* 25, no. 33 (August 13, 1929): 239. Baumann-Dittersbach found Lania's film "good," but noted that it did not find a wide reception.

6. Baumann-Dittersbach, "Waldenburg (I)," 241.

7. See Leo Lania, "Das deutsche Hungergebiet," *Die Weltbühne* 21, no. 21 (May 26, 1925): 769.

8. See W. John Koch, *Daisy, Princess of Pless, 1873–1943: A Discovery* (Edmonton, Can.: W. J. Koch, 2003), 111.

9. "Aufzeichnung des Filmreferenten vom Reichsinnenministerium über das Zulassungsverfahren zu 'Hunger in Waldenburg,'" in *Film und revolutionäre Arbeiterbewegung in Deutschland 1918–1932*, ed. Gertraude Kühn, Karl Tümmler, and Walter Wimmer (Berlin: Henschel, 1975), 2:74.

10. See Martin Wagner, *Das sanitäre Grün der Städte: Ein Beitrag zur Freiflächentheorie* (Berlin: Carl Heymanns Verlag, 1915), 1–3.

11. Martin Wagner, "Urban Open-Space Policy," in *Metropolis Berlin, 1880–1940*, ed. Iain Boyd Whyte and David Frisby, trans. Iain Boyd Whyte (Berkeley: University of California Press, 2012), 267.

12. Matthew Gandy, *The Fabric of Space: Water, Modernity, and the Urban Imagination* (Cambridge, MA: MIT Press, 2014), 62–69.

13. Julius Moses, *Arbeitslosigkeit: Ein Problem der Volksgesundheit* (Berlin: Arthur Scholem, 1931), 13.

14. Moses, *Arbeitslosigkeit*, 6.

15. Willi Münzenberg, *Erobert den Film! Winke aus der Praxis für die Praxis proletarischer Filmpropaganda* (Berlin: Neuer Deutscher Verlag, 1925), 6.

16. On the various aid groups active in Germany after the war, see Mary Elizabeth Cox, "Hunger Games: Or How the Allied Blockade in the First World War Deprived German Children of Nutrition, and Allied Food Aid Subsequently Saved Them," *Economic History Review* 68, no. 2 (2015): 600–631.

17. Leo Lania, "Die Internationale Arbeiterhilfe," *Die Weltbühne* 19, no. 51 (December 20, 1923): 637.

18. On housing inspection, see Rath, "Wohnungsaufsicht."

19. See, for example, Gesine Asmus, "'Mißstände . . . an das Licht des Tages zerren': Zu den Photographien der Wohnungs-Enquête," in *Hinterhof, Keller und Mansarde: Einblicke in Berliner Wohnungselend 1901–1920*, ed. Gesine Asmus (Reinbek bei Hamburg: Rowohlt, 1982), 32–43.

20. Lania, "Das deutsche Hungergebiet," 770.

21. I thank Carl Gelderloos for making this connection.

22. The reviewer for the KPD paper *Die rote Fahne* found the commercial director Zelnik's emulation of *Battleship Potemkin* unconvincing in its overly theatrical staging. He did, however, praise *The Weavers'* clear depiction of conflict and exploitation. Unlike *Metropolis*, "the film does not bring any class reconciliation to the screen." Doorwien, "'Die Weber' im Film," in *Film und revolutionäre Arbeiterbewegung in Deutschland 1918–1932*, ed. Gertraude Kühn, Karl Tümmler, and Walter Wimmer (Berlin: Henschel, 1975), 1:186.

23. Willi Bredel, "Hunger in Waldenburg," in *Film und revolutionäre Arbeiterbewegung in Deutschland 1918–1932*, ed. Gertraude Kühn, Karl Tümmler, and Walter Wimmer (Berlin: Henschel, 1975), 2:91.

24. Kristin Poling, "Shantytowns and Pioneers beyond the City Wall: Berlin's Urban Frontier in the Nineteenth Century," *Central European History* 47 (2014): 258.

25. Theodore F. Rippey, "*Kuhle Wampe* and the Problem of Corporal Culture," *Cinema Journal* 47, no. 1 (2007): 13.

26. On the film's editing, see Christoph Schaub, "Labor-Movement Modernism: Proletarian Collectives between *Kuhle Wampe* and Working-Class Performance Culture," *Modernism/modernity* 25, no. 2 (2018): 327–48.

27. Since its growth in the nineteenth century, the city's edges "became places where the residents of Berlin projected both their utopian and dystopian ideas about themselves and their nation," writes Eli Rubin. "This became heightened and accentuated by the fact that Berlin was the national capital; but it also was a function of the flatness and perceived emptiness of the landscape around Berlin, which allowed Germans in Berlin to conceive of the surrounding land as a blank slate—a tabula rasa—onto which they could project their dreams and their nightmares." Rubin, "From the Grünen Wiesen to Urban Space: Berlin, Expansion, and the Longue Durée," *Central European History* 47 (2014): 236.

28. Michael Hau notes that "Paragraph 120 of the Weimar constitution declared it the responsibility of parents and the state to ensure the 'physical, mental and social fitness' (*Tüchtigkeit*) of the younger generation." Hau, "Constitutional Therapy and Clinical Racial Hygiene in Weimar and Nazi Germany," *Journal of the History of Medicine and Allied Sciences* 71, no. 2 (2015): 118.

29. On these and other sexual hygiene films, see chapter 4 of Killen, *Homo Cinematicus*. Michael Cowan traces biopolitics in the director's work in *Walter Ruttmann*, chap. 3, which includes a section on *Feind im Blut* (102–18).

30. Knowing transmission was legally prohibited by the 1918 Verordnung zur Bekämpfung der Geschlechtskrankheiten (Ordinance for Combatting Venereal Diseases), followed by a 1927 law. Thomalla and Kaufmann's 1920 film *Die Geschlechtskrankheiten und ihre Folgen* (*Venereal Diseases and Their Consequences*) warned viewers of possible imprisonment.

31. Weindling, *Health, Race and German Politics*, 339.

32. Weindling, *Health, Race and German Politics*, 444.

33. Atina Grossmann, *Reforming Sex: The German Movement for Birth Control & Abortion Reform, 1920–1950* (New York: Oxford University Press, 1995), 78–79.

34. Friedrich Wolf, *Cyankali von Friedrich Wolf: Eine Dokumentation mit dem berühmten Theaterstück gegen den "Abtreibungsparagraphen,"* ed. Emmi Wolf and Klaus Hammer (West Berlin: das europäische buch, 1986). Hans Tintner's screen adaptation of *Cyankali* starring Grete Mosheim was released in 1930.

35. Cornelie Usborne, *Cultures of Abortion in Weimar Germany* (New York: Berghahn, 2007), 58–59.

36. Usborne, *Cultures of Abortion*, 3.

37. Grossmann, *Reforming Sex*, 95.

38. Karl Kautsky, *Vermehrung und Entwicklung in Natur und Gesellschaft* (Stuttgart: J.H.W. Dietz, 1910), 266–67.

39. Karl Marx, *Capital: A Critique of Political Economy*, trans. Ben Fowkes (New York: Vintage Books, 1977), 1:786.

40. Marx, *Capital*, 1:794–97.

41. Marx, *Capital*, 1:797.

42. Hau, *Performance Anxiety*, 51.

43. W. L. Guttsman, *Workers' Culture in Weimar Germany: Between Tradition and Commitment* (New York: Berg, 1990), 136.

44. Schaub, "Labor-Movement Modernism," 338.

45. See again Cowan, *Walter Ruttmann*, chap. 3.

46. Lekan, *Imagining the Nation in Nature*, 160–61.

47. "Reichserbhofgesetz. Vom 29. September 1933," *Reichsgesetzblatt*, September 30, 1933, 685.

48. Lekan, *Imagining the Nation in Nature*, 164.

Afterword

1. Polygon staff, "What to Know about Movie Theaters and COVID-19 in Your State," *Polygon* (blog), June 10, 2021, https://www.polygon.com/2020/8/27/21402474/movie-theaters-rules-coronavirus-states-new-cdc-guidelines-covid-19.

2. In June 2021, for instance, the Berlinale Film Festival's "Summer Special" hosted events in sixteen open-air cinemas throughout Berlin. "Berlinale Summer Special: Tickets, Films and Info," *visitBerlin Blog* (blog), June 1, 2021, https://www.visitberlin.de/en/blog/berlinale-summer-special-tickets-films-and-info.

3. Owen Evans and Graeme Harper, "The Healing Power of Cinema," *Studies in European Cinema* 18, no. 1 (2021): 2.

Der letzte Mann (1924; *The Last Laugh*). Directed by Friedrich Wilhelm Murnau. Kino Classics, 2017. Blu-ray disc.

Die Frankfurter Küche (1927; *The Frankfurt Kitchen*). Directed by Paul Wolff. *Das Neue Frankfurt*. Absolut MEDIEN, 2015. DVD.

Die Stadt von Morgen: Ein Film vom Städtebau (1930; *The City of Tomorrow: An Urban Planning Film*). Directed by Maximilian von Goldbeck and Erich Kotzer. *Die moderne Stadt*. Absolut MEDIEN, 2015. DVD.

Die Straße (1923; *The Street*). Directed by Karl Grune.

Faust (1926). Directed by Friedrich Wilhelm Murnau. Kino Classics, 2015. Blu-ray disc.

Hunger in Waldenburg, or *Um's tägliche Brot* (1929; *Hunger in Waldenburg*). Directed by Phil Jutzi. Absolut MEDIEN, 2018. DVD.

Im Strudel des Verkehrs: Ein Film für Jedermann (1925; *In the Vortex of Traffic: A Film for Everyone*). Directed by Leo Peukert. *Die Stadt der Millionen*. Absolut MEDIEN, 2014. DVD.

Krüppelnot und Krüppelhilfe (1920; *The Plight and Care of the Disabled*). Directed by Nicholas Kaufmann. 35mm.

Kuhle Wampe oder Wem gehört die Welt? (1932; *Kuhle Wampe, or Who Owns the World?*). Directed by Slatan Dudow. DEFA Film Library, 2008. DVD.

Wie bleibe ich gesund? 1. Teil: Hygiene des häuslichen Lebens (1922; *How Do I Stay Healthy? Part 1: Hygiene of Domestic Life*). Directed by Curt Thomalla and Nicholas Kaufmann. 35mm.

Wo wohnen alte Leute (1932; *Where Old People Live*). Directed by Ella Bergmann-Michel. *Ella Bergmann-Michel: Dokumentarische Filme 1931–1933*. Edition Filmmuseum, 2010. DVD.

Zeitprobleme: Wie der Arbeiter wohnt (1930; *How the Berlin Worker Lives*). Directed by Slatan Dudow. *Kuhle Wampe, or Who Owns the World?* DEFA Film Library, 2008. DVD.

WORKS CITED

Abel, Rudolf. "Die nächsten Aufgaben der öffentlichen Gesundheitspflege." *Öffentliche Gesundheitspflege* 51, no. 1 (1919): 1–10.

Albera, François, and Maria Tortajada, eds. *Cine-Dispositives: Essays in Epistemology across Media.* Amsterdam: Amsterdam University Press, 2015.

———, eds. *Cinema Beyond Film: Media Epistemology in the Modern Era.* Amsterdam: Amsterdam University Press, 2010.

———. "Introduction to an Epistemology of Viewing and Listening Dispositives." In *Cinema beyond Film: Media Epistemology in the Modern Era*, edited by François Albera and Maria Tortajada, 9–22. Amsterdam: Amsterdam University Press, 2010.

Arneil, Barbara. "Disability, Self Image, and Modern Political Theory." *Political Theory* 37, no. 2 (2009): 218–42.

Ascher, Louis, and Ernst Kobbert. "Verhütung von Rauch und Ruß in den Städten." In *Weyl's Handbuch der Hygiene*, 2nd ed., edited by C. Fraenken, vol. 2, *Städtereinigung*, 25–72. Leipzig: J. A. Barth, 1914.

Asmus, Gesine. "'Mißstände . . . an das Licht des Tages zerren': Zu den Photographien der Wohnungs-Enquête." In *Hinterhof, Keller und Mansarde: Einblicke in Berliner Wohnungselend 1901–1920*, edited by Gesine Asmus, 32–43. Reinbek bei Hamburg: Rowohlt, 1982.

"Aufzeichnung des Filmreferenten vom Reichsinnenministerium über das Zulassungsverfahren zu 'Hunger in Waldenburg.'" In *Film und revolutionäre Arbeiterbewegung in Deutschland 1918–1932*, edited by Gertraude Kühn, Karl Tümmler, and Walter Wimmer, 2:74-76. Berlin: Henschel, 1975.

Barnard, Timothy. "The 'Machine Operator': Deus Ex Machina of the Storefront Cinema." *Framework* 43, no. 1 (2002): 40–75.

Basile, Salvatore. *Cool: How Air Conditioning Changed Everything.* New York: Fordham University Press, 2014.

Baudry, Jean-Louis. "The Apparatus." Translated by Jean Andrews and Bertrand Augst. *Camera Obscura* 1, no. 1 (1976): 104–26.

Baumann-Dittersbach, Emil. "Waldenburg (I)." *Die Weltbühne* 25, no. 33 (August 13, 1929): 239–44.

Behne, Adolf. *Neues Wohnen – Neues Bauen.* Leipzig: Hesse & Becker, 1927.

Benjamin, Walter. "Das Kunstwerk im Zeitalter seiner technischen Reproduzierbarkeit (zweite Fassung)." In *Gesammelte Schriften*, edited by Rolf Tiedemann and Hermann Schweppenhäuser, 7.1:350–84. Frankfurt am Main: Suhrkamp, 1991.

———. "On Some Motifs in Baudelaire." In *Walter Benjamin: Selected Writings*, edited by Howard Eiland and Michael William Jennings, translated by Harry Zohn, vol. 4, *1938–1940*, 313–55. Cambridge, MA: Belknap, 2003.

———. "The Work of Art in the Age of Its Technological Reproducibility: Second Version." In *Walter Benjamin: Selected Writings*, edited by Howard Eiland and Michael William Jennings, translated by Edmund Jephcott and Harry Zohn, vol. 3, *1935–1938*, 101–33. Cambridge, MA: Belknap, 2002.

"Bericht über das Ergebnis der Kinobesuche in Cöln durch Beauftragte von der Volksgemeinschaft zur Wahrung von Anstand und guter Sitte." In *Verhandlungen der verfassungsgebenden Deutschen Nationalversammlung*, vol. 341: 2511–12. Berlin: Julius Sittenfeld, 1920.

"Bericht über die Verwaltung der Feuerwehr." Verwaltungsbericht des Magistrats zu Berlin für das Etatsjahr 1908. Berlin: Magistrat zu Berlin, 1910.

"Bericht über die Verwaltung der Feuerwehr." Verwaltungsbericht des Magistrats zu Berlin für das Etatsjahr 1909. Berlin: Magistrat zu Berlin, 1911.

"Bericht über die Verwaltung der Feuerwehr." Verwaltungsbericht des Magistrats zu Berlin für das Etatsjahr 1912. Berlin: Magistrat zu Berlin, 1914.

Bignens, Christoph. *Kinos: Architektur als Marketing*. Zürich: Hans Rohr, 1988.

Blankenship, Janelle. "'Film-Symphonie vom Leben und Sterben der Blumen': Plant Rhythm and Time-Lapse Vision in *Das Blumenwunder*." *Intermédialités*, no. 16 (2010): 83–103.

Bock, Hans-Michael, and Michael Töteberg, eds. *Das Ufa-Buch: Kunst und Krisen, Stars und Regisseure, Wirtschaft und Politik: Die internationale Geschichte von Deutschlands grösstem Film-Konzern*. Frankfurt am Main: Zweitausendeins, 1992.

Boeger, Peter. *Architektur der Lichtspieltheater in Berlin: Bauten und Projekte 1919–1930*. Berlin: Arenhövel, 1993.

Bredel, Willi. "Hunger in Waldenburg." In *Film und revolutionäre Arbeiterbewegung in Deutschland 1918–1932*, edited by Gertraude Kühn, Karl Tümmler, and Walter Wimmer, 2:90–92. Berlin: Henschel, 1975.

Cahill, James Leo. "How It Feels to Be Run Over: Early Film Accidents." *Discourse* 30, no. 3 (2008): 289–316.

Cartwright, Lisa. *Screening the Body: Tracing Medicine's Visual Culture*. Minneapolis: University of Minnesota Press, 1995.

Chivers, Sally, and Nicole Markotić. "Introduction." In *The Problem Body: Projecting Disability on Film*, edited by Sally Chivers and Nicole Markotić, 1–21. Columbus: Ohio State University Press, 2010.

Cioc, Mark. "The Impact of the Coal Age on the German Environment: A Review of the Historical Literature." *Environment and History* 4, no. 1 (1998): 105–24.

Cowan, Michael. *Walter Ruttmann and the Cinema of Multiplicity: Avant-Garde – Advertising – Modernity*. Amsterdam: Amsterdam University Press, 2014.

Cox, Mary Elizabeth. "Hunger Games: Or How the Allied Blockade in the First World War Deprived German Children of Nutrition, and Allied Food Aid Subsequently Saved Them." *Economic History Review* 68, no. 2 (2015): 600–631.

Crary, Jonathan. *Suspensions of Perception: Attention, Spectacle, and Modern Culture*. Cambridge, MA: MIT Press, 1999.

———. *Techniques of the Observer: On Vision and Modernity in the Nineteenth Century*. Cambridge, MA: MIT Press, 1990.

Crook, Tom. *Governing Systems: Modernity and the Making of Public Health in England, 1830–1910*. Berkeley: University of California Press, 2016.

Curtis, Scott. *The Shape of Spectatorship: Art, Science, and Early Cinema in Germany*. New York: Columbia University Press, 2016.

Davis, Lennard J. *Enforcing Normalcy: Disability, Deafness, and the Body*. London: Verso, 1995.

Der Preussische Minister für Volkswohlfahrt. "Erlass, betreffend die Überwachung der Lichtspieltheater." *Zentralblatt der Bauverwaltung* 43, no. 33/34 (April 25, 1923): 204.

———. *Vorschriften über die Anlage und Einrichtung von Lichtspieltheatern sowie für die Sicherheit bei Lichtspielvorführungen*. Berlin: Carl Heymanns Verlag, 1926.

Dickinson, Edward Ross. "Biopolitics, Fascism, Democracy: Some Reflections on Our Discourse about 'Modernity.'" *Central European History* 37, no. 1 (2004): 1–48.

Doane, Mary Ann. *The Emergence of Cinematic Time: Modernity, Contingency, the Archive*. Cambridge, MA: Harvard University Press, 2002.

Doorwien. "'Die Weber' im Film." In *Film und revolutionäre Arbeiterbewegung in Deutschland 1918–1932*, edited by Gertraude Kühn, Karl Tümmler, and Walter Wimmer, 1:186–87. Berlin: Henschel, 1975.

Douglas, Mary. *Purity and Danger: An Analysis of Concepts of Pollution and Taboo*. New York: Praeger, 1966.

Drigalski, Wilhelm von. "Deutsche Jugendnot." *Öffentliche Gesundheitspflege* 6, no. 11 (1921): 361–88.

Eckart, Wolfgang U. "Kino, Hunger, 'Rassenschmach': Exemplarische Dokumentar- und Propagandafilme aus dem Nachkriegsdeutschland, 1919–1924." In *Das Vorprogramm: Lehrfilm / Gebrauchsfilm / Propagandafilm / unveröffentlichter Film in Kinos und Archiven am Oberrhein 1900–1970*, edited by Philipp Osten, Gabriele Moser, Christian Bonah, Alexandre Sumpf, Tricia Close-Koenig, and Joël Danet, 315–36. Heidelberg: A25 Rhinfilm, 2015.

Effenberger, Gustav. *Die Welt in Flammen: Eine Geschichte der großen und interessanten Brände aller Jahrhunderte*. Hannover: Rechts-, Staats- und Sozialwissenschaftlicher Verlag, 1913.

Eghigian, Greg. *Making Security Social: Disability, Insurance, and the Birth of the Social Entitlement State in Germany*. Ann Arbor: University of Michigan Press, 2000.

Eisner, Lotte H. *Murnau*. Berkeley: University of California Press, 1973.

Ekici, Didem. "The Physiology of the House: Modern Architecture and the Science of Hygiene." In *Healing Spaces, Modern Architecture, and the Body*, edited by Sarah Schrank and Didem Ekici, 47–64. London: Routledge, 2017.

Elcott, Noam M. *Artificial Darkness: An Obscure History of Modern Art and Media*. Chicago: University of Chicago Press, 2016.

Ellenbürger, Judith. *Fun Works: Arbeit in der Filmkomödie von den Lumières bis Chaplin*. Paderborn: Fink, 2015.

Elsaesser, Thomas. "Die Kamera in der Küche: Werben für das neue Wohnen." In *Umwidmungen: Architektonische und kinematographische Räume*, edited by Gertrud Koch, 36–56. Berlin: Vorwerk 8, 2005.

———. "Die Stadt von morgen: Filme zum Bauen und Wohnen." In *Geschichte des dokumentarischen Films in Deutschland*, edited by Peter Zimmermann, vol. 2, *Weimarer Republik (1918–1933)*, edited by Klaus Kreimeier, Antje Ehmann, and Jeanpaul Goergen, 381–409. Stuttgart: Reclam, 2005.

———. "Discipline through Diegesis: The Rube Film between 'Attractions' and 'Narrative Integration.'" In *The Cinema of Attractions Reloaded*, edited by Wanda Strauven, 206–23. Amsterdam: Amsterdam University Press, 2006.

Engels, Friedrich. *Dialectics of Nature*. Edited and translated by Clemens Dutt. New York: International Publishers, 1960.

Etzemüller, Thomas. "Social Engineering als Verhaltenslehre des kühlen Kopfes. Eine einleitende Skizze." In *Die Ordnung der Moderne: Social Engineering im 20. Jahrhundert*, edited by Thomas Etzemüller, 11–39. Bielefeld: transcript, 2009.

Evans, Owen, and Graeme Harper. "The Healing Power of Cinema." *Studies in European Cinema* 18, no. 1 (2021): 1–3.

Fack, Dietmar. *Automobil, Verkehr und Erziehung: Motorisierung und Sozialisation zwischen Beschleunigung und Anpassung 1885–1945*. Leverkusen: Leske + Budrich, 2000.

Fay, Jennifer. *Inhospitable World: Cinema in the Time of the Anthropocene*. Oxford: Oxford University Press, 2018.

Forty, Adrian. *Objects of Desire*. New York: Pantheon Books, 1986.

Foucault, Michel. "The Confession of the Flesh." In *Power/Knowledge: Selected Interviews and Other Writings 1972–1977*, edited by Colin Gordon, translated by Colin Gordon, Leo Marshall, John Mepham, and Kate Soper, 194–228. New York: Pantheon Books, 1980.

———. *The History of Sexuality*. Vol. 1, *An Introduction*, translated by Robert Hurley. New York: Pantheon Books, 1978.

———. *Security, Territory, Population: Lectures at the Collège de France, 1977–78*. Translated by Graham Burchell. New York: Palgrave Macmillan, 2007.

Frederick, Christine. *Household Engineering: Scientific Management in the Home*. Chicago: American School of Home Economics, 1923.

Gad, Urban. *Der Film: Seine Mittel – seine Ziele*. Schuster & Loeffler, 1921.

Gandy, Matthew. *The Fabric of Space: Water, Modernity, and the Urban Imagination*. Cambridge, MA: MIT Press, 2014.

———. "Rethinking Urban Metabolism: Water, Space and the Modern City." *City* 8, no. 3 (2004): 363–79.

Garland-Thomson, Rosemarie. *Extraordinary Bodies: Figuring Physical Disability in American Culture and Literature*. New York: Columbia University Press, 1997.

———. "Seeing the Disabled: Visual Rhetorics of Disability in Popular Photography." In *The New Disability History*, edited by Paul K. Longmore and Lauri Umansky, 335–74. New York: New York University Press, 2001.

Garncarz, Joseph. "Perceptual Environments for Films: The Development of Cinema in Germany, 1895–1914." In *Film 1900: Technology, Perception, Culture*, edited by Klaus Kreimeier and Annemone Ligensa, 141–50. New Barnet, UK: John Libbey, 2009.

Gärtner, August. *Leitfaden der Hygiene für Studierende, Ärtze, Architekten, Ingenieure und Verwaltungsbeamte*. 8th ed. Berlin: S. Karger, 1920.

Gaupp, Robert. "The Dangers of Cinema." In *The Promise of Cinema: German Film Theory, 1907–1933*, edited by Anton Kaes, Nicholas Baer, and Michael

Cowan, translated by Eric Ames, 223–26. Berkeley: University of California Press, 2016.

Gleeson, Brendan. *Geographies of Disability*. London: Routledge, 1999.

Goergen, Jeanpaul. "Werben für eine neue Stadt: Stadtplanung und Dokumentarfilm im Wiederaufbau der Bundesrepublik." In *Architektur im Film: Korrespondenzen zwischen Film, Architekturgeschichte und Architekturtheorie*, edited by Christiane Keim and Barbara Schrödl, 115–46. Bielefeld: transcript, 2015.

Goldbeck, Maximilian von, and Erich Kotzer. "Die Stadt von Morgen: Ein Film vom Städtebau." *Städtebau 25*, no. 12 (1930): 237–39.

Goodbody, Axel. *Nature, Technology and Cultural Change in Twentieth-Century German Literature: The Challenge of Ecocriticism*. Basingstoke, UK: Palgrave Macmillan, 2007.

Greve, Ludwig, Margot Pehle, and Heidi Westhoff, eds. *Hätte ich das Kino! Deutsche Schriftsteller und der Stummfilm*. Munich: Kösel, 1976.

Grossmann, Atina. *Reforming Sex: The German Movement for Birth Control and Abortion Reform, 1920–1950*. New York: Oxford University Press, 1995.

Guerin, Frances. *A Culture of Light: Cinema and Technology in 1920s Germany*. Minneapolis: University of Minnesota Press, 2005.

Gunning, Tom. "An Aesthetic of Astonishment: Early Film and the (In)Credulous Spectator." In *Viewing Positions: Ways of Seeing Film*, edited by Linda Williams, 114–33. New Brunswick, NJ: Rutgers University Press, 1994.

———. "The Cinema of Attractions: Early Film, Its Spectator and the Avant-Garde." In *Early Cinema: Space—Frame—Narrative*, edited by Thomas Elsaesser, 56–62. London: British Film Institute, 1990.

———. "'Primitive' Cinema—A Frame-up? Or The Trick's on Us." *Cinema Journal 28*, no. 2 (1989): 3–12.

Guttmann, Richard. *Die Kinomenschheit: Versuch einer prinzipiellen Analyse*. Vienna: Anzengruber, 1916.

Guttsman, W. L. *Workers' Culture in Weimar Germany: Between Tradition and Commitment*. New York: Berg, 1990.

Haemmerling, Konrad. *Sittengeschichte des Kinos*. Dresden: P. Aretz, 1926.

Hake, Sabine. *The Cinema's Third Machine: Writing on Film in Germany, 1907–1933*. Lincoln: University of Nebraska Press, 1993.

———. *Topographies of Class: Modern Architecture and Mass Society in Weimar Berlin*. Ann Arbor: University of Michigan Press, 2008.

———. "Who Gets the Last Laugh? Old Age and Generational Change in F. W. Murnau's *The Last Laugh* (1924)." In *Weimar Cinema: An Essential Guide to Classic Films of the Era*, edited by Noah Isenberg, 115–33. New York: Columbia University Press, 2009.

Hall, Sara. "Open Your Eyes! Public Ordering and the Policing Gaze." *Modernism/modernity 15*, no. 2 (2008): 277–96.

Halle, Randall. *The Europeanization of Cinema: Interzones and Imaginative Communities*. Urbana: University of Illinois Press, 2014.

Hans, Anjeana. *Gender and the Uncanny in the Films of the Weimar Republic*. Detroit, MI: Wayne State University Press, 2014.

Hardy, Anne I. *Ärtze, Ingenieure und städtische Gesundheit: Medizinische Theorien in der Hygienebewegung des 19. Jahrhunderts*. Frankfurt: Campus Verlag, 2005.

Hau, Michael. "Constitutional Therapy and Clinical Racial Hygiene in Weimar and Nazi Germany." *Journal of the History of Medicine and Allied Sciences* 71, no. 2 (2015): 115–43.

———. *The Cult of Health and Beauty in Germany: A Social History, 1890–1930*. Chicago: University of Chicago Press, 2003.

———. *Performance Anxiety: Sport and Work in Germany from the Empire to Nazism*. Toronto: University of Toronto Press, 2017.

Hauptmann, Gerhart. "Worte zu Faust." In *Hätte ich das Kino! Deutsche Schriftsteller und der Stummfilm*, edited by Ludwig Greve, Margot Pehle, and Heidi Westhoff, 265–66. Munich: Kösel, 1976.

Hediger, Vinzenz, and Patrick Vonderau, eds. *Films That Work: Industrial Film and the Productivity of Media*. Amsterdam: Amsterdam University Press, 2009.

Heim, and Nier. "Die Bekämpfung des Staubes im Hause und auf der Strasse." *Deutsche Vierteljahrsschrift für öffentliche Gesundheitspflege* 39, no. 1 (1907): 107–57.

Helmholtz, Hermann von. "On the Interaction of Natural Forces." *London, Edinburgh and Dublin Philosophical Magazine and Journal of Science* 11 (4th series), no. 75: Supplement (1856): 489–518.

Henderson, Susan R. *Building Culture: Ernst May and the New Frankfurt Initiative, 1926–1931*. New York: Peter Lang, 2013.

Hermand, Jost. *Grüne Utopien in Deutschland: Zur Geschichte des ökologischen Bewusstseins*. Frankfurt am Main: Fischer Taschenbuch Verlag, 1991.

———. *Im Wettlauf mit der Zeit: Anstösse zu einer ökologiebewussten Ästhetik*. Berlin: Edition Sigma, 1991.

Heynen, Robert. *Degeneration and Revolution: Radical Cultural Politics and the Body in Weimar Germany*. Leiden: Brill, 2015.

Holland, Lotar. "Universum." *Filmtechnik* 4, no. 24 (November 24, 1928): 468–70.

Hoormann, Anne. *Lichtspiele: Zur Medienreflexion der Avantgarde in der Weimarer Republik*. Munich: Fink, 2003.

Horn, Eva. "Air Conditioning: Die Zähmung des Klimas als Projekt der Moderne." *Sinn und Form* 67, no. 4 (2015): 455–62.

Hueppe, Ferdinand. "Wohnung und Gesundheit." In *Weyl's Handbuch der Hygiene*, 2nd ed., edited by C. Fraenken, vol. 4, *Bau- und Wohnungshygiene*, 3–51. Leipzig: J. A. Barth, 1914.

International Hygiene Exhibition. Guide. Dresden, 1911.

Jacobson, Brian R. "Fire and Failure: Studio Technology, Environmental Control, and the Politics of Progress." *Cinema Journal* 57, no. 2 (2018): 22–43.

———. "Introduction: Studio Perspectives." In *In the Studio: Visual Creation and Its Material Environments*, 1–15. Berkeley: University of California Press, 2020.

———. *Studios before the System: Architecture, Technology, and the Emergence of Cinematic Space*. New York: Columbia University Press, 2015.

Jakob, Hanns. "Form und Hygiene des Filmtheaterbaues." *Filmtechnik* 2, no. 26 (December 25, 1926): 512–13.

Kade. "Zur Frage der Verkehrsbeschulung der Jugend." *Die Polizei* 24 (1927): 593–94.

Kaes, Anton. "29 November 1923: Karl Grune's *Die Straße* Inaugurates 'Street Film,' Foreshadows Film Noir." In *A New History of German Cinema*, edited by Jennifer M. Kapczynski and Michael D. Richardson, 124–28. Rochester, NY: Camden House, 2012.

———. *Shell Shock Cinema: Weimar Culture and the Wounds of War*. Princeton, NJ: Princeton University Press, 2009.

Kautsky, Karl. *Vermehrung und Entwicklung in Natur und Gesellschaft*. Stuttgart: J. H. W. Dietz, 1910.

Keim, Christiane. "'Neue Welten der Sichtbarkeit schaffen': Der Lehrfilm 'Die Frankfurter Küche' als Teil der medialen Repräsentation des 'Neuen Frankfurt' in den 1920er-Jahren." In *Architektur im Film: Korrespondenzen zwischen Film, Architekturgeschichte und Architekturtheorie*, edited by Christiane Keim and Barbara Schrödl, 69–89. Bielefeld: transcript, 2015.

Kessler, Frank. "The Cinema of Attractions as Dispositif." In *The Cinema of Attractions Reloaded*, edited by Wanda Strauven, 57–69. Amsterdam: Amsterdam University Press, 2006.

Kienitz, Sabine. *Beschädigte Helden: Kriegsinvalidität und Körperbilder 1914–1923*. Paderborn: Ferdinand Schöningh, 2008.

Killen, Andreas. "Accidents Happen: The Industrial Accident in Interwar Germany." In *Catastrophes: A History and Theory of an Operative Concept*, edited by Nitzan Lebovic and Andreas Killen, 75–92. Berlin: De Gruyter, 2014.

———. *Homo Cinematicus: Science, Motion Pictures, and the Making of Modern Germany*. Philadelphia: University of Pennsylvania Press, 2017.

Koch, W. John. *Daisy, Princess of Pless, 1873–1943: A Discovery*. Edmonton, Can.: W. J. Koch, 2003.

Kohlschütter, Volkmar. *Nebel, Rauch und Staub*. Bern: Akadem. Buchhandl. v. Drechsel, 1918.

Kondratowitz, Hans-Joachim von. "Das Alter – eine Last: Die Geschichte einer Ausgrenzung, dargestellt an der institutionellen Versorgung des Alters 1880–1933." *Archiv für Sozialgeschichte* 30 (1990): 105–44.

Kossowsky, Alex. "Das Filmgelände der Decla-Bioscop." In *Babelsberg: Ein Filmstudio 1912–1992*, edited by Wolfgang Jacobsen, 33–43. Berlin: Argon, 1992.

Kracauer, Siegfried. "Calico-World: The UFA City in Neubabelsberg." In *The Mass Ornament: Weimar Essays*, edited and translated by Thomas Y. Levin, 281–88. Cambridge, MA: Harvard University Press, 1995.

———. *The Mass Ornament: Weimar Essays*. Edited and translated by Thomas Y. Levin. Cambridge, MA: Harvard University Press, 1995.

———. *The Salaried Masses: Duty and Distraction in Weimar Germany*. Translated by Quintin Hoare. London: Verso Books, 1998.

Kraszna-Krausz, Andor. "Das moderne Lichtspielhaus." *Filmtechnik* 2, no. 26 (December 25, 1926): 509.

———. "Faust." *Filmtechnik*, no. 22 (1926): 443–45.

Kreimeier, Klaus. "Ein deutsches Paradigma: Die Kulturabteilung der Ufa." In *Geschichte des dokumentarischen Films in Deutschland*, edited by Peter Zimmermann, vol. 2, *Weimarer Republik (1918–1933)*, edited by Klaus Kreimeier, Antje Ehmann, and Jeanpaul Goergen, 67–86. Stuttgart: Reclam, 2005.

———. "Komplex-starr: Semiologie des Kulturfilms." In *Geschichte des dokumentarischen Films in Deutschland*, edited by Peter Zimmermann, vol. 2, *Weimarer Republik (1918–1933)*, edited by Klaus Kreimeier, Antje Ehmann, and Jeanpaul Goergen, 87–119. Stuttgart: Reclam, 2005.

Kreuzer, Gundula. "Wagner-Dampf: Steam in *Der Ring des Nibelungen* and Operatic Production." *The Opera Quarterly* 27, no. 2 (2011): 179–218.

Krüger, K. "Zeitlupe und Zeitraffer." In *Das Kulturfilmbuch*, edited by Edgar Beyfuss and Alexander Kossowsky, 186–93. Berlin: Carl P. Chryselius'scher Verlag, 1924.

Labisch, Alfons. "Doctors, Workers and the Scientific Cosmology of the Industrial World: The Social Construction of 'Health' and the 'Homo Hygienicus.'" *Journal of Contemporary History* 20 (1985): 599–615.

———. *Homo Hygienicus: Gesundheit und Medizin in der Neuzeit*. Frankfurt: Campus Verlag, 1992.

Lachmund, Jens. *Greening Berlin: The Co-Production of Science, Politics, and Urban Nature*. Cambridge, MA: MIT Press, 2013.

Lania, Leo. "Das deutsche Hungergebiet." *Die Weltbühne* 21, no. 21 (May 26, 1925): 768–70.

———. "Die Internationale Arbeiterhilfe." *Die Weltbühne* 19, no. 51 (December 20, 1923): 637–38.

Laquer, B. "Der Einfluss der sozialen Lage auf den Alkoholismus." In *Krankheit und soziale Lage*, edited by M. Mosse and Gustav Tugendreich, 473–95. Munich: J. F. Lehmanns Verlag, 1913.

Laukötter, Anja. *Sex-richtig! Körperpolitik und Gefühlserziehung im Kino des 20. Jahrhunderts*. Göttingen: Wallstein, 2021.

———. "Wissen als Animation: Zur Transformation der Anschaulichkeit im Gesundheitsaufklärungsfilm." *montage AV: Zeitschrift für Theorie und Geschichte audiovisueller Kommunikation* 22, no. 2 (2013): 79–96.

Lebovic, Nitzan, and Andreas Killen. "Introduction." In *Catastrophes: A History and Theory of an Operative Concept*, edited by Nitzan Lebovic and Andreas Killen, 1–14. Berlin: De Gruyter, 2014.

Leendertz, Ariane. "Ordnung, Ausgleich, Harmonie: Koordinaten raumplanerischen Denkens in Deutschland, 1920 bis 1970." In *Die Ordnung der Moderne: Social Engineering im 20. Jahrhundert*, edited by Thomas Etzemüller, 129–50. Bielefeld: transcript, 2009.

Lees, Andrew. *Cities, Sin, and Social Reform in Imperial Germany*. Ann Arbor: University of Michigan Press, 2002.

Lefebvre, Martin, and André Gaudreault, eds. "Cinema & Technology." Special issue, *Recherches Sémiotiques / Semiotic Inquiry* 31, no. 1–2–3 (2011).

Lehmann, K. B. *Arbeits- und Gewerbehygiene*, vol. 4.2 of *Handbuch der Hygiene*, edited by Max Rubner, M. v. Gruber, and M. Ficker. Leipzig: S. Hirzel, 1919.

"Lehrfilme zum Krüppelkongreß." *Film-Kurier* 2, no. 196 (September 3, 1920): n.p.

Leitfaden für Kinooperateure und Kinobesitzer. 4th ed. Leipzig: Otto Klemm, 1919.

Lekan, Thomas M. *Imagining the Nation in Nature: Landscape Preservation and German Identity, 1885–1945*. Cambridge, MA: Harvard University Press, 2004.

Ligensa, Annemone. "Triangulating a Turn: Film 1900 as Technology, Perception and Culture." In *Film 1900: Technology, Perception, Culture*, edited by Klaus Kreimeier and Annemone Ligensa, 1–7. New Barnet, UK: John Libbey, 2009.

Lorenz, Friedrich H. "Soziale Tuberkulosebekämpfung." *Öffentliche Gesundheitspflege* 52, no. 2 (1920): 43–54.

Luke, Megan R. "Our Life Together: Collective Homemaking in the Films of Ella Bergmann-Michel." *Oxford Art Journal* 40, no. 1 (2017): 27–48.

Maase, Kaspar. "Massenkunst und Volkserziehung: Die Regulierung von Film und Kino im deutschen Kaiserreich." *Archiv für Sozialgeschichte* 41 (2001): 39–77.

Marion, Fulgence. *The Wonders of Optics*. Translated by Charles W. Quin. New York: Charles Scribner's Sons, 1869.

Marx, Karl. *Capital: A Critique of Political Economy*. Vol. 1, translated by Ben Fowkes. New York: Vintage Books, 1977.

Maxwell, James Clerk. *Theorie der Wärme*. Translated by Felix Auerbach. Breslau: Maruschke & Berendt, 1877.

———. *Theory of Heat*. London: Longmans, 1871.

McNeill, John Robert. *Something New under the Sun: An Environmental History of the Twentieth-Century World*. New York: W. W. Norton, 2000.

McRuer, Robert. *Crip Theory: Cultural Signs of Queerness and Disability*. New York: New York University Press, 2006.

Michels, Eckard. "Die 'Spanische Grippe' 1918/19: Verlauf, Folgen und Deutungen in Deutschland im Kontext des Ersten Weltkriegs." *Vierteljahrshefte für Zeitgeschichte* 58, no. 1 (2010): 1–33.

Moser, Gabriele, and Jochen Fleischhacker. "People's Health and Nation's Body: The Modernisation of Statistics, Demography and Social Hygiene in the Weimar Republic." In *The Politics of the Healthy Life: An International Perspective*, edited by Esteban Rodríguez-Ocaña, 151–79. Sheffield, UK: European Association for the History of Medicine and Health Publications, 2002.

Moses, Julius. *Arbeitslosigkeit: Ein Problem der Volksgesundheit*. Berlin: Arthur Scholem, 1931.

Müller, Eckhard. "Entwicklung des baulichen Brandschutzes bei Versammlungsstätten." *Schadenprisma* 6, no. 4 (1977): 53–56.

Mumford, Lewis. *Technics and Civilization*. New York: Harcourt, Brace, 1934.

Münsterberg, Hugo. *Psychology and Industrial Efficiency*. Boston: Houghton Mifflin, 1913.

Münzenberg, Willi. *Erobert den Film! Winke aus der Praxis für die Praxis proletarischer Filmpropaganda*. Berlin: Neuer Deutscher Verlag, 1925.

Murnau, Friedrich Wilhelm. ". . . der frei im Raum zu bewegende Aufnahmeapparat." In *Friedrich Wilhelm Murnau*, edited by Fred Gehler and Ullrich Kasten, 141. Berlin: Henschel, 1990.

Murray, Bruce. *Film and the German Left in the Weimar Republic: From Caligari to Kuhle Wampe*. Austin: University of Texas Press, 1990.

Neumann, Boaz. "Being Prosthetic in the First World War and Weimar Germany." *Body & Society* 16, no. 3 (2010): 96–126.

Noack, Victor. *Der Kino: Etwas über sein Wesen und seine Bedeutung*. Gautzsch b. Leipzig: Felix Dietrich, 1913.

———. "'Schlafburschen' und 'Möblierte.'" *Sexual-Probleme*, no. 6 (1912): 384–98.

———. *Wohnungsnot und Mieterelend: Ein Erbstück des alten Staates*. Berlin: Ernst Wasmuth, 1918.

Norden, Martin F. *The Cinema of Isolation: A History of Physical Disability in the Movies.* New Brunswick, NJ: Rutgers University Press, 1994.

Osten, Philipp. "Ärzte als Filmregisseure: Ein Ufa-Kulturfilm aus dem Berliner Oskar-Helene-Heim für die Heilung und Erziehung gebrechlicher Kinder, aufgenommen in den Jahren 1910 bis 1920." *Filmblatt*, no. 37 (2008): 36–55.

————. *Die Modellanstalt: Über den Aufbau einer "modernen Krüppelfürsorge," 1905–1933.* Frankfurt am Main: Mabuse-Verlag, 2012.

Ostherr, Kirsten. *Cinematic Prophylaxis: Globalization and Contagion in the Discourse of World Health.* Durham, NC: Duke University Press, 2005.

Ostwald, Wilhelm. *Energetische Grundlagen der Kulturwissenschaft.* Leipzig: Dr. Werner Klinkhardt, 1909.

Otter, Chris. "Making Liberalism Durable: Vision and Civility in the Late Victorian City." *Social History* 27, no. 1 (2002): 1–15.

————. *The Victorian Eye: A Political History of Light and Vision in Britain, 1800–1910.* Chicago: University of Chicago Press, 2008.

Peabody, Seth. "Environmental Fantasies: Mountains, Cities, and Heimat in Weimar Cinema." PhD diss., Harvard University, 2015. https://dash.harvard.edu/handle/1/17467382.

————. "Infrastructure, Water, Ecology: Fritz Lang's *Metropolis* as Ecological Archive." *Colloquia Germanica: Internationale Zeitschrift für Germanistik* 53, no. 2–3 (2021): 249–67.

Perry, Heather R. *Recycling the Disabled: Army, Medicine, and Modernity in WWI Germany.* Manchester, UK: Manchester University Press, 2014.

Peukert, Detlev J. K. *Max Webers Diagnose der Moderne.* Göttingen: Vandenhoeck & Ruprecht, 1989.

Pfitzner, Felix. "Das moderne Filmatelier." *Der Film* 10, no. 39 (September 27, 1925): 52–58.

Poling, Kristin. "Shantytowns and Pioneers beyond the City Wall: Berlin's Urban Frontier in the Nineteenth Century." *Central European History* 47 (2014): 245–74.

"Polizei-Verordnung betreffend die bauliche Anlage und die innere Einrichtung von Theatern, Circusgebäuden und öffentlichen Versammlungsräumen." *Centralblatt der Bauverwaltung*, November 30, 1889.

"Polizeiverordnung über die bauliche Anlage, die innere Einrichtung und den Betrieb von Theatern, öffentlichen Versammlungsräumen und Zirkusanlagen." *Zentralblatt der Bauverwaltung*, April 21, 1909.

Pollmann, Inga. *Cinematic Vitalism: Film Theory and the Question of Life.* Amsterdam: Amsterdam University Press, 2018.

Polthier, Konrad. "Brandsicherheitswachen der Feuerwehr in Versammlungsstätten mit Bühnen und Szenenflächen." *Schadenprisma* 6, no. 4 (1977): 56–59.

Polygon staff. "What to Know about Movie Theaters and COVID-19 in Your State." *Polygon* (blog), June 10, 2021. https://www.polygon.com/2020/8/27/21402474/movie-theaters-rules-coronavirus-states-new-cdc-guidelines-covid-19.

Poore, Carol. *Disability in Twentieth-Century German Culture.* Ann Arbor: University of Michigan Press, 2007.

Rabinbach, Anson. *The Human Motor: Energy, Fatigue, and the Origins of Modernity.* New York: Basic Books, 1990.

Radkau, Joachim. *The Age of Ecology: A Global History.* Translated by Patrick Camiller. Cambridge: Polity, 2014.

Rath, Adolf. "Wohnungsaufsicht." In *Weyl's Handbuch der Hygiene,* 2nd ed., edited by C. Fraenken, vol. 4, *Bau- und Wohnungshygiene,* 53–84. Leipzig: J. A. Barth, 1914.

Reich, Eduard. *System der Hygieine.* Vol. 1. Leipzig: Friedrich Fleischer, 1870.

Reichenbach, H. "Beleuchtung." In *Weyl's Handbuch der Hygiene,* 2nd ed., edited by C. Fraenken, vol. 4, *Bau- und Wohnungshygiene,* 89–166. Leipzig: J. A. Barth, 1914.

"Reichserbhofgesetz. Vom 29. September 1933." *Reichsgesetzblatt,* September 30, 1933.

Retlow, K. "Die Projektionswand." *Filmtechnik* 2, no. 26 (December 25, 1926): 518–22.

Richardson, Benjamin Ward. *Hygeia: A City of Health.* London: Macmillan, 1876.

Rigby, Catherine E. *Topographies of the Sacred: The Poetics of Place in European Romanticism.* Charlottesville: University of Virginia Press, 2004.

Rippey, Theodore F. "*Kuhle Wampe* and the Problem of Corporal Culture." *Cinema Journal* 47, no. 1 (2007): 3–25.

Ritzheimer, Kara L. *"Trash," Censorship, and National Identity in Early Twentieth-Century Germany.* New York: Cambridge University Press, 2016.

Rollins, William. "A Nation in White: Germany's Hygienic Consensus and the Ambiguities of Modernist Architecture." *German Politics and Society* 19, no. 4 (2001): 1–42.

Rosen, George. "What Is Social Medicine? A Genetic Analysis of the Concept." *Bulletin of the History of Medicine* 21 (1947): 674–733.

Rubin, Eli. "From the Grünen Wiesen to Urban Space: Berlin, Expansion, and the Longue Durée." *Central European History* 47 (2014): 221–44.

Sandahl, Carrie. "Considering Disability: Disability Phenomenology's Role in Revolutionizing Theatrical Space." *Journal of Dramatic Theory and Criticism* 2, no. 2 (2002): 17–32.

Sarasin, Philipp. *Reizbare Maschinen: Eine Geschichte des Körpers, 1765–1914.* Frankfurt am Main: Suhrkamp, 2001.

Schaub, Christoph. "Labor-Movement Modernism: Proletarian Collectives between *Kuhle Wampe* and Working-Class Performance Culture." *Modernism/modernity* 25, no. 2 (2018): 327–48.

Schivelbusch, Wolfgang. *Disenchanted Night: The Industrialization of Light in the Nineteenth Century.* Translated by Angela Davies. Berkeley: University of California Press, 1995.

Schliepmann, Hans. *Lichtspieltheater: Eine Sammlung ausgeführter Kinohäuser in Gross-Berlin.* Berlin: Ernst Wasmuth, 1914.

Schmidt, Ulf. "'Der Blick auf den Körper': Sozialhygienische Filme, Sexualaufklärung und Propaganda in der Weimarer Republik." In *Geschlecht in Fesseln: Sexualität zwischen Aufklärung und Ausbeutung im Weimarer Kino 1918–1933,* edited by Malte Hagener, 23–46. Munich: edition text & kritik, 2000.

Schott, Dieter. "The *Handbuch der Hygiene*: A Manual of Proto-Environmental Science in Germany of 1900?" In *Environment, Health and History,* edited by Virginia Berridge and Martin Gorsky, 69–92. Basingstoke, UK: Palgrave Macmillan, 2012.

———. "Industrialisierung und städtische Umwelt in Deutschland." In *Umwelt und Geschichte in Deutschland und Großbritanien*, edited by Franz Bosbach, Jens Ivo Engels, and Fiona Watson, 91–104. Munich: K. G. Saur, 2006.

Schroeder, Julius von, and Carl Reuss. *Die Beschädigung der Vegetation durch Rauch und die Oberharzer Hütterauchschäden*. Berlin: Paul Parey, 1883.

Schütte-Lihotzky, Margarete. "Rationalisierung im Haushalt." *Das neue Frankfurt* 1, no. 5 (1927): 120–23.

Schweisheimer, Waldemar. *Die Bedeutung des Films für die soziale Hygiene und Medizin*. Munich: Georg Müller Verlag, 1920.

Seeber, Guido. "Rauch und Nebel." *Filmtechnik* 4, no. 14 (1928): 262–63.

Sellmann, Adolf. "Das Geheimnis des Kinos." *Bild und Film* 1, no. 3 (1912): 65–67.

Serres, Michel. "Turner Translates Carnot." In *Hermes: Literature, Science, Philosophy*, edited by Josué V. Harari and David F. Bell. Baltimore, MD: Johns Hopkins University Press, 1982.

Shakespeare, Tom. *Disability: The Basics*. New York: Routledge, 2018.

Shildrick, Margrit. *Embodying the Monster: Encounters with the Vulnerable Self*. London: Sage, 2002.

Siegert, Bernhard. "Cultural Techniques: Or the End of the Intellectual Postwar Era in German Media Theory." *Theory, Culture & Society* 30, no. 6 (2013): 48–65.

Silberman, Marc. "Political Cinema as Oppositional Practice: Weimar and Beyond." In *The German Cinema Book*, edited by Tim Bergfelder, Erica Carter, and Deniz Göktürk, 165–72. London: British Film Institute, 2002.

Smith, Crosbie. *The Science of Energy: A Cultural History of Energy Physics in Victorian Britain*. Chicago: University of Chicago Press, 1998.

Smith, Jill Suzanne. *Berlin Coquette: Prostitution and the New German Woman, 1890–1933*. Ithaca, NY: Cornell University Press, 2013.

Snyder, Sharon L., and David T. Mitchell. *Cultural Locations of Disability*. Chicago: University of Chicago Press, 2006.

Spode, Hasso. *Die Macht der Trunkenheit: Kultur- und Sozialgeschichte des Alkohols in Deutschland*. Opladen: Leske und Budrich, 1993.

Stam, Mart, and Werner Moser. "Das Altersheim der Henry und Emma Budge-Stiftung in Frankfurt a. M." *Das neue Frankfurt* 4, no. 7 (1930): 157–76.

Steakley, James D. "Cinema and Censorship in the Weimar Republic: The Case of *Anders als die Andern*." *Film History* 11, no. 2 (1999): 181–203.

Stindt, Georg Otto. *Das Lichtspiel als Kunstform: Die Philosophie des Films, Regie, Dramaturgie und Schauspieltechnik*. Oldenburg i. O.: Gerhard Stalling, 1924.

———. "Die Luft im Kino." *Filmtechnik* 2, no. 26 (December 25, 1926): 513–14.

———. "Kalte und warme Farben." *Filmtechnik* 3, no. 16 (August 6, 1927): 304–5.

Street, Sarah, and Joshua Yumibe. *Chromatic Modernity: Color, Cinema, and Media of the 1920s*. New York: Columbia University Press, 2019.

Sullivan, Heather I. "Ecocriticism, the Elements, and the Ascent/Descent into Weather in Goethe's *Faust*." *Goethe Yearbook* 17 (2010): 55–72.

Szczepaniak-Gillece, Jocelyn. *The Optical Vacuum: Spectatorship and Modernized American Theater Architecture.* Oxford: Oxford University Press, 2018.

Taut, Bruno. *Die neue Wohnung: Die Frau als Schöpferin.* 3rd ed. Leipzig: Klinkhardt & Biermann, 1925.

Thielemann, Walter. "Notausgänge in Kinotheatern." *Kinematograph*, May 28, 1919.

Thomalla, Curt. "The Development of the Medical Film and of Those Dealing with Hygiene and General Culture in Germany." *International Review of Educational Cinematography* 1, no. 4 (1929): 440–54.

———. "Film Propaganda in Favour of Protection against Accidents." *International Review of Educational Cinematography* 2, no. 7–8 (1930): 949–56.

———. "Hygiene und soziale Medizin im Volksbelehrungsfilm (I)." *Zeitschrift für Medizinalbeamte* 35, no. 21 (1922): 589–93.

———. "Hygiene und soziale Medizin im Volksbelehrungsfilm (II)." *Zeitschrift für Medizinalbeamte* 35, no. 22 (1922): 606–10.

———. "Hygiene und soziale Medizin im Volksbelehrungsfilm (III)." *Zeitschrift für Medizinalbeamte* 35, no. 23 (1922): 631–35.

Thomann, Klaus-Dieter. "Der 'Krüppel': Entstehen und Verschwinden eines Kampfbegriffs." *Medizinhistorisches Journal* 27, no. 3-4 (1992): 221–71.

Toepfer, Georg. "Konkurrenz." In *Historisches Wörterbuch der Biologie: Geschichte und Theorie der biologischen Grundbegriffe*, 2:277–89. Stuttgart: J. B. Metzler, 2011.

———. "Umwelt." In *Historisches Wörterbuch der Biologie: Geschichte und Theorie der biologischen Grundbegriffe*, 3:566–607. Stuttgart: J. B. Metzler, 2011.

Tramm, Karl. "Die Verhütung der Unfälle durch Propaganda." *Industrielle Psychotechnik* 1, no. 5–6 (1924): 148–56.

Treitel, Corinna. *Eating Nature in Modern Germany: Food, Agriculture and Environment, c. 1870 to 2000.* Cambridge: Cambridge University Press, 2017.

———. "Max Rubner and the Biopolitics of Rational Nutrition." *Central European History* 41, no. 1 (2008): 1–25.

Tuszkai, Ödön. "Menschenökonomie: Die öffentliche Hygiene auf volkswirtschaftlicher Grundlage." *Archiv für soziale Hygiene und Demographie* 15 (1924): 1–12.

Uekötter, Frank. *The Age of Smoke: Environmental Policy in Germany and the United States, 1880–1970.* Pittsburgh, PA: University of Pittsburgh Press, 2009.

———. *Umweltgeschichte im 19. und 20. Jahrhundert.* Munich: Oldenbourg, 2007.

Usborne, Cornelie. *Cultures of Abortion in Weimar Germany.* New York: Berghahn, 2007.

v. d. Hude, and Hennicke. "Das Central-Hôtel in Berlin." *Zeitschrift für Bauwesen* 31 (1881): 175–88.

visitBerlin Blog. "Berlinale Summer Special: Tickets, Films and Info," June 1, 2021. https://www.visitberlin.de/en/blog/berlinale-summer-special-tickets-films-and-info.

Wagner, Anselm. "Historie versus Hygiene: Staub in der Architektur(theorie)." In *Staub: Eine interdisziplinäre Perspektive*, edited by Daniel Gethmann and Anselm Wagner, 75–106. Vienna: Lit, 2013.

Wagner, Martin. *Das sanitäre Grün der Städte: Ein Beitrag zur Freiflächentheorie*. Berlin: Carl Heymanns Verlag, 1915.

———. "Urban Open-Space Policy." In *Metropolis Berlin, 1880–1940*, edited by Iain Boyd Whyte and David Frisby, translated by Iain Boyd Whyte, 267–68. Berkeley: University of California Press, 2012.

Weber, Richard, ed. "Der Volksfilmverband: Von einer bürgerlichen Bündnisorganisation zur proletarischen Kulturorganisation." In *Film und Volk: Organ des Volksfilmverbandes*, 5–27. Cologne: Gaehme, Henke, 1975.

Weindling, Paul. *Health, Race and German Politics between National Unification and Nazism, 1870–1945*. Cambridge: Cambridge University Press, 1989.

Weist, Caroline. "Castration and Critique: Resisting Rehabilitation in Ernst Toller's *Hinkemann*." *Monatshefte* 112, no. 3 (2020): 367–91.

Wernicke, Erich. "Die Wohnung in ihrem Einfluss auf Krankheit und Sterblichkeit." In *Krankheit und soziale Lage*, edited by M. Mosse and Gustav Tugendreich, 45–120. Munich: J. F. Lehmanns Verlag, 1913.

Weyl, Theodor. *Die Einwirkung hygienischer Werke auf die Gesundheit der Städte mit besonderer Rücksicht auf Berlin*. Jena: Gustav Fischer, 1893.

———. "Die Ursachen der Luftverschlechterung in bewohnten Räumen." In *Weyl's Handbuch der Hygiene*, 2nd ed., edited by C. Fraenken, vol. 4, *Bau- und Wohnungshygiene*, 258–66. Leipzig: J. A. Barth, 1914.

Wilms, Fritz. *Lichtspieltheaterbauten*. Berlin: Friedrich Ernst Hübsch Verlag, 1928.

Witlin, Leo. "Das Aufbauprinzip von großen Lichtspielhäusern." *Filmtechnik* 2, no. 26 (December 25, 1926): 510–11.

———. "Mercedes-Palast in Neukölln." *Filmtechnik* 3, no. 6 (March 19, 1927): 105–7.

Wolf, Friedrich. *Cyankali von Friedrich Wolf: Eine Dokumentation mit dem berühmten Theaterstück gegen den "Abtreibungsparagraphen."* Edited by Emmi Wolf and Klaus Hammer. West Berlin: das europäische buch, 1986.

INDEX

Abel, Rudolf, 49
able-bodiedness, 112–15, 118–23, 125
abortion, 137, 149, 150
accident prevention, 62–63, 76, 83–84
administrative intervention: charity and,
    139; hygiene and, 11; and linking of
    apparatuses, 77
aesthetics: of cleanliness, 7–8; fascist, 152–
    53; and film studies, 11; particulate,
    17–18, 80–81, 85–89, 98–101, 133
aging: and disability, 113–26; and housing,
    108–12; and modernity, 18–19
air: cooling of, 43; and disease, 24, 38, 90;
    and entropy, 95; in housing, 55, 56; in
    movie theaters, 38–39, 42–43; pollution
    of, 79–80, 82–85
"Air in the Cinema" (Stindt), 43–44
Albera, François, 10–11
alcoholism, 51, 75, 116–18
animation, 53, 70, 73, 77
apparatus: cinema as, 18–19, 46–48,
    162n25; of hygiene, 50, 155, 160; and
    modernism, 10–12
architecture: in Berlin, 3–4; environmental
    control in, 4; of film studio, 17;
    historicist, 39; and hygiene, 7–8, 15,
    111–12; modernism in, 38–48, 50, 79; of
    movie theaters, 15, 21–22, 37–48; and
    rationalization, 13, 58–62
Arneil, Barbara, 113
Ascher, Louis, 82
attention and distraction, 95–100
audience: experience of, 52; and filmic space,
    105, 123; gaze of, 101; growth of, 19; and
    illusion, 101; for Kulturfilme, 50, 155; and
    oligoptic visual regime, 77; professional,
    76; and reform imaginary, 37; urban, 54;
    working-class, 46, 52–53
authority: and expertise, 16, 19, 21–23, 53,
    55–57, 59, 67, 78, 130, 159; and oligoptic
    visual relations, 77; of police, 66–68; of
    scientific hygiene, 140

Babelsberg Studio, 83
Balázs, Béla, 130

Battleship Potemkin (Eisenstein), 131,
    181n22
Baudry, Jean-Louis, 10, 46
Baumann-Dittersbach, Emil, 131
Bedeutung des Films für die soziale Hygiene
    und Medizin, Die (Film's Significance
    for Social Hygiene and Medicine)
    (Schweisheimer), 29–30
Behne, Adolf, 39–40, 59
Benjamin, Walter: on Umwelt, 12; on
    Zerstreuung (distraction/dissipation), 95,
    175n49
Bergmann-Michel, Ella: and Budge Home,
    108; Wo wohnen alte Leute (Where Old
    People Live), 108–13, 121–22
Berlin: green periphery of, 19, 70–76, 135–
    36, 181n27; improvised settlements
    around, 142–46; modernization of city
    center, 3–4; municipal health office of, 54;
    regulation of movie theaters in, 33–34
Berlin (Ruttmann), 155
Berlin Alexanderplatz (Jutzi), 131
Berlin Fichte Workers' Sport Association,
    152
Biesalski, Konrad, 105–8
biopolitics: and dust, 79–80; and film, 75–
    76; and media, 15
Black Imp, The (Méliès), 87–88
Blumenwunder, Das (The Miracle of
    Flowers), 74
Blut und Boden (Blood and Soil) (Sonjevski-
    Jamrowski, Passavant, and Ruttmann),
    153–54
body: able, 104–5, 113, 114–15, 118–
    22; aged, 103, 109–26; disabled, 75,
    103–9, 113–26; and entropy, 89, 133;
    and environment, 6–7, 8–9, 18, 50, 85;
    health education films about, 53–54, 75;
    improper contact with, 22–23; insurance
    of, 52–53; and modernity, 107, 114; of
    nation, 16, 23, 139; and particulates, 85;
    and physical fitness, 19, 75, 108, 119, 147,
    152–53; social, 38; as source of disorder,
    101; vs. spirit, 96–97; white, 75
Brecht, Bertolt, 19